ABOUT THE AUTHOR

Sally Wise is the author of seven cookbooks. She is a regular guest on ABC Local Radio 936 Tasmania.

Sally has recently opened the Sally Wise Cooking School in Molesworth in the picturesque Derwent Valley in Tasmania. Sally's classes feature how to transform the best of seasonal produce into delicious dishes and preserves.

Sally regularly gives presentations for events such as Sustainable Living, The Essential Ingredient, Open Gardens Australia and the Melbourne Food and Wine Festival as well as many and varied community groups.

In October 2011 *The Weekend Australian* listed Sally as the sixth top selling cookbook author in Australia, just below Jamie Oliver.

The Complete
Slow Cooker

Two bestselling books in one

Sally Wise

ABC
Books

The ABC 'Wave' device is a trademark of the Australian Broadcasting Corporation and is used under licence by HarperCollins*Publishers* Australia.

First published in Australia in 2013
by HarperCollins*Publishers* Australia Pty Limited
ABN 36 009 913 517
harpercollins.com.au

The Complete Slow Cooker is a revised, compilation edition of *Slow Cooker* (2009) and *Slow Cooker 2* (2012)

Text copyright © Sally Wise 2013

HarperCollins*Publishers*
Level 13, 201 Elizabeth Street, Sydney NSW 2000, Australia
Unit D1, 63 Apollo Drive, Rosedale, Auckland 0632, New Zealand
A 53, Sector 57, Noida, UP, India
77–85 Fulham Palace Road, London W6 8JB, United Kingdom
2 Bloor Street East, 20th floor, Toronto, Ontario M4W 1A8, Canada
10 East 53rd Street, New York NY 10022, USA

National Library of Australia Cataloguing-in-Publication data:

Wise, Sally.
   The complete slow cooker / Sally Wise.
   978 0 7333 3146 6 (hbk.)
   Includes index.
   Electric cooking, slow.
641.588

Cover design by Matt Stanton, HarperCollins Design Studio
Cover images by shutterstock.com
Typeset in 11.5/15pt Centaur MT by Kirby Jones
Printed and bound in China
The papers used by HarperCollins in the manufacture of this book are a natural, recyclable product made from wood grown in sustainable plantation forests. The fibre source and manufacturing processes meet recognised international environmental standards, and carry certification.

6 5 4   14 15 16

This book is dedicated to my husband and children and to all those who share a love of slow-cooking.

CONTENTS

ACKNOWLEDGEMENTS

Thanks to my wonderful family who share a passion for food and cooking and a love for working with seasonal produce.

Special thanks to ABC presenter Chris Wisbey for his ongoing encouragement and support.

Much appreciation goes to the people who visit our house and become test tasting conscripts.

Thanks to Bev and Phil from Doolishus Food Van at Eaglehawk Neck for their generous help in providing the best quality fresh fish for developing the seafood recipes in this book. Thanks also to Pauline O'Carolan.

To the exceptional team at ABC Books/HarperCollins who do such a great job in the publishing and promotion of my books — with special thanks to Amruta Slee, Karen Penning, Julia Collingwood, Julie Bullock, Helen Biles, Matt Stanton and Nicola Wood.

INTRODUCTION

For a time, there seemed to be a common perception that slow cookers (once more commonly known as crock pots) were a thing of the past, a fad that came and went in the 1970s. For those of us who were young housewives at the time, however, there was hardly a benchtop that was not adorned with a resplendent orange slow cooker, put to good use in making casseroles, soups and other culinary delights for our families.

With the advent of the microwave, and with women returning in ever greater numbers to the workforce, and the growth of ever-so-convenient fast food outlets, slow cookers faded into the background. They were eventually relegated to the depths of our cupboards and were often to be seen sitting forlornly on garage sale tables, discarded and unappreciated. But there is now a resurgence of interest in slow cookers that is causing many of us to think once more about their advantages.

They make good economic sense. Most models available today only cost a few cents per hour to operate. They also allow for forward planning in the preparation of meals. For working families, it means that dinner can be on the table in a matter of minutes after arriving home, when often the last thing we feel like doing is preparing a meal. In this way it also saves money by removing the temptation to buy pre-prepared meals on the way home.

The slow-cooking process retains maximum nutrients, as all the delicious juices are kept in the food, and the extended cooking time results in better distribution of flavours. The cooker is very versatile in that it cooks soups, seafood, chicken and meat to perfection. Vegetables are far less likely to become mushy and unpalatable, and desserts are moist and delicious. It frees up the oven for other uses, and needs little or no tending as it cooks. In summer, the kitchen does not become overheated through using the oven and in winter the kitchen is not filled with steam from pans cooking on the stove. Food is very unlikely to burn, and if we are held up at an appointment, rarely is any harm done to the food as it slowly simmers away in our absence.

Not to be neglected is the fact that almost daily we receive a barrage of information about the dangers of eating processed and takeaway foods. We are looking more closely at the number of food additives on labels, suspecting that even if they do no harm, they certainly are not doing us a lot of good. With slow cookers, we can easily control the contents of our food, all the more important for those with food allergies or intolerances, or people on special diets. Fats need to be removed from meats and poultry before adding to the slow cooker, which is also good news for our health.

Slow cookers are amazingly adaptable. They are wonderful for having a hot meal to come home to after work or recreation. Even on a day at home, I find it's so good to put something in the slow cooker early, leaving the rest of the day free in the sure knowledge that dinner is organised. I admit to being a messy cook, so it also allows time for a clean-up. A dinner can be started hours in advance so that by mealtime, all you need to do is serve.

A healthy breakfast is easy – you can cook porridge, a fruit compote or rancher's eggs overnight, ready to serve as soon as you get up. I wondered for a long time how to accomplish the porridge factor – it always turned to stodge using regular rolled oats; however, if you use steel cut oats, available from health food stores, the porridge is perfect – and is also very economical and healthy.

It is for all these reasons that I recently pulled my old slow cooker from the depths of the cupboard, feeling a little guilty for neglecting it for so long. Alongside it were three others, purchased at garage sales on a whim, in memory of how useful my old faithful had once been, promising myself to soon go back to slow-cooking with renewed enthusiasm.

I recalled with fondness how my slow cooker had been associated with markers in my life. After bringing my third baby home from hospital, I used it each day, putting a simple meal into it in the relative calm of the morning, knowing that even if the sky fell in, I could rely on having a meal on the table that night. As my children went to school, I would make soup so that when they came home in the afternoon there was always a welcoming aroma and something good and nourishing to eat. Then, when I went back into the workforce, I would spend a mere few minutes before I left preparing something in the slow cooker, switching it to the Low setting, guaranteed to come home to the wonderful smell of a meal well cooked, with time to spare for a cup of tea or glass of wine before serving.

It is especially helpful when members of a household arrive home at different times. Each person can help themselves to dinner directly from the slow cooker.

All these thoughts ran through my head as I looked at the chips in the orange paintwork and dings in the shell of my old slow cooker. It surely deserved better for all its hard work, and I immediately determined to bring it back to its former usefulness. This indeed has happened, and the slow cooker once again never leaves my benchtop and is constantly in use. I now wonder how I ever did without it. It has been joined by others I've purchased more recently

As I used the slow cookers more, I developed new recipes that have led to this book coming into existence. These recipes are designed specifically for slow-cooking, made with common everyday ingredients. They show that slow-cooking does not need to be confined to mere soups and stews, and showcase the flavours that can be attained so easily in our quest for tasty and wholesome food. I hope you enjoy preparing and eating them as much as I have enjoyed putting them together.

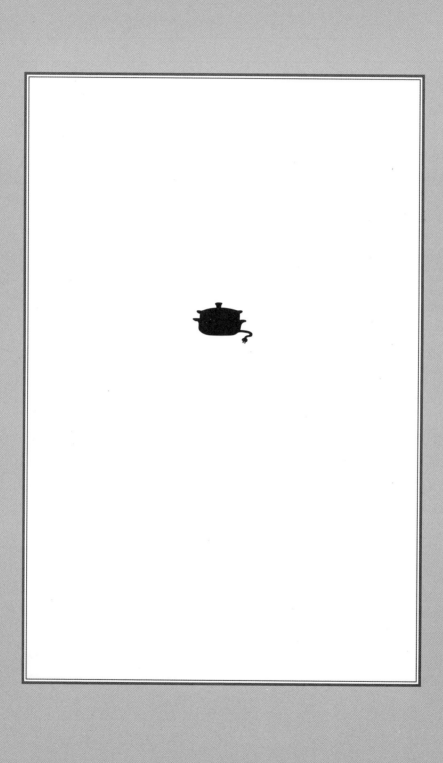

General
Helpful
Hints

Recipes in this book have been prepared in a range of slow cookers, using either a 3.5- or 4.5-litre capacity cooker. Cookers with greater capacity are suitable for larger quantities and are ideal for soups and casserole style dishes to feed a crowd, or to provide enough to freeze for later use.

Many slow cookers have two or more temperature settings. These settings can vary from one cooker to the next, so it is very important to read the manufacturer's instructions carefully.

Most modern cookers have a 'Low' and a 'High' setting. Some will have an 'Auto' option, which means it starts cooking at High, then switches automatically to Low. If a cooker has a 'Keep Warm' setting, it means that after the food is cooked it will hold the food at a safe temperature until serving time. Some cookers have timers, which cook the food for a specified time, then switch automatically to 'Keep Warm' until serving time. Some have the option to brown the meat in a removable insert, before returning it to the cooker to complete cooking.

When purchasing a slow cooker and wondering about the right size for your needs, think about what you will be using the cooker for. A small family? Entertaining? Is one enough? Also consider if you want one with a round or oval shape – the latter is better for cooking certain roasts, such as a leg of lamb.

Most of the recipes in this book serve four to six people and the recommended capacity of the slow cooker is indicated at the beginning of the recipe. To feed more, use a larger cooker and increase the quantities of ingredients correspondingly. Keep in mind that the cooker should not be filled to more than 3 centimetres from the top.

A very handy size is the smaller 1.5 litre capacity cooker (serves two to three people). I find that the food tends to cook in a shorter amount of time, so if I'm going out I will use the Low setting. If you are using this smaller cooker, reduce the quantities of ingredients correspondingly in the recipe.

Is Slow-cooking Safe?

Yes, slow cookers cook foods at a lower temperature for an extended period of time, but the temperatures reach a level far above the recommended food safety levels. Any bacteria are destroyed by the multi-directional heat combined with the steam created in the tightly sealed container.

Times and Temperatures

The amount of time dishes take to cook can vary, so always allow plenty of time. It is highly unlikely that the food will overcook, especially on Low. Even on High an extra hour will have no detrimental effect. I've cooked some meals for several hours extra on Low with no ill effect. The meat and vegetables were still intact and the meat delightfully tender.

As a general rule, the Low setting is approximately 94°C (200°F) and the High setting is approximately 149°C (300°F).

One hour on High is more or less equivalent to 2 hours on Low. This may vary to a degree in some recipes, which will have instructions to this effect. Some recipes require cooking on a specific setting. For meat dishes, as a general guide only, you can use the following table. Check the instruction manual for your cooker for any variations.

Conventional recipe times	Slow Cooker – Low	Slow Cooker – High
15 to 30 minutes	4 to 7 hours	1½ to 2½ hours
35 to 50 minutes	6 to 9 hours	3 to 4 hours
50 minutes to 3 hours	8 to 16 hours	4 to 6 hours

Note: *Recipes can be cooked for 1 to 2 hours on High and then reduced to Low if this is convenient.*

For Safety's Sake

If the power goes off when you are not at home, you will unfortunately need to discard the food because the temperature may have dropped to unsafe levels, causing the food to spoil.

If you have an old cooker, you can quite easily test to see if it is cooking to temperature. Fill the cooker with about 2 litres of cool water (less of course for a smaller cooker), cover with the lid, then heat on Low for 8 hours. Remove the lid and immediately check the temperature with a food thermometer. The temperature should be about 85°C (185°F). If the temperature is lower, the cooker may not be heating effectively enough to be safe.

Always defrost foods before adding them to the slow cooker. And certainly don't use the slow cooker to defrost foods.

If you wish to prepare foods the night before to set on to cook the next morning, it is best not to put the prepared ingredients into the cooker insert and then refrigerate it overnight. This is because the chilled insert takes longer to come up to the required temperature in the cooker. Instead, store the ingredients in containers in the fridge (keep meat and vegetables separate). It only takes a few moments to combine them in the cooker the next day. Make sure also to wipe away any food on the rim of the cooker insert after preparing ingredients in the cooker, so that a good seal forms with the lid during cooking.

When cooking foods in the cooker at altitudes over 1067 metres above sea level, you will need to extend the recommended cooking time by 50 per cent.

According to food experts, food should not be reheated in the slow cooker.

It is best not to leave leftovers in the cooker as they take a long time to cool down, meaning that bacteria could potentially grow in the food during this time. Instead, place them in containers and store in the fridge or freezer. Leftovers are very tasty indeed the next day and make wonderful fillings for pies. Leftovers can usually be frozen for up to 3 months.

Some people recommend using an external timer for the cooker. This means that the food is placed in the cooker and set to turn on at a specific time if anyone is away from the house. Although this may be very convenient, it does carry significant risks – for instance, the food left standing at room temperature may develop harmful bacteria. As a general rule, don't leave food waiting to be cooked at room temperature.

General Tips

Preheating on High may be recommended for your brand of slow cooker. Follow the manufacturer's directions in the instruction manual that comes with your cooker. If someone has donated a cooker to you minus the accompanying manual, it would be best to preheat for 15 minutes.

Always make sure not to overfill the cooker – no more than halfway to two-thirds full – otherwise the seal may not form effectively.

When lifting the lid from your cooker, lift straight up and away from the cooker so that the moisture on the lid doesn't fall back into the food.

Oven bags can be used to line the slow cooker insert, which will reduce washing up, although some instruction manuals carry a warning that they should not be used with chicken, lamb, pork or beef.

Some slow cooker inserts can be placed in the oven preheated to 160°C to brown toppings etc at the end of the cooking time. Again, check the manufacturer's manual to be sure.

Slow cookers don't like fat, so cut visible fat and skin from meat and poultry before adding to the cooker.

Generally it is not necessary to stir during cooking time, so don't be tempted to lift the lid unless it is to add dumplings or toppings, soft or thawed frozen vegetables, or dairy in the latter stages of cooking. Each time the lid is lifted, an extra 20–30 minutes must be added onto the cooking time. This is because the steam that results from slow-cooking creates a seal with the lid, and when the lid is lifted this seal is broken and needs to form again. Heat is also lost each time the lid is lifted.

If the dish is not cooked, replace the lid, set the cooker to High and cook in 30-minute increments. Always allow plenty of time.

Don't place the hot slow cooker insert on a cold surface, nor a very cold slow cooker insert into a hot unit.

Don't pour cold water into a hot slow cooker or hot water into a cold slow cooker.

Liquid Content

Use about half the recommended amount as you would in a conventional recipe, unless otherwise stated. One cup of liquid for a casserole-style dish is generally more than ample. If you find that the dish has too much liquid for your liking, simply turn the setting to High during the last hour of cooking. Some books recommend taking off the lid and turning the cooker to High for a time, to reduce the excess liquid, but I've not always found this to be successful as heat is lost. It is more successful if the lid is placed back on the slow cooker. Often, I instead take out most of the excess liquid with a soup ladle and put it into a small saucepan. I cook it over high heat on the stovetop until it reduces right down, and then return it to the slow cooker. It only takes a few minutes and needs little attention. In this way the flavours are retained and intensified.

Another trick is to thicken the sauce in the saucepan with cornflour paste (up to 1 tablespoon of cornflour mixed to a paste with a little cold water), stirring constantly while adding, and using only as much as is needed to thicken to the desired consistency. Then return the resulting gravy to the cooker.

Many casseroles can be thickened in the cooker itself quite effectively (particularly on the High setting) by merely stirring in some cornflour paste, as the density and heat of the food is enough to induce the thickening in conjunction with the cornflour.

Some cookbooks advise rolling the meat for casseroles and braises in flour before adding to the slow cooker to help thicken the pan juices during cooking. I steer away from this as I have childhood memories of dinners at the house of an aunt, not a particularly good cook, whose gravies tasted like flavoured glue and had much the same consistency.

The Flavour Factor

It is sometimes claimed that during long slow-cooking some of the flavours of the food are diminished. In fact, I have rarely found this to be the case, but I have a range of simple products on stand-by as flavour enhancers, should they ever be necessary. It is really important to taste the food before serving (as with any form of cooking), so that flavours can be adjusted if necessary.

Although I generally refrain from using anything reeking of artificiality, I do keep on hand top-quality beef, vegetable and chicken stock powders.

The other items on the list of (good-quality) flavourings include:

soy sauce
Worcestershire sauce
sweet chilli sauce
barbecue sauce
fish sauce

chutney or relish

tomato sauce (ketchup)

quince or redcurrant jelly

raspberry jam

marmalade

apricot jam

honey

You can use the commercial product or make your own (except for the soy sauce) – there are many easy recipes in my book *A Year in a Bottle*.

Soups

Only add enough water to barely cover the ingredients and add extra (hot) water later if necessary. To make a cream soup, I make a cheese or cream sauce on the stovetop and add this at the end. This sauce can be made any time and reheated before adding to the slow cooker. Another method is to add cream or evaporated milk at the end of cooking time, replacing the lid on the cooker, turning the setting to High and reheating for approximately 20 minutes.

For a really rich soup, a combination of cream and egg yolks can be stirred in at the end of cooking time. This is indicated in specific recipes in this book.

Rice and Pasta

The same amount of water can be used as for conventional cooking, or reduce by one-third at most.

Rice and pasta should never be cooked for an extended period of time; 2 hours is usually ample. For pasta and rice dishes, cooked rice or pasta should be added during the last hour to half-hour of cooking time.

Fish and Seafood

When cooking a whole fish, it is a good idea to line the cooker with a piece of baking paper large enough to reach up the side, then place the fish on top. This makes lifting out the cooked fish much easier.

I have found cooking seafood highly successful in the slow cooker; it retains its shape, nutritional value and delicate flavour. It is ideal for squid, for instance, which benefits greatly from the slow-cooking process.

I had read that fish will go rubbery, mushy and unpalatable when cooked in the slow cooker. I have simply not found this to be the case, so long as it is cooked for no longer than 2–3 hours. Use the seafood recipes in this book as a guide.

Vegetables

In the slow cooker, some vegetables tend to take longer to cook than meat. Generally speaking, root vegetables, such as carrots, parsnips and onions, should be cut into pieces no larger than 2 centimetres.

Soft vegetables, such as tomatoes and zucchini, should be added in the last hour of cooking, unless you want them to break down. Frozen vegetables should be thawed and added during the last half-hour.

Green vegetables, such as peas and beans, lose their characteristic bright colour if slow cooked too long.

Dried beans should be soaked overnight, and some beans, such as red kidney beans, need to be cooked for 15 minutes and drained before adding to the cooker. Certain varieties of dried beans can be poisonous if not cooked first. If you are unsure about the type of bean you are using, it is best to cook them in this way before using them in a slow cooker recipe.

I often use drained canned chickpeas or beans, and add them during the last hour to half-hour of cooking time.

Herbs and Spices

During cooking, herbs and spices may diminish in flavour. This particularly applies to dried herbs, so it is better to use fresh. I often use a combination of both. If you think the dish could do with a little more flavour when tasting at the end of the cooking time, just add extra at this point.

Be careful with adding cayenne pepper and Tabasco sauce – they can become bitter over a long period of cooking. Add them towards the end.

Dairy Products

Dairy products do not handle long periods of slow-cooking particularly well. Generally, they should be added during the last hour to half-hour of cooking.

Cheese or white sauces reputedly break down, though I have not found this to be a real issue if a combination of cornflour and eggs is added to the sauce mixture.

Low-fat cream or evaporated milk can be used instead of regular cream, and sometimes they perform better than the full-fat varieties.

Meat

Cheaper cuts of meat, such as casserole steaks, are a good choice for the slow cooker, as they break down to become very tender indeed.

Some people brown meat before adding it to the cooker. Generally, this is not necessary (I certainly don't bother), not even for roasts – it will just take extra time and effort and means extra cleaning up. In many recipes in this book, I have eliminated the need to brown meat for the sake of convenience.

However, if you want to sear the meat first, then that's fine too. If you have the luxury of a cooker insert that gives this option, by all means include this step if you want.

All visible fat and gristle should be cut off meat for the slow cooker. Use smaller whole roasts or cut a roast beef, for example, to fit comfortably in the cooker. Any lean trimmings from the meat can be used later in a casserole-type dish.

Meat should be thawed before placing in the cooker. This is because foods should reach 60°C (140°F) as soon as possible, and the inclusion of frozen meat could hamper this process.

Roasting meats is simple – just place them straight into the slow cooker. No liquid is necessary – the gravy develops during the cooking process. Herbs and spices can be used to season the meat if desired.

In some recipes an amount of sausage meat will be specified. Instead of buying sausage mince especially, use the required weight in sausages. Simply slit the skins lengthways and they easily peel off, leaving the filling ready to use.

To heat frankfurters or similar in the slow cooker, just pour in about ½ cup of water and place the frankfurters in the cooker. Heat on High or Low until hot enough to serve.

Chicken

For whole chicken, use a chicken no larger than 1.5 kilograms.

Although not absolutely necessary, for best results remove skin and visible fat from chicken. Opinions now vary on whether it is necessary to cook chicken on High – some manufacturers' instruction manuals indicate this should be so, others indicate that to cook chicken on Low is perfectly fine. Always check your cooker's instruction manual to be sure. What I do is cook the chicken dish on High at the outset – even if only for a few minutes or half an hour, then reduce the setting to Low and cook for several hours more as indicated in the recipe.

Stocks

Slow-cooking is an ideal way to make stocks and saves buying expensive commercially made preparations. However, for convenience use commercial preparations by all means or even a good-quality stock powder mixed with water (generally ¾ teaspoon per cup of liquid).

Desserts

It is always a good idea to preheat the cooker for a few minutes on High before adding a pudding, especially if the recipe contains self-raising flour so that the raising ingredient is activated.

Slow cookers make wonderful desserts. Steamed puddings cook without filling the kitchen with steam and without needing constant attention to see if their surrounding water has run dry. It is always a good idea to preheat the cooker for a few minutes on High before adding a pudding, especially if the recipe contains self-raising flour, so that the raising agent is activated.

Cookers with wrap-around side-elements can even be persuaded to make custard and meringue puddings very successfully on the Low setting.

Poached fruits are far more likely to keep their shape during cooking, and the colour developed with quinces over the slow-cooking time is a sight and taste that must be experienced.

Having said all this, there are a number of dessert recipes in this book which are recommended for using a specific capacity slow cooker, usually a 3.5 litre cooker. The reason for this is that the ingredient quantities better cater for a smaller size slow cooker.

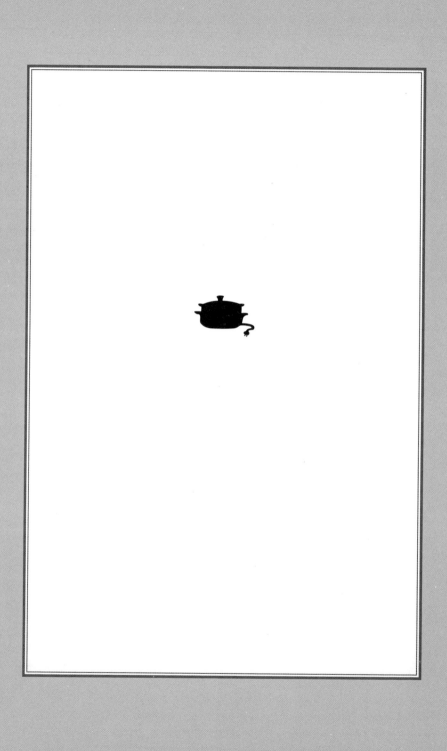

SOUPS

CAULIFLOWER, CARROT AND CUMIN SOUP

Serves 6
(for a 3.5–4.5 litre slow cooker)

½ cauliflower, 450g approximately
2 onions, diced
800g carrots, diced
2½ cups chicken or vegetable stock (or 2½ cups water with
    1½ teaspoons stock powder)
2 teaspoons ground cumin
3 teaspoons fish sauce
1 tablespoon tomato sauce (ketchup)
1 tablespoon sweet chilli sauce
3 teaspoons cornflour mixed to a paste with 1 tablespoon
    cold water
1 cup grated tasty cheese
½ cup grated parmesan cheese
½ cup cream
chopped parsley or coriander, to serve

Cut the cauliflower into small florets and place in the base of the slow cooker. Add the onion and carrot.

Mix together the stock, cumin and sauces and pour over the vegetables. Do not stir or the cauliflower on the surface may discolour to an unattractive brown as it is exposed to the air.

Place the lid on the cooker and cook for 4 hours on High or 7–8 hours on Low.

Purée the soup with a stick blender. Mix in the cornflour paste and cook for 5 minutes on High, then stir in the cheeses and cream. Replace the lid and cook for a further 3 minutes on High, or until the cheese has melted. Add salt and pepper to taste.

Serve sprinkled with the parsley or coriander.

CHICKEN AND VEGETABLE SOUP

Serves 4–6
(for a 3.2–4.5 litre slow cooker)

You can vary the vegetables used in this recipe. Personally, I like about ½ cup of fresh or thawed frozen peas added about 30 minutes from the end of cooking time.

> 600g chicken drumsticks
> 2 onions
> 1 leek, white part only (optional)
> ½ red capsicum, deseeded
> 1 large stalk celery
> 2 carrots
> 420g can creamed corn
> 2 cups chicken or vegetable stock (or 2 cups water with
>   2 teaspoons stock powder)
> garlic bread, to serve

Remove the skin from the chicken legs (it should just pull back – it doesn't matter if a little is left on), and place the legs in the slow cooker.

Dice the vegetables and add to the cooker with the creamed corn and stock.

Place the lid on the cooker and cook for 4 hours on High or 7–8 hours on Low.

Remove the drumsticks and shred the meat, returning this to the cooker. Add salt and pepper to taste.

This soup is nice served with garlic bread.

COUNTRY CHICKEN SOUP

Serves 6
(for a 3.5–4.5 litre slow cooker)

1kg chicken drumsticks
1 onion
1 carrot
½ parsnip
60g sweet potato
1 stalk celery
2 tablespoons green split peas
2 tablespoons pearl barley
3 cups chicken stock (or 3 cups water with
    1 tablespoon chicken stock powder)
white pepper, to taste

Remove as much skin from the chicken as possible. Peel and chop the onion, carrot, parsnip and sweet potato, and chop the celery. Place chicken and vegetables in the slow cooker with the split peas, barley and stock. Stir to combine.

Place lid on cooker and cook for 4 hours on High.

Add salt and white pepper to taste.

COURTNEY'S CREAM OF CORN AND BACON SOUP

Serves 6
(for a 3.5–4.5 litre slow cooker)

1 small onion
3 rashers bacon
1 cup fresh or frozen corn kernels
400g canned creamed corn
1 cup milk, plus 2 tablespoons extra
½ teaspoon stock powder
2 teaspoons sweet chilli sauce
2 teaspoons cornflour
90g grated tasty cheese

Peel and finely dice the onion. Remove rind from bacon and dice finely. Place in the slow cooker with the corn kernels, creamed corn, stock powder, sweet chilli sauce and 1¼ cups of water.

Place lid on cooker and cook for 2 hours on High or 4 hours on Low.

Meanwhile, make the cheese sauce.* Mix the cornflour with the extra 2 tablespoons of milk to a paste. Place the milk in a small saucepan and bring to the boil. Thicken with the cornflour paste, then mix in the tasty cheese.

About 1 hour before the end of cooking time, mix the cheese sauce into the soup. Replace the lid and allow the soup to heat through completely on High.

Hint: *If you have any cheese sauce left over from another meal, this is a great way to use it up.*

Cream of Carrot Soup

Serves 4
(for a 3.2–3.5 litre slow cooker)

1kg carrots
2 onions
4 cups chicken stock (or 4 cups water with 2 teaspoons
   stock powder)
2 teaspoons sweet paprika
½ teaspoon brown sugar
½ teaspoon salt (optional)
½ cup cream

Chop the carrots and onions into 1.25cm pieces and place in the slow cooker. Add the stock, paprika, sugar and salt and stir to combine.

Place the lid on the cooker and cook for 4 hours on High or 7–8 hours on Low.

Purée the soup with a stick blender, then stir in the cream. Add salt and pepper to taste.

CREAM OF CAULIFLOWER AND LEEK SOUP

Serves 6
(for a 3.5–4.5 litre slow cooker)

The main part of this soup is cooked in the slow cooker. About 5 minutes work at the end involves making a quick cheese sauce that is stirred into the slow cooker to make a delicious creamy soup.

    250g leeks, white part only, diced
    1 cauliflower, roughly chopped
    4 cups chicken or vegetable stock (or 4 cups water with
        3 teaspoons stock powder)
    ¾ cup milk
    1 cup cream
    1 tablespoon cornflour mixed to a paste with ¼ cup milk
    1 cup grated tasty cheese
    1–2 teaspoons chicken or vegetable stock powder
        (optional)

Place the leek, cauliflower, and stock in the slow cooker, cover with the lid and cook for 4 hours on High or 7–8 hours on Low. Purée with a stick blender.

In a saucepan, combine the milk and cream and bring to the boil, stirring occasionally. Mix in the cornflour paste, stirring with a whisk until thickened. Stir in the cheese until melted. Add the stock powder, if using, or salt and pepper to taste. Stir into the cauliflower soup.

CREAM OF CELERIAC AND PARSNIP SOUP

Serves 4–6
(for a 4.5–5 litre slow cooker)

2kg celeriac, approximately
3 teaspoons olive oil
1 tablespoon lemon juice
300g parsnips
1 onion
1 leek, white part only
3 cloves garlic
4 cups chicken or vegetable stock (or 4 cups water with
    3 teaspoons stock powder)
1 cup cream
white pepper, to taste

Cut the top and base from the celeriac and peel. Cut into 1.25cm cubes and place in the slow cooker. Add the olive oil and lemon juice and stir to coat the celeriac (this stops it discolouring).

Peel the parsnips and cut into 1cm chunks, dice the onion and leek, chop the garlic and add them all to the cooker, together with the stock. Do not stir.

Place the lid on the cooker and cook for 6–7 hours on High or 10–11 hours on Low.

Purée the soup with a stick blender, then stir in the cream and add salt and white pepper to taste.

CREAM OF MUSHROOM SOUP

Serves 4
(for a 3.5–4.5 litre slow cooker)

375g mushrooms
½ small onion
1 clove garlic
¾ cup chicken stock (or ¾ cup water with
    2 teaspoons stock powder)
½ cup cream, light cream or evaporated milk
½ teaspoon Dijon mustard (optional)

Wipe the mushrooms and slice finely. Peel the onion and garlic and dice finely. Place in the slow cooker with the stock.

Place lid on cooker and cook for 4 hours on High or 8 hours on Low.

Purée the ingredients until the desired consistency is reached. Stir through the cream. Add the mustard, if you think it is needed, and salt and freshly ground black pepper to taste.

CREAM OF PARSNIP AND BACON SOUP

Serves 4–6
(for a 3.5–4.5 litre slow cooker)

The sweetness of parsnip is contrasted beautifully by the saltiness of bacon in this soup. If I have the time and inclination, I sauté 2 tablespoons of diced bacon in a little oil and sprinkle over the top of each bowl of soup to garnish.

> 1 leek (or small onion), white part only
> 750g parsnips
> 1 large onion, diced
> 125g lean bacon, rind removed, diced, plus extra to
>   serve (optional)
> 4 cups chicken stock (or 4 cups water with 2 teaspoons
>   stock powder)
> ¼ teaspoon salt (optional)
> ⅓ cup pouring or thickened cream
> chopped parsley, to serve (optional)

Wash the leek well, then dice. Peel the parsnips and chop into 2cm pieces. If there is any tough core, remove it and, if possible, replace its weight with more parsnip.

Place the leek and parsnip in the slow cooker with the onion, bacon, stock and salt. Cover with the lid and cook for 4 hours on High or 7–8 hours on Low. Mix in the cream and add salt and pepper to taste.

Serve topped with a little chopped parsley and/or crispy bacon pieces.

FENNEL AND POTATO SOUP

Serves 6–8
(for a 3.5–4.5 litre slow cooker)

1kg fennel bulbs
900g potatoes
1 small onion
100g diced bacon
3 cups chicken stock
90ml sour cream
2 tablespoons finely chopped mint

Remove and discard any tough sections* from the fennel and dice finely. Peel and dice the potatoes. Peel and dice the onion. Place all in the slow cooker with the bacon and stock.

Place lid on cooker and cook for 4 hours on High.

Purée or sieve until very smooth, then add the sour cream.

Serve topped with a little chopped mint.

Hint: *The tough sections of the fennel can be used later in a stock.*

Goulash Soup

Serves 6–8
(for a 4.5–5 litre slow cooker)

This hearty soup is great for a winter's day, ideal to set and forget when you leave home for recreational activities or work. When you come home you can add the dumplings if liked, but this is by no means necessary. It is really a meal unto itself and is delicious served with fresh crusty bread or garlic bread.

600g beef cheeks or chuck or blade steak
2 x 400g cans diced tomatoes (or 800g fresh or bottled
    tomatoes)
3 cloves garlic, crushed
2 onions, diced
90g mushrooms, diced
1 large capsicum, deseeded and diced
1 carrot, diced
1 stalk celery, diced (optional)
2 tablespoons tomato paste
2 tablespoons tomato sauce (ketchup)
1 teaspoon brown sugar
1 tablespoon sweet chilli sauce
1 teaspoon Dijon mustard
2½ cups chicken, beef or vegetable stock (or 2½ cups
    water with 1½ teaspoons stock power)
2 sprigs fresh thyme or ½ teaspoon dried thyme
1 teaspoon salt (optional)

Herb Dumplings (optional)

2 teaspoons butter, softened

1 cup self-raising flour

¼ teaspoon salt

1 tablespoon snipped chives

1 tablespoon chopped parsley

milk or water to mix

Remove all visible fat from the meat and cut into small dice. Place in the slow cooker with the rest of the soup ingredients and stir to combine. Place the lid on the cooker and cook for 5 hours on High or 10 hours on Low. Add salt and pepper to taste.

To make the dumplings, rub the butter into the flour and salt with your fingertips (or do this in the food processor). Mix in the herbs and then add enough milk or water to make a soft dough. Shape teaspoonfuls of the dough into small balls.

Drop the dumplings into the simmering soup. Grease a piece of baking paper slightly larger than the cooker and place, greased side down, over the top of the cooker. Replace the lid and cook for 20 minutes more on High until the dumplings are puffed and light.

Hearty Lamb and Vegetable Soup

Serves 6
(for a 3.5–4.5 litre slow cooker)

125g sweet potato
2 carrots
1 onion
2 lean lamb shanks
2 tablespoon green split peas
1 cup fresh, canned or frozen corn kernels
1 teaspoon salt
4 cups water

Peel and dice the sweet potato, carrots and onion. Place in the slow cooker with the remaining ingredients and stir.

Place lid on cooker and cook for 4 hours on High or 8 hours on Low.

Add salt and pepper to taste.

HERBED PUMPKIN AND BACON SOUP

Serves 6
(for a 3.5–4.5 litre slow cooker)

800g dark-fleshed pumpkin (such as Kent, Jap or
    butternut), peeled and diced
125g lean bacon, rind removed, diced
1 large onion, diced
2 cups chicken stock (or 2 cups water with 1½ teaspoons
    stock powder)
2 tablespoons chopped parsley, plus 1 tablespoon extra
2 teaspoons chopped thyme
1 cup milk
2 teaspoons tomato paste
1 teaspoon Dijon mustard
½ teaspoon salt (optional)
½ cup grated parmesan cheese

Place the pumpkin, bacon, onion, stock, parsley, thyme, milk, tomato
paste, mustard and salt in the slow cooker.

Place the lid on the cooker and cook for 4 hours on High or 7–8 hours on
Low.

Purée the soup using a stick blender. Mix in the extra parsley and the
parmesan and stir until the cheese has melted. Add salt and pepper to
taste.

ITALIAN MUSHROOM SOUP

Serves 4
(for a 3.2–3.5 litre slow cooker)

400g mushrooms, thinly sliced
2½ cups chicken stock (or 2½ cups water with
    1½ teaspoons stock power)
1 onion, diced
2 cloves garlic, crushed
1½ tablespoons dry or medium-dry sherry
1½ tablespoons tomato paste
¾ teaspoon salt (optional)
3 egg yolks
½ cup cream
⅓ cup finely grated parmesan cheese

Place the mushrooms, stock, onion, garlic, sherry, tomato paste and salt
in the slow cooker and cover with the lid. Cook for 4 hours on High or
7–8 hours on Low.

Turn the cooker to High (if set on Low). Whisk together the egg yolks,
cream and parmesan and stir into the soup to thicken slightly. Add salt
and pepper to taste.

ITALIAN TOMATO AND BASIL SOUP WITH MEATBALLS

Serves 6
(for a 3.5–4.5 litre slow cooker)

2 x 400g cans diced tomatoes
1 onion
10 basil leaves
2 cloves garlic, crushed
1 teaspoon salt
2 teaspoons Worcestershire sauce
2 teaspoons sweet chilli sauce or 1 long red chilli,
    deseeded and roughly chopped
2 teaspoons tomato sauce (ketchup)
2 cups chicken stock (or 2 cups water with 1½ teaspoons
    stock powder)
½ teaspoon brown sugar

Meatballs
250g pork and veal mince
1 small onion, grated
1 slice of bread, crumbed
1 egg yolk
1 teaspoon soy sauce
1 teaspoon Worcestershire sauce
2 teaspoons smooth-textured chutney (any sort)
½ teaspoon salt
¼ cup grated parmesan cheese, plus extra, to serve
¼ teaspoon finely grated lemon rind (optional)
crusty bread or garlic bread, to serve

Place all the soup ingredients in the bowl of a food processor and process until smooth. Pour into the slow cooker. Turn the cooker onto High and heat while the meatballs are being made.

To make the meatballs, mix all the ingredients together until well combined. Roll teaspoonfuls of the mixture into balls and place in the liquid in the cooker.

Place the lid on the cooker and cook for 4 hours on High or 7–8 hours on Low.

Serve with a little extra parmesan sprinkled on top and some fresh crusty bread or garlic bread.

LEEK AND CORN CHOWDER

Serves 6
(for a 3.5–4.5 litre slow cooker)

3 leeks
2 carrots
1 small sweet potato
1 small potato
6 rashers lean bacon, rind removed
1½ cups fresh, canned or frozen corn kernels
1½ cups canned creamed corn
2½ cups stock or water
1½ teaspoons salt
3–4 teaspoons cornflour
1¼ cups milk
½ cup cream
1 cup grated tasty cheese
½ teaspoon Dijon mustard

Remove and discard the green parts of the leeks. Wash the white parts carefully and dice finely. Peel and dice the carrots, sweet potato and potato. Dice the bacon. Place all the ingredients in the slow cooker with the corn, stock or water and salt. Stir to combine.

Place lid on cooker and cook for 5 hours on High or 8–9 hours on Low.

Near end of cooking time, mix the cornflour with ¼ cup of cold milk to a paste. Combine remaining milk and the cream in a saucepan and bring to the boil. Thicken with the cornflour paste, stirring to stop lumps forming. Stir in the cheese until melted. Add the mustard. Mix the cheese sauce into the chowder and add salt and pepper to taste.

Leek and Potato Soup

Serves 6
(for a 3.5–4.5 litre slow cooker)

1kg leeks
600g potatoes
2 cups chicken stock (or 2 cups water with
    3 teaspoons chicken stock powder)
¾ cup cream, light cream or evaporated milk
½ cup grated tasty cheese (optional)
white pepper, to taste

Remove the green section of the leeks and discard them (these would make the soup bitter). Wash the white section of the leeks well and cut into 1cm dice. Place in the slow cooker.

Peel the potatoes and cut into 1cm dice. Add to the cooker with the chicken stock.

Place lid on cooker and cook for 4 hours on High or 8 hours on Low.

Purée with a stick blender or in a food processor.

Turn off the heat, then add the cream and cheese, if using. Stir well to combine. Add salt and white pepper to taste. If the soup is too thick for your liking, simply thin it down with a little more cream or milk until it reaches the desired consistency.

LENTIL SOUP WITH CHORIZO

Serves 6
(for a 4–4.5 litre slow cooker)

250g chorizo, diced
125g lean bacon, rind removed, diced
300g dried red lentils
5 cups chicken stock (or 5 cups water with 2 teaspoons
    chicken stock powder)
2 onions, diced
2 carrots, diced

Place all the ingredients in the slow cooker and stir to combine.

Place the lid on the cooker and cook for 4–5 hours on High or 8–10 hours on Low. Add salt and pepper to taste.

MINESTRONE

Serves 6–8

(for a 3.5–4.5 litre slow cooker)

2 carrots
1 onion
1 small potato
1 small zucchini
3 cloves garlic
⅓ cup chopped bacon
½ cup tomato paste
1½ cups diced fresh, canned or bottled tomatoes
2 cups water with 2 teaspoons stock powder
410g can red kidney beans, drained
1 teaspoon dried oregano
2 cups cooked small macaroni
grated parmesan, to serve

Peel and dice the carrots, onion and potato. Dice the zucchini. Peel and crush the garlic. Place in the slow cooker with the remaining ingredients, except the macaroni and parmesan, and mix well.

Place lid on cooker and cook for 4 hours on High or 7–8 hours on Low. About 30 minutes before the end of cooking time, heat the cooked macaroni and add to the cooker. Replace the lid and cook for a further 30 minutes.

Add salt and pepper to taste and serve topped with grated parmesan.

MULLIGATAWNY SOUP

Serves 6
(for a 3.5–4.5 litre slow cooker)

500g chicken pieces, fat and skin removed
½ cup dried red lentils
2 onions, diced
2 carrots, diced
2 stalks celery, diced
2 teaspoons curry powder
1 teaspoon sweet paprika
½ teaspoon garam masala
1 teaspoon grated green ginger root
2 cloves garlic, crushed
1 long red chilli or 3 teaspoons sweet chilli sauce (optional)
2 teaspoons Worcestershire sauce
2 teaspoons chutney (any sort)
4 cups chicken stock (or 4 cups water with 3 teaspoons
    stock powder)
65ml coconut milk
crusty bread or naan, to serve

Place all the ingredients in the slow cooker. Cover with the lid and cook for 4 hours on High or 8 hours on Low.

Remove the chicken from the cooker and dice or shred the meat, discarding the bones. Return the chicken to the slow cooker. Add salt and pepper to taste.

Serve with fresh crusty bread or naan.

OXTAIL SOUP WITH BARLEY

Serves 6–8
(for a 3.5–4.5 litre slow cooker)

750g oxtail pieces

2 onions, diced

2 carrots, diced

1 stalk celery, diced

125g lean bacon, rind removed, diced

½ cup pearl barley

½ teaspoon salt (optional)

4 cups chicken or beef stock (or 4 cups water with
    3 teaspoons stock powder)

Place all the ingredients in the slow cooker. Stir to combine.

Place the lid on the cooker and cook for 5 hours on High or 10 hours on Low. Add salt and pepper to taste.

PARSNIP AND BLUE CHEESE SOUP

Serves 4
(for a 3.5–4.5 litre slow cooker)

This unusual soup is my personal favourite. Choose your audience well with this one, but it is a real treat for those who love blue cheese.

500g young parsnips
1½ cups chicken stock
2 teaspoons lemon juice
50g blue cheese (a hard variety, not a brie or camembert)
½ cup cream
white pepper, to taste

Peel and chop the parsnips, removing any sign of woody core. Place in the slow cooker with the chicken stock and lemon juice.

Place lid on cooker and cook for 4 hours on High or 7 hours on Low, or until the parsnip is tender.

Add the blue cheese and purée until very smooth.

Stir in the cream and add salt and a little white pepper to taste.

Note: *Reduce the amount of stock and eliminate the cream to turn this into a parsnip and blue cheese dip.*

PEA AND HAM SOUP

Serves 4–6
(for a 3.5–4.5 litre slow cooker)

3 carrots
½ parsnip (optional)
1 onion
300g green split peas
300g bacon bones or ham hock
1½ teaspoons salt
5 cups water

Peel and dice the carrots and parsnip, if using. Peel and finely dice the onion. Place in the slow cooker with the remaining ingredients and stir.

Place lid on cooker and cook for 4 hours on High or 8 hours on Low.

POTATO AND BACON CHOWDER

Serves 8
(for a 3.5–4.5 litre slow cooker)

I had read in many books that dairy does not fare well in a slow cooker, but some did mention that if light cream were used, this would work out well. So one day I decided to put this to the test by making the family favourite "Potato Bake" in my slow cooker.

I layered the potato, onion and bacon with the cream and garlic as specified, and left it to cook. However, it turned out a disaster, with lumps of cream sitting on top of a watery mass of potato, onion and bacon. Disgusted, I told my husband to feed it to the chickens the next morning. What a waste of ingredients.

As I was heading to bed, I once more caught sight of the offending dish sitting complacently on the benchtop. It suddenly occurred to me that if I blitzed it with my stick blender, there just may be a chance to retrieve it by making it into a soup.

In actual fact, it turned the mixture into a sensational creamy soup, and has since then been prepared as potato and bacon chowder with much less fuss in the making, for as a bonus I no longer need to painstakingly layer the ingredients. It is totally in keeping with our family philosophy that there is no such thing as a failure, only something we haven't found a use for yet.

1kg potatoes (not the waxy kind)
150g lean bacon
1 onion
2 cloves garlic
300ml light cream
3 teaspoons stock powder
2 cups hot milk, approximately
2 tablespoons chopped parsley, to serve
2 tablespoons chopped chives, to serve

Peel the potatoes and cut into 1cm dice. Remove the rind from the bacon and dice. Peel and dice the onion. Place in the slow cooker.

Peel and crush the garlic and mix into the cream with the stock powder. Pour over the ingredients in the cooker.

Place lid on cooker and cook for 4 hours on High or 8 hours on Low.

Purée ingredients, adding milk until the desired consistency is reached. Add salt and pepper to taste.

Sprinkle with chopped parsley and chives to serve.

PUMPKIN SOUP

Serves 4
(for a 3.5–4.5 litre slow cooker)

750g dark-fleshed pumpkin (such as Jap or butternut)
1 onion
1½ cups vegetable stock (or 1½ cups water with
   3 teaspoons vegetable stock powder)
½ cup cream
½ cup grated tasty cheese

Peel the pumpkin and cut into 2cm squares. Peel and dice the onion. Place in the slow cooker with the stock. Stir to combine.

Place lid on cooker and cook for 4 hours on High or 8 hours on Low.

At the end of cooking time, purée and stir through the cream and grated cheese. Add salt and pepper to taste.

Hint: *Sweet potato can be substituted for the pumpkin. In this case, add the diced flesh of half a peeled cooking apple, such as Granny Smith.*

PUMPKIN, SWEET POTATO AND APPLE SOUP

Serves 6
(for a 3.2–4.5 litre slow cooker)

500g diced sweet potato
1 cooking apple (such as Granny Smith), peeled, cored and
    diced
500g diced pumpkin
1 large onion, diced
2 cups chicken or vegetable stock (or 2 cups water with
    1½ teaspoons stock powder)
1 teaspoon salt (optional)
½ cup cream (optional)
⅔ cup grated tasty cheese (optional)
white pepper, to taste

Place the sweet potato in the base of the slow cooker, then add the apple, followed by the rest of the ingredients.

Place the lid on the cooker and cook for 4–5 hours on High or 8–9 hours on Low.

Purée the soup with a stick blender. Stir in the cream and cheese, if using. Add salt and white pepper to taste.

ROASTED RED CAPSICUM AND PUMPKIN SOUP

Serves 6
(for a 3.5–4.5 litre slow cooker)

1kg dark-fleshed pumpkin (such as Jap or butternut)
500g red capsicums
1 tablespoon tomato paste
3 cups chicken stock (or 3 cups water with 2 teaspoons
    stock powder)
1 teaspoon paprika
½ cup coconut cream
½ cup cream

Peel the pumpkin and cut the flesh into 3cm dice.

Cut the capsicums into quarters and remove the seeds then roast, skin side up, under a hot grill until the skin blackens. Wrap in plastic wrap until cool enough to handle, then remove and discard the skin.

Add the capsicum to the slow cooker with the pumpkin, tomato paste, stock and paprika. Place the lid on the cooker and cook for 4–5 hours on High or 8–9 hours on Low.

Purée the soup with a stick blender. Stir in the coconut cream and cream and add salt and pepper to taste.

Scotch Broth

Serves 6
(for a 3.5–4.5 litre slow cooker)

800g lamb forequarter pieces or chops
¼ cup pearl barley
2 onions, diced
2 carrots, diced
1 parsnip, diced
1 stalk celery, diced
5 cups chicken or vegetable stock (or 5 cups water with
    2 teaspoons stock powder)
¾ teaspoon salt
fresh crusty bread, to serve

Trim all visible fat from the meat and place in the slow cooker, along with the rest of the ingredients. Cover with the lid and cook for 4 hours on High or 8 hours on Low, or until the meat is falling off the bones.

Remove the meat pieces from the cooker with a slotted spoon. Shred the meat, discarding the bones, and return the meat to the soup. Add salt and pepper to taste.

Serve with fresh crusty bread.

SUBTERFUGE SOUP

Serves 6
(for a 3.5–4.5 litre slow cooker)

As any parent is well aware, children can be fussy about eating vegetables. With six children in our household, there was always someone who didn't like something at some stage. For instance, our youngest, Courtney, loved broccoli, calling it 'trees' from the age of 9 months, but most of the others loathed it.

To avoid major or minor conflict at the dinner table, I invented this soup as a subtle form of subterfuge to maximise the chance of getting a range of vegetables into them. It worked really well. For instance, if the broccoli remained untouched on the main course plate, it didn't matter too much as they had unknowingly consumed it in the soup. I don't use the florets, but would peel and chop the stalk for the purpose so specks of the head of broccoli weren't evident. This saved wastage as well.

It is a really tasty soup in its own right and I still make it often. If you are feeding fussy children, just remember to be discreet. Don't use strong vegetables such as swede or turnip – they will be spotted in a moment. I often used sweet potato and pumpkin, so should I be asked if pumpkin were in the soup, I could evasively reply that the colour was from the sweet potato, which was technically correct.

Including a small piece of cooking apple also gives the soup a subtle sweetness.

1 onion

1kg mixed fresh vegetables*

3 cups chicken or vegetable stock (or 3 cups water with
    3 teaspoons stock powder)

½ cup cream, light cream or evaporated milk

½ cup grated tasty cheese (optional)

Peel the onion and other vegetables and cut into 1cm dice. Place in the slow cooker. Add the stock and mix well.

Place lid on cooker and cook for 3 hours on High or 6 hours on Low.

Purée until very smooth. Stir in the cream and cheese, if using. Add salt and pepper to taste.

*   *A good combination of vegetables could include pumpkin, sweet potato, a small piece of parsnip, peeled broccoli stalks, potato, carrot (which should be finely diced) and even a few celery leaves.*

SWEET POTATO AND CORIANDER SOUP

Serves 4–6
(for a 3.5–4.5 litre slow cooker)

800g sweet potato
1 onion, diced
1 clove garlic, crushed
1 tablespoon fish sauce
3 cups chicken stock (or 3 cups water with 2 teaspoons
    stock powder)
¼ teaspoon ground cumin
4 tablespoons chopped coriander
65ml coconut milk

Peel the sweet potato, cut into 2cm cubes and add to the slow cooker with the onion, garlic, fish sauce, stock, cumin and 2 tablespoons of the coriander. Stir to combine.

Place the lid on the cooker and cook for 4 hours on High or 8–9 hours on Low.

Purée the soup with a stick blender.

Stir in the remaining coriander and the coconut milk and cook for 10 minutes more on High. Add salt and pepper to taste.

Swiss Chicken Soup

Serves 4

(for a 3.2–3.5 litre slow cooker)

250–300g skinless chicken breast fillets

90g sliced ham

2 onions

1 tablespoon Dijon mustard

4 cups chicken stock (or 4 cups water with 2½ teaspoons
    stock powder)

410g can creamed corn

2 teaspoons cornflour mixed to a paste with 3 teaspoons
    cold water

1 cup grated tasty cheese

½ cup cream

4 egg yolks

crusty bread, to serve

Finely dice the chicken, ham and onions. Place in the slow cooker with the mustard, stock and corn. Stir to combine, place the lid on the cooker and cook for 4 hours on High or 8 hours on Low.

Stir the cornflour paste into the soup and cook for 5 minutes on High, then stir in the cheese until melted.

Whisk together the cream and egg yolks and mix into the soup. Add salt and pepper to taste. Replace the lid and cook for 5 minutes more on High.

Serve with fresh crusty bread.

THAI CHICKEN, CORN AND CHILLI SOUP

Serves 4
(for a 3.2–4 litre slow cooker)

400ml tin coconut milk
1 cup chicken stock (or 1 cup water with ½ teaspoon
    stock powder)
1 tablespoon lime juice
rind of ½ lime, grated
125g button mushrooms, sliced thinly
1½ teaspoons grated fresh green ginger
3 teaspoons fish sauce
2 teaspoons sweet chilli sauce
1 cup creamed corn
½ cup corn kernels
3 long red chillies, seeds removed and finely chopped
250g skinless chicken breast fillet, diced

Place all the ingredients in the slow cooker and stir to combine. Place
the lid on the cooker and cook for 3 hours on High or 5–6 hours on Low.
Add salt and white pepper to taste.

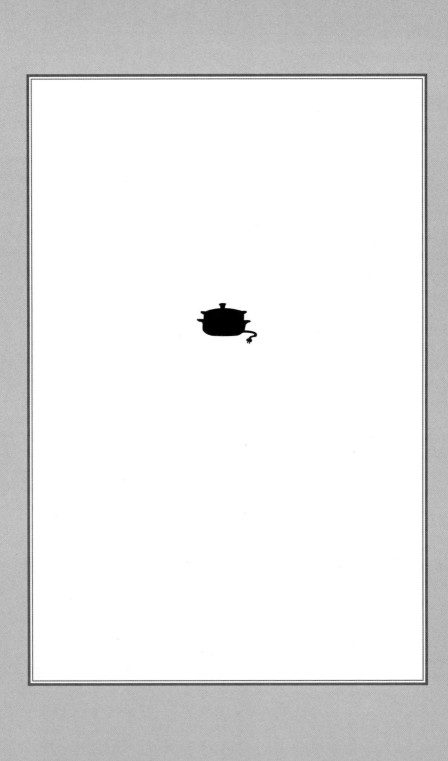

CHICKEN

APRICOT CHICKEN WITH HERBED FORCEMEAT BALLS

Serves 6
(for a 4.5 litre slow cooker)

1.5kg chicken, skin removed

Forcemeat Balls
125g good quality lean sausage mince
½ cup fresh breadcrumbs
2 teaspoons grated onion
¼ teaspoon chopped thyme or sage
½ teaspoon chopped parsley
¼ teaspoon salt
1 teaspoon chutney (any sort)
1 teaspoon soy sauce
1 teaspoon tomato sauce (ketchup)
1 tablespoon chopped dried apricots
1 tablespoon finely chopped pine nuts

Sauce
1 cup apricot nectar
1 teaspoon chicken or vegetable stock powder
2 teaspoons sweet chilli sauce
2 teaspoons soy sauce
2 teaspoons cornflour mixed to a paste with 1 tablespoon
    cold water (optional)

Place the chicken in the slow cooker.

Place all the ingredients for the forcemeat balls in a bowl and mix until very well combined. Shape into walnut-sized balls and place around the chicken.

Mix all the sauce ingredients except the cornflour paste together and pour over the chicken and forcemeat balls.

Place the lid on the cooker and cook for 4 hours on High or 7–8 hours on Low.

Lift the forcemeat balls out of the cooker with a slotted spoon and keep warm. Lift out the chicken, cover with foil and leave to stand for 10 minutes before carving.

Turn the cooker to High (if set on Low) and stir in some or all of the cornflour paste to thicken, if needed. Add salt and pepper to taste. Replace the lid on the cooker and cook for 10 minutes more.

Serve with seasonal vegetables.

ASIAN SPICED ROAST CHICKEN

Serves 4–6
(for a 3.5–4.5 litre slow cooker)

1.5kg chicken
3 tablespoons dry or medium-dry sherry
1½ tablespoons honey
2 teaspoons grated green ginger root
1 clove garlic, crushed
1 tablespoon sweet chilli sauce
3 teaspoons vinegar (any sort)
½ teaspoon salt
¼ teaspoon five-spice powder
2 teaspoons cornflour mixed to a paste with 1 tablespoon
    cold water
2 spring onion tops, thinly sliced (optional)
boiled or steamed rice, to serve

Remove the skin from the chicken (don't worry too much about the wings, it's too difficult). Just slip your fingers under the breast skin and work the skin off the flesh. Place the chicken in the slow cooker.

Mix together the sherry, honey, ginger, garlic, sweet chilli sauce, vinegar, salt and five-spice powder. Pour over the chicken.

Place the lid on the cooker and cook for 4 hours on High or 6 hours on Low.

Remove the chicken from the cooker and tip the juices into a small saucepan. Bring to the boil, whisk in the cornflour paste and continue to boil until the sauce has reduced and thickened slightly. Add salt and pepper to taste.

Serve portions of the chicken, drizzled with the sauce and sprinkled with the spring onion, if using, over plain rice.

BEDEVILLED CHICKEN

Serves 4–6
(for a 3.5–4.5 litre slow cooker)

1kg skinless chicken fillets
1 tablespoon tomato sauce (ketchup)
1 tablespoon plum sauce
1 tablespoon sweet chilli sauce
1 tablespoon lemon juice
2 teaspoons Worcestershire sauce
2 teaspoons chutney
2 teaspoons brown sugar
1 teaspoon mustard powder
1 teaspoon salt
2 teaspoons cornflour (optional)

Cut chicken into 4cm pieces. Place in the slow cooker. Combine the remaining ingredients, except cornflour, and pour over the chicken.

Place lid on cooker and cook for 3 hours on High.

If necessary, mix the cornflour with about 1 tablespoon of cold water to a paste and use a little or all of it to thicken the dish. Add salt and pepper to taste.

BUTTER CHICKEN

Serves 4–6
(for a 3.5–4 litre slow cooker)

1 large onion, diced
750g skinless chicken breast or thigh fillets
3 teaspoons ground coriander
4 teaspoons ground cumin
1 teaspoon sweet paprika
¼ teaspoon grated lemon rind
1 tablespoon lemon juice
½ cup Greek-style yoghurt
½ cup coconut milk
1 teaspoon chicken stock powder
1 teaspoon salt
2 teaspoons redcurrant or quince jelly or apricot jam
½ teaspoon ground turmeric
1½ tablespoons tomato sauce (ketchup)
1 tablespoon tomato paste
2 teaspoons sweet chilli sauce

Place the onion in the slow cooker.

Remove all visible fat from the chicken and cut into 1.25cm pieces. Place on top of the onion.

Mix the rest of the ingredients together in a bowl and pour over the chicken. Stir to combine.

Cover with the lid and cook for 3 hours on High or 6 hours on Low.

CHICKEN AND ALMONDS

Serves 6
(for a 3.5–4.5 litre slow cooker)

1kg skinless chicken breast or thigh fillets
250g mushrooms
1 onion
2 cloves garlic
3 tablespoons slivered almonds
1 teaspoon salt
1 teaspoon chicken stock powder (optional)
3 teaspoons Dijon mustard
¼ cup sherry
3 teaspoons cornflour (optional)
½ cup sour cream
¼ cup cream

Remove any visible fat from the chicken and cut into 1cm dice. Place in the slow cooker.

Wipe and slice the mushrooms. Peel and slice the onion. Peel and crush the garlic. Place in the cooker with the almonds, salt, stock powder, if using, mustard, sherry and ¼ cup of water. Stir to combine.

Place lid on cooker and cook for 3 hours on High.

If necessary, mix the cornflour with about 2 tablespoons of cold water to a paste and use a little or all of it to thicken the dish. Add salt and pepper to taste. Stir in the sour cream and cream.

CHICKEN WITH APRICOTS

Serves 4–6

(for a 3.5–4.5 litre slow cooker)

14 canned or bottled apricot halves

1 onion

1 clove garlic

800g skinless chicken breast fillets

½ teaspoon grated green ginger root

2 teaspoons chicken or vegetable stock powder

1 teaspoon soy sauce

2 teaspoons lemon juice

1 teaspoon brown sugar

½ cup apricot nectar

½ teaspoon salt

3 teaspoons cornflour (optional)

Place apricot halves in base of the slow cooker.

Peel and finely dice the onion. Peel and crush the garlic. Cut each chicken fillet into four pieces. Place all on top of the apricot.

Mix together the ginger, stock powder, soy sauce, lemon juice, brown sugar, apricot nectar and salt. Pour over the chicken, then stir gently to combine all ingredients.

Place lid on cooker and cook for 3 hours on High.

If necessary, mix the cornflour with about 2 tablespoons of cold water to a paste and use a little or all of it to thicken the dish. Add salt and pepper to taste.

CHICKEN BIRYANI

Serves 4
(for a 3.2–3.5 litre slow cooker)

1kg skinless chicken breast fillets
1½ tablespoons grated green ginger root
4 cloves garlic, crushed
1 onion, diced
¼ teaspoon salt
½ teaspoon ground turmeric
1 teaspoon ground coriander
1½ teaspoons ground cumin
½ teaspoon ground cardamom
½ teaspoon ground cinnamon
¾ teaspoon garam masala
½ cup chicken stock (or ½ cup water with ½ teaspoon
    stock powder)
3 teaspoons cornflour mixed to a paste with 2 tablespoons
    cold water (optional)
2 tablespoons chopped coriander

Cut the chicken into 1.25cm cubes and place in the slow cooker with the rest of the ingredients except the cornflour paste and coriander. Stir to combine.

Cover with the lid and cook for 3 hours on High or 6 hours on Low.

If the mixture needs thickening, remove the lid and add the cornflour, stirring thoroughly. Replace the lid and cook for a further 10 minutes on High. Add salt and pepper to taste.

Sprinkle with the chopped coriander and serve over plain boiled or steamed rice.

CHICKEN CACCIATORE WITH PARMESAN CRUST

Serves 4–6
(for a 3.5–4.5 litre slow cooker)

750g skinless chicken breast fillets
1 onion, diced
90g lean bacon, rind removed, diced
400g tomatoes, diced
1 red capsicum, deseeded and diced
1½ tablespoons tomato paste
1½ teaspoons chicken stock powder
1 teaspoon brown sugar
2 teaspoons chopped sage
2 teaspoons chopped rosemary
1 bay leaf
3 teaspoons sweet chilli sauce
½ cup white wine
2 teaspoons cornflour mixed to a paste with 3 teaspoons
    cold water (optional)

Crust

1 cup self-raising flour
30g butter, diced
¼ cup grated parmesan cheese
½ teaspoon salt
1 egg
1 tablespoon white wine
1 tablespoon milk

Cut the chicken into 1cm cubes and place in the slow cooker with the onion. Add the bacon, tomato and capsicum to the slow cooker with the tomato paste, stock powder, sugar, sage, rosemary, bay leaf, sweet chilli sauce and wine.

Place the lid on the cooker and cook for 3–4 hours on High or 6–8 hours on Low.

Add salt and pepper to taste. Stir in the cornflour paste, if the mixture needs thickening (turning the cooker to High). Place the lid back on the cooker while preparing the crust.

To make the crust, mix together the flour, butter, parmesan and salt and rub together with the fingertips until the mixture resembles breadcrumbs. Mix in the egg, wine and enough milk to make a soft dough. Roll out on a lightly floured surface to the size of the cooker and lift onto the surface of the cacciatore. Place the lid on the cooker and cook for 30 minutes until the crust is cooked through.

Serve the chicken with seasonal vegetables and/or Peppered Rice with Peas (page 284).

CHICKEN AND CHORIZO RAGOUT

Serves 4–6
(for a 3.5–4 litre slow cooker)

750g skinless chicken breast fillets
2 onions, diced
200g tomatoes, diced
90g lean bacon, rind removed, diced
1 chorizo, diced
1½ tablespoons tomato paste
1½ tablespoons tomato sauce (ketchup)
1 teaspoon sweet paprika
½ teaspoon salt
2 tablespoons chopped parsley
2 teaspoons cornflour mixed to a paste with 1 tablespoon
    cold water (optional)

Cut the chicken into 2cm cubes and place in the slow cooker with the onion, tomato, bacon, chorizo, tomato paste, tomato sauce, paprika, salt and 1 tablespoon of the parsley.

Place the lid on the cooker and cook for 3 hours on High or 6 hours on Low.

Stir in the remaining parsley and thicken by stirring in some or all of the cornflour paste, if necessary. Add salt and pepper to taste. Replace the lid and cook for a further 10 minutes on High.

Serve with plain boiled or steamed rice and/or seasonal vegetables.

CHICKEN WITH FENNEL AND LEMON SAUCE

Serves 4–6
(for a 3.5–4.5 litre slow cooker)

½ cup chopped capsicum
½ cup chopped fennel, plus sprigs to garnish
½ cup chopped semi-dried tomato
juice of 1 lemon
½ cup white wine
1kg skinless chicken maryland fillets
2 teaspoons tomato paste
2 teaspoons quince or cranberry jelly
1 teaspoon chicken stock powder
2 teaspoons cornflour

Stuffing
1 large onion
1 small clove garlic
1 cup basil leaves
¾ cup semi-dried tomatoes
½ cup chopped red, yellow or green capsicum
1½ cups fresh breadcrumbs
½ teaspoon salt
2 teaspoons finely grated lemon rind
1 tablespoon lemon juice
1 egg, lightly beaten

Combine the capsicum, fennel and semi-dried tomato and place in the base of the slow cooker. Pour over the lemon juice and white wine.

To make the stuffing, peel and very finely dice or grate the onion. Peel and crush the garlic. Shred the basil and chop the semi-dried tomatoes. Combine with the remaining stuffing ingredients. Taste to see if more salt is needed.

Open the chicken fillets out on a board and remove any visible fat. Divide the stuffing between them, placing it along the centre of each and rolling the sides around to enclose the filling. Place the chicken fillets in the slow cooker, packed together tightly.

Place lid on cooker and cook for 4 hours on High.

Remove the chicken from the cooker and place in a serving dish.

Place a sieve over a medium saucepan and strain the juices from the cooker. Place the pan over medium heat on the stovetop and bring the juices to the boil. Add the tomato paste, quince or redcurrant jelly and stock powder. Bring to the boil and reduce to two-thirds of its original volume.

Mix the cornflour with about 2 tablespoons of cold water to a paste and use a little or all of it to thicken the sauce to a coating consistency. Add salt and pepper to taste.

Pour the fennel and lemon sauce over the chicken. Garnish with fennel sprigs.

CHICKEN À LA KING

Serves 4

(for a 3.2–3.5 litre slow cooker)

750g skinless chicken breast fillets
125g mushrooms
1 red capsicum, deseeded
1 small onion, diced
1 tablespoon lemon or lime juice
½ teaspoon sweet paprika
¾ cup chicken stock (or ¾ cup with ½ teaspoon stock
    powder)
2 tablespoons dry or medium-dry sherry
½ teaspoon salt
½ cup cream
3 egg yolks, whisked
white pepper, to taste

Cut the chicken breast into 1cm cubes and place in the slow cooker.

Slice the mushrooms and capsicum into thin strips and place in the slow cooker with the onion. Add the lemon or lime juice, paprika, stock, sherry and salt and stir to combine.

Place the lid on the cooker and cook for 3 hours on High or 5–6 hours on Low.

Remove the lid and stir in the cream and egg yolks. Add salt and white pepper to taste.

Serve the chicken over plain steamed or boiled rice.

CHICKEN MARENGO WITH BACON

Serves 6
(for a 3.5–4.5 litre slow cooker)

1.5kg chicken
1 onion, diced
125g lean bacon, rind removed, diced
200g mushrooms, sliced
1 sprig fresh thyme or ½ teaspoon dried thyme
3 tablespoons tomato paste
juice of ½ lemon
2 tablespoons dry or medium-dry sherry
3 teaspoons cornflour mixed to a paste with 1 tablespoon
    cold water

Remove the skin from the chicken (don't worry too much about the wings, it's too difficult). Just slip your fingers under the breast skin and work the skin off the flesh.

Place the chicken in the slow cooker. Sprinkle over the onion, bacon, mushrooms and thyme. In a bowl, mix together the tomato paste, lemon juice and sherry. Spoon over the contents of the cooker. Cover with the lid and cook for 4 hours on High or 8 hours on Low.

Remove the chicken from the cooker and leave to stand in a warm place while making the sauce. You can do this in the cooker if the dish has been cooked on High, or if cooked on Low, transfer the sauce to a small saucepan and heat to boiling. Remove any excess fat from the surface with a spoon. Stir some or all of the cornflour paste into the sauce until thickened. Add salt and pepper to taste.

Cut the chicken into portions and serve with the sauce and seasonal vegetables.

CHICKEN PAPRIKA

Serves 4
(for a 3.5–4.5 litre slow cooker)

1 teaspoon butter
1 tablespoon paprika
3 teaspoons sugar
2 teaspoons salt
½ teaspoon ground oregano
½ teaspoon mustard powder
¼ teaspoon ground black pepper
900g–1kg skinless chicken breast fillets
mashed potato, to serve

Grease the inside of the slow cooker with the butter.

Combine the paprika, sugar, salt, oregano, mustard powder and pepper in a bowl. Cut each chicken breast in two, lengthways, and coat with the paprika mixture. Place chicken in the slow cooker.

Place lid on cooker and cook for 2 hours on High.

Serve chicken with creamy mashed potato, drizzled with a little of the juices left in the cooker.

CHINESE CHICKEN WITH VEGETABLES

Serves 4
(for a 3.2–3.5 litre slow cooker)

600g skinless chicken breast fillets
1 onion
2 carrots
1 large red capsicum
1 large stalk celery
¼ cup tomato sauce (ketchup)
¼ cup soy sauce
¼ cup white or cider vinegar
1 tablespoon honey
1 tablespoon sweet chilli sauce
1 tablespoon brown sugar
½ teaspoon salt
3 teaspoons cornflour mixed to a paste with
    1½ tablespoons cold water (optional)
1 cup baby English spinach leaves or 2 silverbeet leaves,
    shredded
boiled or steamed rice, to serve

Slice the chicken into thin strips and place in the slow cooker.

Cut the onion in half, then cut into thin strips. Cut the carrots in half crossways, then cut into thin strips. Remove the seeds and core from the capsicum and cut into strips the same size as the carrot strips. Cut celery into thin strips the same size as the carrot strips. Place all the vegetables in the slow cooker with the rest of the ingredients except the cornflour paste and spinach or silverbeet. Stir to combine.

Place the lid on the cooker and cook for 3 hours on High or 6 hours on Low.

If needed, turn the cooker to High and stir in some or all of the cornflour paste to thicken.

Stir in the spinach or silverbeet and cook on HIgh with the lid on for 5 minutes more. Add salt and pepper to taste.

Serve with plain rice.

CITRUS CHICKEN

Serves 4–6
(for a 3.5–4.5 litre slow cooker)

900g skinless chicken breast or thigh fillets
1 teaspoon finely grated orange rind
1 teaspoon finely grated lemon rind
juice of 1 orange
¼ cup white wine
1 teaspoon apricot jam (or similar)
2 teaspoons quince jelly
1 teaspoon stock powder
1 teaspoon mild-flavoured honey
½ teaspoon salt (optional)
3 teaspoons cornflour
3 teaspoons sour cream

Remove any visible fat from the chicken and cut into 10cm x 5cm pieces. Place in the slow cooker. Mix together the orange and lemon rind, orange juice, white wine, apricot jam, quince jelly, stock powder, honey and salt, if using. Pour over the chicken and stir to combine.

Place lid on cooker and cook for 3 hours on High.

Mix the cornflour with about 2 tablespoons of cold water to a paste and stir through the mixture. Add salt and pepper to taste.

Replace lid, turn cooker setting to High and cook for a further 10 minutes.

Stir through the sour cream just before serving.

COQ AU VIN

Serves 6—8
(for a 4.5 litre slow cooker)

1.5kg chicken drumsticks
12 pickling onions, peeled; or 3 medium onions,
    quartered
180g lean bacon, rind removed, diced
200g mushrooms, sliced
1 cup red wine
2 tablespoons tomato paste
2 teaspoons chutney (any sort)
2 teaspoons redcurrant or quince jelly or brown sugar
2 teaspoons sweet chilli sauce
1½ teaspoons chicken stock powder or ¾ teaspoon salt
3 teaspoons cornflour mixed to a paste with 1 tablespoon
    cold water (optional)
2 tablespoons chopped parsley, to serve (optional)

Remove the skin from the chicken drumsticks.

Place the chicken in the slow cooker with the rest of the ingredients except the cornflour paste and parsley. Stir to combine.

Place the lid on the cooker and cook for 3–4 hours on High or 6–7 hours on Low.

Remove the lid from the cooker, turn to High (if set on Low) and thicken with some or all of the cornflour paste, if necessary. Add salt and pepper to taste.

Sprinkle with the parsley, if liked, and serve with plain steamed or boiled rice or seasonal vegetables.

Hints: *You can use a jointed 1.5kg chicken, or 1.5kg of chicken pieces of your choice instead of drumsticks. You could also buy chicken lovely legs, which have had the skin removed.*

CORONATION CHICKEN

Serves 4–6
(for a 3.2–4 litre slow cooker)

750g skinless chicken breast fillets
2 onions, finely diced
3 teaspoons curry powder
1 teaspoon Dijon mustard
3 tablespoons white wine
3 teaspoons tomato paste
1 tablespoon sweet chilli sauce
3 teaspoons chutney (any sort)
½ cup chicken stock or water
2 teaspoons cornflour mixed to a paste with 3 teaspoons
    cold water (optional)
1½ tablespoons sour cream (optional)

Cut the chicken into 8mm strips and place in the slow cooker with the onion.

Mix together the curry powder, mustard, wine, tomato paste, sweet chilli sauce, chutney and stock or water. Pour over the chicken and stir to combine.

Cover with the lid and cook for 3 hours on High or 6 hours on Low.

Thicken with the cornflour paste, if needed, then mix in the sour cream, if using. Add salt and pepper to taste.

Serve with plain boiled or steamed rice and salad or seasonal vegetables.

CREAMY PAPRIKA CHICKEN WITH KUMARA

Serves 4–6

(for a 3.2–3.5 litre slow cooker)

750g skinless chicken breast fillets

2 onions, diced

250g kumara, peeled and diced

1½ tablespoons sweet paprika

1 teaspoon sugar

1 bay leaf

2 teaspoons Worcestershire sauce

1 cup diced fresh, canned or bottled tomatoes

¼ cup water

1½ tablespoons dry or medium-dry sherry

1 teaspoon salt

1 bay leaf

3 teaspoons cornflour mixed to a paste with 1 tablespoon
cold water

½ cup sour cream

Cut the chicken into 1.5cm cubes, then place in the slow cooker with the rest of the ingredients except the cornflour paste and sour cream, and stir to combine.

Place the lid on the cooker and cook for 3½–4 hours on High or 7–8 hours on Low.

Remove the lid from the cooker, turn to High (if set on Low) and stir in the cornflour paste to thicken. Cook for 5 minutes with the lid on, then stir in the sour cream. Add salt and pepper to taste.

Serve with pasta, rice or seasonal vegetables.

EASY CHICKEN, LEEK AND VEGETABLE CURRY

Serves 4
(for a 3.5–4.5 litre slow cooker)

You can increase or decrease the amount of curry powder in this recipe according to taste. Curry paste can be substituted for the curry powder. You can also substitute a large diced onion for the leek.

    750g skinless chicken breast fillets, diced
    2–3 teaspoons curry powder
    250g leek, white part only, thinly sliced
    1 cooking apple (such as Granny Smith),
        cored and diced
    1 large carrot, finely diced
    200g cauliflower florets
    1 tablespoon soy sauce
    2 teaspoons Worcestershire sauce
    3 teaspoons chutney (any sort) or tomato sauce (ketchup)
    3 teaspoons sweet chilli sauce
    2 teaspoons quince, redcurrant jelly or apricot jam
    ½ cup chicken stock or water
    1 teaspoon salt
    3 teaspoons cornflour mixed to a paste with
        2 tablespoons cold water
    65ml coconut cream

Place all the ingredients except the cornflour paste and coconut cream in the slow cooker. Cover with the lid and cook for 4 hours on High or 8 hours on Low.

Stir in the cornflour paste to thicken, then mix in the coconut cream. Add salt and pepper to taste

Serve the curry over plain boiled or steamed rice.

GINGER BARBECUE CHICKEN

Serves 4–6

(for a 3.5–4.5 litre slow cooker)

1.5kg chicken

1 onion, quartered

6 sage leaves (optional)

1 tablespoon grated green ginger root

2 cloves garlic, crushed

1 tablespoon Worcestershire sauce

2 teaspoons chutney (any sort)

1 tablespoon white or cider vinegar

2 teaspoons barbecue sauce

2 teaspoons honey

2 teaspoons Dijon mustard

½ teaspoon salt

3 teaspoons cornflour mixed to a paste with 1 tablespoon
cold water (optional)

Remove the skin from the chicken (don't worry too much about the wings, it's too difficult). Slip your fingers under the breast skin and work the skin off the flesh.

Place the onion and sage, if using, in the cavity of the chicken. Transfer the chicken to the slow cooker.

Mix together the ginger, garlic, Worcestershire sauce, chutney, vinegar, barbecue sauce, honey, mustard and salt and pour evenly over the chicken.

Place the lid on the cooker and cook for 4 hours on High or 6–7 hours on Low.

Remove the chicken from the cooker and set aside to rest in a warm place. If needed whisk in the cornflour paste. Add salt and pepper to taste. Replace the lid and cook for a further 10 minutes.

Dish up the portions of the chicken and pour over the gravy from cooker. Serve with fresh crusty bread and seasonal vegetables or salad.

GREEK CHICKEN STEW WITH FETTA AND OLIVES

Serves 4–6

(for a 3.2–4.5 litre slow cooker)

850g skinless chicken breast fillets
1 onion
1 red capsicum
¼ cup chopped fresh basil
2 teaspoons apricot jam
3 teaspoons chutney (any sort)
1½ tablespoons tomato paste
400g can diced tomatoes
1½ teaspoons chicken or vegetable stock powder
1 tablespoon sweet paprika
1 tablespoon soy sauce
1 tablespoon tomato sauce (ketchup)
1 teaspoon dried oregano
200g fetta cheese
¾ cup black olives
⅓ cup shredded basil, to serve

Cut the chicken into 2cm cubes and place in the slow cooker. Cut the onion into quarters, then cut each quarter into thin slices. Remove the seeds and core from the capsicum and cut into 1cm cubes. Add the onion and capsicum to the slow cooker with the basil, jam, chutney, tomato paste, tomatoes, stock powder, paprika, sauces and oregano, and stir to combine.

Place the lid on the cooker and cook for 3 hours on High or 6 hours on Low.

Cut 150g of the fetta into 1cm cubes and stir into the mixture, together with the olives. Replace the lid and cook on High for 15 minutes more. Add salt and pepper to taste.

Serve the stew with plain steamed or boiled rice or seasonal vegetables. Crumble the remaining fetta over each serving and top with a little of the shredded basil.

LEMON ROAST CHICKEN

Serves 4–6
(for a 3.5–4.5 litre slow cooker)

1.5kg chicken
2 teaspoons oil (optional)
2 teaspoons butter (optional)
1 small onion
2 large sprigs rosemary
1 lemon
¼ cup chicken stock
8 raisins
2 teaspoons redcurrant or quince jelly
3 teaspoons cornflour (optional)

Remove the skin from the chicken (don't worry about the wings, it's too difficult). Slip your fingers under the breast skin and work the skin off the flesh.

If you wish, heat the oil and butter in a frying pan and brown the chicken, turning once, before placing in the slow cooker.

Peel the onion and cut into quarters. Push into the cavity of the chicken, together with the rosemary.

Juice the lemon, retaining the rind. Pour the juice over the chicken. Cut a quarter-piece rind and place it inside the chicken.

Pour the chicken stock around the base of the chicken (not over the top) and add the raisins.

Place lid on cooker and cook for 3½–4 hours on High.

Remove chicken from cooker, retaining the juices, and leave to rest.

To make the lemon jus, strain the juices from the cooker into a small saucepan. Bring to the boil, add the redcurrant or quince jelly and reduce to about two-thirds its original volume.

If necessary, mix the cornflour with about 2 tablespoons of cold water to a paste and use a little or all of it to thicken the jus. Add salt and pepper to taste.

MEDITERRANEAN CHICKEN

Serves 4–6
(for a 3.5–4.5 litre slow cooker)

1kg chicken fillets (thigh, breast or maryland)
1 onion
1 capsicum
1 cup diced fresh, canned or bottled tomatoes
½ cup tomato paste
2 teaspoons quince jelly or sugar
2 teaspoons salt
1 chorizo sausage
¾ cup pitted kalamata olives
3 teaspoons cornflour (optional)

Remove any visible fat from the chicken fillets and cut into 3cm pieces.
Peel the onion and cut into 1cm pieces. Remove the stalk, seeds and
membrane from the capsicum and chop.

Place the chicken, onion and capsicum in the slow cooker with the
tomato, tomato paste, quince jelly or sugar, salt and ½ cup of water.
Mix well.

Place lid on cooker and cook for 3 hours on High.

Cut the chorizo into 1cm slices. Add to the cooker with the olives and
stir. Replace lid and cook for a further 30 minutes.

If necessary, mix the cornflour with about 2 tablespoons of cold water
to a paste and use a little or all of it to thicken the dish. Add salt and
pepper to taste.

SATAY CHICKEN

Serves 4–6
(for a 3.5–4.5 litre slow cooker)

1kg chicken breast or thigh fillets
2 cloves garlic
2 heaped tablespoons peanut butter
5 teaspoons soy sauce
1 tablespoon Worcestershire sauce
1 tablespoon tomato sauce (ketchup)
1 tablespoon sweet chilli sauce
¾ cup coconut milk
3 teaspoons cornflour (optional)
steamed rice and seasonal vegetables,* to serve

Remove any visible fat from the chicken and cut into strips. Peel and crush the garlic. Place in the slow cooker with the peanut butter, soy sauce, Worcestershire sauce, tomato sauce, sweet chilli sauce and coconut milk. Stir to combine.

Place lid on cooker and cook for 3 hours on High.

If necessary, mix the cornflour with about 2 tablespoons of cold water to a paste and use a little or all of it to thicken the dish. Add salt and pepper to taste.

Serve with steamed rice and seasonal vegetables.

* *Vegetables can be included in the sauce. Peel and finely slice vegetables such as carrot, celery and onion.*

SPICY ROAST CHICKEN

Serves 4–6
(for a 3.5–4.5 litre slow cooker)

1.5kg chicken
1 tablespoon sweet paprika
1 teaspoon ground cumin
1 teaspoon ground ginger
¾ teaspoon ground coriander
½ teaspoon stock powder or salt
½ teaspoon ground cinnamon
½ teaspoon dried mint
½ teaspoon sugar
¼ teaspoon mustard powder
¼ cup chicken stock
2 teaspoons sweet chilli sauce
1 teaspoon cornflour (optional)

Remove the skin from the chicken (don't worry about the wings, it's too difficult). Wash it inside and out and pat dry.

Combine the paprika, cumin, ginger, coriander, stock powder or salt, cinnamon, mint, sugar and mustard powder. Rub spice mixture into the surface of the chicken.

Place chicken in the slow cooker. Carefully pour the stock around the base of the chicken (not over it).

Place lid on cooker and cook for 3½–4 hours on High.

Spoon a little of the cooking juices over the chicken. Remove chicken from cooker.

Add the sweet chilli sauce to the remaining cooking juices. If necessary, mix the cornflour with about 1 tablespoon of cold water to a paste and use a little or all of it to thicken the sauce. Add salt to taste. Serve portions of chicken drizzled with a little of the sauce.

THAI CHICKEN CURRY WITH CORIANDER RICE DUMPLINGS

Serves 4
(for a 3.2–3.5 litre slow cooker)

700g skinless chicken breast fillets
1 stalk lemongrass, white part only
2cm piece of green ginger root, peeled and finely grated
3 cloves garlic, crushed
1 onion, diced
2 teaspoons sweet paprika
1 teaspoon ground turmeric
1 tablespoon soy sauce
3 teaspoons fish sauce
2 teaspoons tomato paste
2 teaspoons brown sugar
1 tablespoon sweet chilli sauce
¾ cup coconut milk
3 teaspoons cornflour mixed to a paste with 1 tablespoon
    cold water

Dumplings

2 cups cooked rice
1 egg, lightly beaten
1 cup fresh breadcrumbs
½ teaspoon salt
1 tablespoon finely chopped coriander, Vietnamese mint or
    parsley

Cut the chicken into strips and place in the slow cooker.

Cut the lemongrass in half lengthways and bruise with the blunt side of a knife, then chop finely. Place in the cooker with the rest of the curry ingredients except the cornflour paste and stir to combine.

Place the lid on the cooker and cook for 3 hours on High or 6 hours on Low. Add salt and pepper to taste.

To make the dumplings, mix all the ingredients together and shape into walnut-sized balls.

Place the dumplings on top of the simmering curry, replace the lid and cook for 20 minutes more on High.

Remove the dumplings and set aside. Thicken the curry with some or all of the cornflour paste, if needed.

Serve with steamed Asian greens.

Hint: *This curry can be made without the dumplings, but I prefer to make them. They are a good way to use up leftover rice, add extra flavour and save cooking rice for serving.*

THYME CHICKEN WITH APRICOT JUS

Serves 4–6
(for a 3.5–4.5 litre slow cooker)

1 cup breadcrumbs
1 small onion
90g diced bacon
1 tablespoon finely chopped pine nuts
1 tablespoon chopped lemon thyme
    or ordinary thyme
½ teaspoon dried thyme
1 egg, lightly whisked
½ teaspoon salt
1kg chicken maryland fillets
1 cup apricot nectar or purée
1 teaspoon sugar (optional)
2 teaspoons cornflour (optional)

Place the breadcrumbs in a bowl. Peel and grate or very finely dice the onion and add to breadcrumbs with the bacon, pine nuts, fresh and dried thyme, egg and salt. Mix very well.

Open out the chicken fillets, remove any fat, and divide the mixture between them. Spread down the centre of each fillet and roll up to enclose filling. Tie each parcel with cooking string.*

Pour half the apricot nectar or purée into the base of the slow cooker and place the chicken parcels on top, packed tightly together. Spread the remaining apricot nectar over the top.

Place lid on cooker and cook for 4 hours on High.

Remove chicken from cooker and leave to rest in a dish. Remove the string from the chicken.

Add sugar to apricot mixture, if needed, and add salt and pepper to taste. If necessary, mix the cornflour with about 1½ tablespoons of cold water to a paste and use a little or all of it to thicken the jus. Serve with the chicken.

*   *Tying them is not really necessary, as long as the parcels are packed tightly together. However, the stuffing is guaranteed not to escape if they are tied securely.*

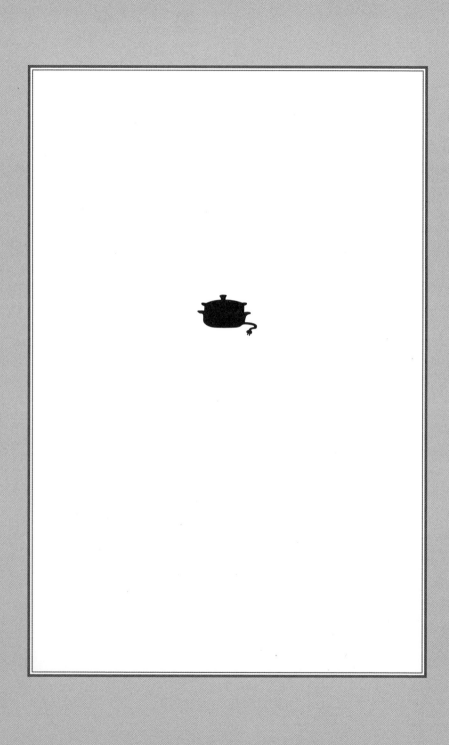

BEEF

ABERDEEN SAUSAGE

Serves 6
(for a 3.2–4.5 litre slow cooker)

Aberdeen sausage is often served cold. It can be made with pork and veal or beef mince.

In this recipe the meat makes its own spicy onion gravy as it cooks.

Aberdeen Sausage
2 onions
300g lean beef mince or pork and veal mince
300g lean sausage mince
250g lean bacon, rind removed, finely diced
2 cups fresh breadcrumbs
3 teaspoons soy sauce
3 teaspoons Worcestershire sauce
1 tablespoon tomato sauce (ketchup)
3 teaspoons plum or barbecue sauce
1 egg, lightly beaten
¼ teaspoon salt

Gravy
¼ cup tomato sauce (ketchup)
2 teaspoons white, cider or malt vinegar
2 teaspoons orange juice
2 teaspoons brown sugar
1 tablespoon sweet chilli sauce

Cut one of the onions into quarters, then cut the quarters into thin slices. Place in the base of the slow cooker. Grate the other onion, place in a bowl with the rest of the sausage ingredients and mix until well combined. Shape into a loaf.

Mix together the gravy ingredients and spread half over the onion in the base of the cooker. Place the sausage loaf on top and spread the remaining gravy mixture over.

Place the lid on the cooker and cook for 4 hours on High or 8 hours on Low.

Remove the sausage from the cooker with a slotted spoon and cut into slices. Drizzle on some of the gravy from the cooker, and serve with creamy mashed potatoes and seasonal vegetables.

BEEF BOURGUIGNON

Serves 6–8
(for a 3.5–4.5 litre slow cooker)

1.5kg lean stewing beef, such as chuck or blade
150g lean rindless bacon
12 small onions
125g mushrooms
1 teaspoon salt
1 teaspoon stock powder
¼ teaspoon dried thyme
¼ teaspoon dried marjoram
1 cup red wine
2 teaspoons tomato sauce (ketchup)
2 teaspoons Worcestershire sauce
1 tablespoon cornflour (optional)

Cut all visible fat from the beef and cut into 1.25cm dice. Dice the bacon and peel the onions. Place all in the slow cooker and stir to combine. Wipe and slice the mushrooms and place on top.

Mix together the salt, stock powder, thyme, marjoram, red wine, tomato sauce and Worcestershire sauce and pour over contents of cooker.

Place lid on cooker and cook for 4–5 hours on High or 8–9 hours on Low.

If necessary, mix the cornflour with about 2 tablespoons of cold water to a paste and use a little or all of it to thicken the dish. Add salt and pepper to taste.

BEEF CANNELLONI

Serves 4–6
(for a 3.5–4.5 litre slow cooker)

1 small onion
1 clove garlic
250g good quality beef mince
1 cup fresh breadcrumbs
2 teaspoons plum sauce
2 teaspoons Worcestershire sauce
2 teaspoons soy sauce
60g fetta, crumbled
1½ teaspoons salt
1 egg
2 tablespoons tomato paste
2½ cups diced canned or bottled tomatoes,
    or passata
1 teaspoon sugar
250g instant cannelloni shells
½ cup grated tasty cheese
¼ cup freshly grated parmesan

Peel and grate the onion. Peel and crush the garlic. Add the onion and garlic to the mince and breadcrumbs, then mix together with the sauces, fetta and ½ teaspoon of salt. Whisk the egg lightly, then add to the meat and mix until very well combined.

In a separate bowl, mix together the tomato paste, tomatoes, sugar, the remaining salt and ½ cup of water. Place one-third of the tomato sauce in the base of the slow cooker.

Fill the cannelloni shells with the meat mixture.*

Put a layer of cannelloni over the tomato sauce base, then spread a small layer of the tomato sauce over it. Add another layer of cannelloni, then spread over the last of the tomato sauce on top.

Mix together the tasty cheese and parmesan and sprinkle over the top of the tomato sauce.

Place lid on cooker and cook for 2½ hours on High.

*   *It is much easier to fill the cannelloni shells using a piping bag. Disposable piping bags are available at most supermarkets.*

BEEF OLIVES

Serves 6
(for a 3.5–4.5 litre slow cooker)

1 onion
125g bacon
2 cups fresh breadcrumbs
¾ teaspoon dried thyme
½ teaspoon salt
1 egg
2 teaspoons sherry
1kg barbecue steak, thinly sliced
½ small red capsicum
¾ cup diced fresh, canned or bottled tomatoes
1 tablespoon tomato sauce (ketchup)
1 tablespoon tomato paste
1 teaspoon stock powder
1 tablespoon brandy

Peel and grate the onion. Remove any rind from the bacon and dice finely. Place in a bowl with the thyme and salt. Lightly whisk the egg and add to the mixture, along with the sherry. Mix well.

Lay the meat out on a board and flatten, if necessary, with a meat hammer. Cut into approximately 10cm x 12cm pieces.

Divide the breadcrumb mixture between the pieces of meat and spread out over each piece. Roll up the meat and tie with butcher's string to secure filling, if you like.* Place in the slow cooker.

Remove the stalk, seeds and membrane from the capsicum. Dice finely and scatter over the meat.

Mix together the tomato, tomato sauce, tomato paste, stock powder and brandy and pour over the contents of the cooker.

Place lid on cooker and cook for 4 hours on High or 7–8 hours on Low.

Remove string from each 'olive' before serving.

*   *This step is a little time consuming. I generally don't do it, but just pack the 'olives' tightly together in the cooker. Inevitably this allows a little of the stuffing to escape, but still equally delicious — the gravy is just a little more textured.*

BOBOTIE

Serves 4–6
(for a 3.5–4.5 litre slow cooker)

2 slices white bread
1 cup milk
1 onion
2 tablespoons olive oil
750g good quality beef mince
2 teaspoons curry powder
1 tablespoon brown sugar
1 tablespoon vinegar
1 tablespoon chutney
1 teaspoon salt
½ teaspoon finely grated lemon rind
2 eggs

Break up the bread into 2cm squares into a bowl and pour the milk over it. Leave to stand for a few minutes.

Meanwhile, peel and dice the onion. Heat the oil and sauté the mince and onion until the mince is lightly browned. Add the curry powder and cook for a further minute. Turn down the heat, then add the sugar, vinegar, chutney, salt and lemon rind. Squeeze the bread, reserving the milk, and add to the mince mixture. Stir as you cook for a further minute. Spoon into the slow cooker.

Beat the eggs with the reserved milk and pour evenly over the mixture in the cooker.

Place lid on cooker and cook for 2 hours on High or 3 hours on Low.

BOLOGNESE SAUCE I

Serves 4–6
(for a 3.5–4.5 litre slow cooker)

2 teaspoons olive oil
600g best quality beef mince
250g pork mince
3 onions
5 cloves garlic
1½ cups diced fresh, canned or bottled tomatoes
¾ cup tomato paste
2 teaspoons dried oregano
2 teaspoons brown sugar
1 tablespoon smooth-textured chutney (any sort)
3 teaspoons Worcestershire sauce
1½ teaspoons salt
½ cup stock or water
3 teaspoons cornflour (optional)

Heat the oil in a large heavy-based saucepan. Add the beef and pork mince and cook until lightly browned, stirring every now and then to break it up.

Peel and chop the onions. Peel and crush the garlic. Add to the pan and cook for a further 2 minutes. Transfer the mince mixture to the slow cooker and add remaining ingredients, except the cornflour. Mix well.

Place lid on cooker and cook for 4 hours on High or 7 hours on Low.

If necessary, mix the cornflour with about 2 tablespoons of cold water to a paste and use a little or all of it to thicken the sauce, stirring through while still hot.

BOLOGNESE SAUCE 2

Serves 6
(for a 3.5–4.5 litre slow cooker)

In this recipe diced beef is used in place of minced meat.

1kg stewing beef (such as gravy beef, chuck or blade
   steak)
60g lean bacon, rind removed, diced
2 onions
1 green or red capsicum, deseeded
125g mushrooms
2 cloves garlic, crushed
3 teaspoons chutney (any sort)
3 teaspoons Worcestershire sauce
2 teaspoons soy sauce
2 teaspoons sweet chilli sauce (optional)
1 teaspoon seedless jam (any sort)
1½ teaspoons brown sugar
2 teaspoons beef or chicken stock powder
2 tablespoons tomato paste
1 sprig rosemary
1 bay leaf
½ teaspoon salt
400g can diced tomatoes
2 teaspoons chopped rosemary
3 teaspoons cornflour mixed to a paste with 1 tablespoon
   cold water
pasta or jacket potatoes, to serve

Remove all visible fat from the meat and cut into small dice (about 6mm). Place in the slow cooker with the bacon.

Peel and dice the onions and dice the capsicum and mushrooms. Place in the cooker with the garlic, chutney, sauces, jam, sugar, stock powder, tomato paste, sprig of rosemary, bay leaf, salt and tomatoes. Stir to combine.

Place the lid on the cooker and cook for 4–5 hours on High or 8–9 hours on Low until meat is tender. Remove the lid, stir in the chopped rosemary and thicken the sauce with the cornflour paste.

Replace the lid on the cooker and cook for 10 minutes more on High. Add salt and pepper and maybe a little extra sugar to taste.

Serve as a pasta sauce or as a topping for jacket potatoes.

Hint: *Any leftovers can be used as a pie filling, or spread on split hamburger bun halves, topped with cheese and baked in the oven at 170°C for 10 minutes until the cheese has melted.*

BRAISED BEEF CHEEKS WITH MUSHROOMS

Serves 4
(for a 3.2–4.5 litre slow cooker)

750g beef cheeks
250g mushrooms
1 onion, diced
1 tablespoon tomato paste
1 cup beef stock (or 1 cup water with ¾ teaspoon stock
    powder)
½ teaspoon salt
2 sprigs thyme (optional)
3 teaspoons cornflour mixed to a paste with 1 tablespoon
    cold water (optional)

Remove all visible fat from the beef cheeks and cut the beef into 1.5cm cubes.

Cut the mushrooms into 1cm pieces.

Add the beef and mushrooms to the slow cooker together with the onion, tomato paste, stock, salt and thyme, if using. Stir to combine.

Place the lid on the cooker and cook for 4–6 hours on High or 8–10 hours on Low until the beef is tender.

If necessary, thicken the mixture with some or all of the cornflour paste, replace the lid and cook for 10 minutes on High. Add salt and pepper to taste.

Serve with creamy mashed potatoes and seasonal vegetables.

BRAISED BEEF WITH CARAWAY PUMPKIN DUMPLINGS

Serves 6
(for a 3.5–4.5 litre slow cooker)

800g–1kg stewing beef, such as chuck, blade
   or gravy beef
2 onions
1 clove garlic
1 tablespoon tomato sauce (ketchup)
2 teaspoons soy sauce
2 teaspoons Worcestershire sauce
1½ tablespoons plum or apricot jam
1 teaspoon salt
½ cup stock or water
3 teaspoons cornflour

Caraway Pumpkin Dumplings
1 cup self-raising flour
½ teaspoon baking powder
½ teaspoon salt
3 teaspoons butter
1 teaspoon caraway seeds
½ cup mashed pumpkin
1 teaspoon lemon juice
1 tablespoon milk

Remove any visible fat from the meat and c-ut into 2cm dice. Peel and chop the onions. Peel and crush the garlic. Place all in the slow cooker with the tomato sauce, soy sauce, Worcestershire sauce, jam, salt and stock or water.

Place lid on cooker and cook for 4–5 hours on High, or until meat is tender.

Mix the cornflour with about 2 tablespoons of cold water to a paste, and use a little or all of it to thicken the mixture. Add salt and pepper to taste, then replace lid.

To make the caraway pumpkin dumplings, mix the flour with the baking powder and salt, then rub in the butter with your fingertips until the mixture resembles fine breadcrumbs. Mix in the caraway seeds. Make a well in the centre and add the pumpkin, lemon juice and enough of the milk to make a soft dough. Place tablespoonfuls of dough on top of the simmering beef.

Take a piece of baking paper slightly larger than the cooker and spray one side with cooking oil or grease with butter. Place the paper greased-side down over the cooker and replace the lid. Cook for 45 minutes on High.

BRAISED STEAK AND MUSHROOMS

Serves 6
(for a 3.5–4.5 litre slow cooker)

2 onions
600g mushrooms
1kg lean diced beef (chuck or blade is ideal)
1 tablespoon lemon juice
1 teaspoon salt
1 tablespoon cornflour (optional)

Peel and dice the onions. Wipe and slice the mushrooms. Add to the slow cooker with the beef, lemon juice, salt and 2 cups of water.

Place lid on cooker and cook for 4 hours on High or 8 hours on Low.

If necessary, mix the cornflour with about 2 tablespoons of cold water to a paste and use a little or all of it to thicken the mixture.

Add salt and pepper to taste.

Hint: *This dish also makes an excellent filling for pies.*

CABBAGE ROLLS

Serves 6
(for a 3.5–4.5 litre slow cooker)

This is a wonderful dish to come home to after a day out. It is a complete meal unto itself, but can be served with steamed seasonal vegetables or fresh crusty chunks of bread to soak up the juices.

Cabbage Rolls
6–8 cabbage leaves
2 rashers lean bacon, rind removed, finely diced
500g beef or pork and veal mince
½ teaspoon salt (optional)
¼ cup short-grain rice
1 onion, grated or finely chopped
½ cup fresh breadcrumbs
1½ teaspoons sweet paprika
1 teaspoon chopped thyme (optional)
2 teaspoons soy sauce
2 teaspoons Worcestershire sauce
1 clove garlic, crushed

Sauce
1 tablespoon tomato paste
½ cup tomato sauce (ketchup)
1 teaspoon chicken stock powder
juice of ½ lemon
2 teaspoons chutney (any sort)
1 tablespoon brown sugar
2 cloves garlic, crushed

½ cup water

½ teaspoon salt

2 teaspoons cornflour mixed to a paste with 1 tablespoon
    cold water (optional)

Remove the tough core from the centre of the cabbage leaves. Bring a saucepan of water to the boil and immerse the cabbage leaves for 3 minutes. Drain while preparing the filling.

Mix together the bacon, mince, salt, rice, onion, breadcrumbs, paprika, thyme, sauces and garlic in a bowl until well combined.

Wrap portions of the meat mixture in the cabbage leaves (you may need to cut them up a bit). Place in the slow cooker.

To make the sauce, mix all the ingredients except the cornflour paste together and pour over the cabbage rolls.

Place the lid on the cooker and cook for 4 hours on High or 7–8 hours on Low.

Remove the rolls to a serving dish and, if needed, whisk some or all of the cornflour paste into the sauce, cook for 10 minutes on High to thicken. Add salt and pepper to taste.

CARBONADE OF BEEF

Serves 4
(for a 3.5–4.5 litre slow cooker)

750g lean stewing beef, such as chuck, blade or gravy beef
2 onions
1½ cups beer
2 teaspoons Worcestershire sauce
1½ teaspoons salt
1 small French bread stick
3 teaspoons seeded mustard
¾ cup grated tasty cheese, or half grated tasty cheese and
    half grated parmesan cheese
2 teaspoons cornflour (optional)
creamy mashed potato, to serve

Cube beef, remove any fat. Peel and finely dice the onions. Place in slow cooker with the beer, Worcestershire sauce and salt. Stir to combine.

Place lid on cooker and cook for 4–5 hours on High or 8 hours on Low.

Cut the bread stick into 2cm slices (you need 8–10 slices). Spread each slice with mustard. Place bread slices mustard-side up on top of the beef mixture and press down into the juices. Scatter the cheese over the top. Replace lid and cook for a further 10 minutes, or until the cheese has melted.

Remove the bread slices with a slotted spoon. If necessary, mix the cornflour with 1 tablespoon of cold water to a paste and use a little or all of it to thicken the carbonade. Add salt and pepper to taste. Top each serve with two slices of the bread and creamy mashed potato.

CHILLI CON CARNE

Serves 6
(for a 3.5–4.5 litre slow cooker)

This dish is more about the flavour of the spices than the heat. However, if you would like to add some heat, try adding I teaspoon dried chilli flakes to the simmering mixture, or a fresh long red chilli or two (diced), or even a tablespoon of sweet chilli sauce.

    1 tablespoon olive oil
    1kg good quality beef mince
    2 onions
    4 cloves garlic
    2 cups diced fresh, canned or bottled tomatoes
    ½ cup tomato paste
    1 tablespoon chutney (preferably tomato)
    3 teaspoons Worcestershire sauce
    1 to 2 tablespoons sweet chilli sauce or ½ to 1 teaspoon
        dried chilli flakes
    2 teaspoons soy sauce
    5 teaspoons ground cumin
    3 teaspoons dried oregano
    2 teaspoons brown sugar
    1½ teaspoons salt
    410g can red kidney beans, drained
    3 teaspoons cornflour (optional)
    couscous, corn chips or baked jacket potatoes,
        to serve

Heat the oil in a heavy-based saucepan and cook the mince until lightly browned.

Peel and finely dice the onion. Peel and crush the garlic. Add to the saucepan and cook for a further 2 minutes. Transfer to the slow cooker. Add the tomato, tomato paste, chutney, Worcestershire sauce, sweet chilli sauce or chilli flakes, soy sauce, cumin, oregano, sugar, salt and 1 cup of water.

Place lid on cooker and cook for 3½ hours on High or 6 hours on Low.

Add the beans and cook for a further 20 minutes on High. Add salt and pepper to taste.

If necessary, mix the cornflour with about 2 tablespoons of cold water to a paste and use a little or all of it to thicken the mixture, stirring it through while very hot. Cook for a further 2 minutes.

Serve with couscous, corn chips or baked jacket potatoes.

COCKTAIL MEATBALLS

Makes 24 meatballs
(for a 3.5–4.5 litre slow cooker)

These meatballs are handy to have as delicious nibbles for a party. However, they are equally suitable to serve as a main meal with seasonal vegetables.

Meatballs

600g good quality beef mince
1 onion, grated
1 egg, lightly whisked
1 slice of bread, crumbed
3 teaspoons soy sauce
3 teaspoons Worcestershire sauce
2 teaspoons chutney (any sort), mashed with a fork if
    chunky
½ teaspoon salt

Sauce

½ cup tomato sauce (ketchup)
juice of ½ orange
½ teaspoon salt
1 tablespoon balsamic vinegar
1 tablespoon soy sauce
¼ cup firmly packed brown sugar
1½ teaspoons cornflour mixed to a paste with 1 tablespoon
    cold water (optional)

To make the meatballs, mix together the mince, onion, egg, breadcrumbs, sauces, chutney and salt. Roll into walnut-sized balls and place in the slow cooker.

To make the sauce, mix together the tomato sauce, orange juice, salt, vinegar, soy sauce and sugar.

Spoon the sauce over the meatballs and place the lid on the cooker. Cook for 3½ hours on High or 6–7 hours on Low.

Lift out the meatballs with a slotted spoon. If desired, while the sauce is still hot, thicken it slightly by stirring in some or all of the cornflour paste, replace the lid and cook for 10 minutes on High. Add salt and pepper to taste.

CORNED BEEF

Serves 6
(for a 3.5–4.5 litre slow cooker)

1 onion
1 carrot
1 stalk celery
1.5kg piece corned silverside
1 teaspoon mixed spice
8 cloves
10 peppercorns
2 tablespoons brown sugar
2 tablespoons vinegar

Peel and chop the onion. Peel the carrot and cut into chunks. Slice the celery. Place the silverside, vegetables, mixed spice, cloves, peppercorns, brown sugar and vinegar in the slow cooker.

Add enough water to come two-thirds up the silverside.

Place lid on cooker and cook for 4–5 hours on High or 8–9 hours on Low.

Cumberland Beef

Serves 6
(for a 3.5–4.5 litre slow cooker)

1.5kg roasting beef (such as topside or blade)
juice of 1 lemon
juice of 1 orange
1 tablespoon Dijon mustard
1 tablespoon tomato sauce (ketchup)
2 teaspoons Worcestershire sauce
3 tablespoons Marsala
3 tablespoons redcurrant jelly
1 teaspoon beef stock powder
1 sprig rosemary
3 teaspoons cornflour mixed to a paste with 1 tablespoon
   cold water (optional)

Remove all visible fat from the beef. Place the beef in the slow cooker.

Mix together the rest of the ingredients except the rosemary and cornflour paste and pour over the beef. Place the sprig of rosemary on top. Cover with the lid and cook for 5–6 hours on High or 10–12 hours on Low until the meat is tender.

Remove the beef to a plate, cover with foil and leave to rest for 15 minutes before slicing.

Meanwhile, turn the cooker to High (if set on Low) and stir in the cornflour paste, if needed. Replace the lid and cook for 10 minutes. Add salt and pepper to taste.

Drizzle the sauce from the cooker over the sliced meat and serve with seasonal vegetables.

DEVILLED BEEF

Serves 4–6
(for a 3.5–4.5 litre slow cooker)

1kg gravy beef or similar
⅓ cup tomato sauce (ketchup)
2 tablespoons vinegar
1 tablespoon Worcestershire sauce
1 tablespoon brown sugar
2 teaspoons seeded mustard
2 teaspoons lemon juice
2 teaspoons sherry
1½ teaspoons salt
3 teaspoons cornflour
mashed potato and seasonal vegetables, to serve

Remove all visible fat from the beef and cut into approximately
7cm x 4cm pieces.

Mix together the tomato sauce, vinegar, Worcestershire sauce, brown
sugar, mustard, lemon juice, sherry and salt. Pour 3 tablespoons of the
mixture over the base of the slow cooker and place the beef on top.
Pour the remaining liquid over the beef.

Place lid on cooker and cook for 4–5 hours on High or 8–9 hours
on Low.

Meanwhile, mix the cornflour with about 2 tablespoons of cold water to
a paste.

Remove the meat and pour the juices from cooker into a small saucepan. Cook over high heat on stovetop until it has reduced to about half its original volume. Thicken with a little or all of the cornflour paste to make a smooth gravy. Add salt and pepper to taste.

Return meat to cooker and cover with the gravy. Place lid on cooker and cook on High for a few more minutes.

Serve with creamy mashed potato and seasonal vegetables.

FRUITY BEEF OLIVES

Serves 6–8

(for a 4.5 litre slow cooker)

I usually make this amount to feed quite a few. By all means halve the quantities and cook it in a 3.2–3.5 litre capacity slow cooker.

850g thinly sliced beef (such as topside or round) (about
    8–10 slices)

500g sausage mince

1 onion, grated

½ cup diced dried apricots

1 tablespoon chopped fresh rosemary or 1 teaspoon dried
    rosemary

½ teaspoon salt

3 teaspoons chutney (any sort)

3 teaspoons soy sauce

3 teaspoons tomato sauce (ketchup), plus ½ cup extra

3 teaspoons Worcestershire sauce

1 cup fresh breadcrumbs (about 2 slices of bread, crumbed)

¼ cup sherry

½ teaspoon mustard powder

½ teaspoon stock powder (any sort)

2 teaspoons white or cider vinegar

2 tablespoons water

3 teaspoons cornflour mixed to a paste with 1 tablespoon
    cold water

Remove all visible fat from the beef.

Mix together the sausage mince, onion, apricots, rosemary, salt, chutney, soy sauce, tomato sauce, Worcestershire sauce and breadcrumbs.

Lay each slice of beef out flat and spread with the sausage meat filling. Roll up and place, seam side down, in the slow cooker, layering as needed.

Mix together the extra tomato sauce, the sherry, mustard powder, stock powder, vinegar and water and pour over the beef rolls.

Place the lid on the cooker and cook for 4–5 hours on High or 8–10 hours on Low until meat is tender.

Remove the rolls from the cooker with a slotted spoon and keep warm.

Stir the cornflour paste into the sauce, replace the lid and cook for 5–10 minutes more on High until thickened slightly. Add salt and pepper to taste.

Serve with seasonal vegetables.

GINGER AND RED CAPSICUM BEEF

Serves 4–6
(for a 3.5–4.5 litre slow cooker)

1 large red capsicum
1kg blade steak
1 tablespoon grated green ginger root
½ tablespoon crushed garlic
2 tablespoons tomato sauce (ketchup)
2 tablespoons plum sauce
1 tablespoon Worcestershire sauce
1 tablespoon soy sauce
2 tablespoons cider vinegar
1 tablespoon sherry
1½ teaspoons salt
1 tablespoon cornflour (optional)
steamed rice, to serve

Remove stalk, seeds and membrane from capsicum and cut into strips.
Remove any visible fat from the steak and cut into strips. Place in the
cooker. Add remaining ingredients, except the cornflour. Stir to
combine.

Place lid on cooker and cook for 4 hours on High or 7–8 hours on Low.

If necessary, mix the cornflour with about 2 tablespoons of cold water
to a paste and use a little or all of it to thicken the dish. Add salt and
pepper to taste. Serve with steamed rice.

GLAZED SCOTCH EGG MEATLOAF

Serves 4–6

(for a 4.5 litre slow cooker)

6 eggs
250g carrots
1½ teaspoons chopped thyme
750g beef mince
1 onion, coarsely grated or very finely chopped
1 cup fresh breadcrumbs
1 tablespoon chutney (any sort)
1 teaspoon salt
3 teaspoons barbecue sauce
3 teaspoons Worcestershire sauce
3 teaspoons soy sauce
3 teaspoons tomato sauce (ketchup)

Topping

¼ cup tomato sauce (ketchup)
1 tablespoon sweet chilli sauce
½ cup grated tasty cheese

Place 5 of the eggs in a small saucepan and cover with cold water. Bring to the boil, then immediately reduce the heat and simmer for 4 minutes. Drain and cover with cold water. Leave to stand for 4 minutes, then remove the shells by lightly tapping all around and peeling off. Rinse in cold water to remove any shell that clings and set aside while preparing the meatloaf.

Peel and thinly slice the carrots. Grease the slow cooker then place the carrots on the base and sprinkle with the thyme.

In a large bowl, combine the beef, onion, the remaining egg (lightly whisked), the breadcrumbs, chutney, salt and sauces and mix until well combined.

Place a large piece of plastic wrap on the work surface. Shape the meat mixture into a rectangle approximately 23 x 19cm. Place the boiled eggs end to end along the centre. Using the plastic wrap, roll up the meat Swiss-roll style to enclose the eggs completely and evenly, shaping it into a loaf. Again, using the plastic wrap for support, place the loaf in the slow cooker on top of the carrots, then carefully remove the plastic wrap.

To make the topping, mix together the tomato sauce and sweet chilli sauce and spoon over the top of the meatloaf.

Place the lid on the cooker and cook for 3 hours on High or 6 hours on Low.

Remove the lid from the cooker and sprinkle the grated cheese over the top of the meatloaf. Replace the lid and cook for 5 minutes on High until the cheese has melted.

While still in the cooker, cut the meatloaf into thick slices and lift out of the cooker with a slotted spoon or egg flip.

Serve with seasonal vegetables and tomato sauce (ketchup) or chutney, if desired.

GOULASH WITH HERB DUMPLINGS

Serves 4–6

(for a 3.5–4.5 litre slow cooker)

2 onions

3 cloves garlic

750g lean chuck or blade beef

2 cups diced fresh, canned or bottled tomatoes

3 tablespoons tomato paste

2 tablespoons sweet paprika

2 teaspoons vegetable or beef stock powder

Herb Dumplings

2 teaspoons butter

1 cup self-raising flour

½ teaspoon salt

1½ teaspoons chopped thyme

1 tablespoon finely chopped parsley

milk, to combine

Peel and dice the onions. Peel and crush the garlic. Trim all visible fat from the meat and dice. Place the onion and garlic in the slow cooker, then put the meat on top with the tomato, tomato paste, paprika, stock powder and 1 cup of water. Mix to combine.

Place lid on cooker and cook for 4 hours on High or 8 hours on Low. Add salt and pepper to taste. Replace lid on cooker.

About 30 minutes before the end of cooking time, turn the cooker setting to High (if it has been cooking on Low), in preparation for cooking the dumplings.

To make the herb dumplings, rub the butter into the combined flour and salt with your fingertips until the mixture resembles fine breadcrumbs. Add the thyme and parsley, and mix to a soft dough with a little milk. Roll into walnut-size balls.

Remove lid from cooker. Place dumplings on top of goulash. Have ready a piece of baking paper slightly larger than the cooker and spray one side with cooking oil. Place paper greased-side down over the cooker. Place lid on top and cook for 30 minutes on High.

HEDGEHOGS

Serves 6
(for a 3.5–4.5 litre slow cooker)

A popular dish with children. The meatballs contain long grain rice which stick out the sides of the meatballs when the rice swell with the heat and moisture of the soup, hence the name 'Hedgehogs'.

500g can good quality tomato soup
½ cup diced canned or bottled tomatoes
1 large or 2 smaller onions
1 egg
½ cup fresh breadcrumbs
700g good quality beef mince
1 tablespoon Worcestershire sauce
2 teaspoons soy sauce
3 teaspoons chutney
1 teaspoon salt
⅔ cup long grain rice

Pour the soup into the slow cooker. Add 2¼ cups of water and the tomato and stir to combine. Turn the cooker setting to High while preparing the meatballs.

Peel and grate the onion. Whisk the egg until well broken up. Combine all with the remaining ingredients. Roll into walnut-size balls and drop into the soup mixture. Make sure the liquid covers all the meatballs.

Place lid on cooker and cook for 4 hours on High or 7–8 hours on Low.

Honey Spiced Corned Beef with Honey Mustard Glaze

Serves 6–8
(for a 3.5–5 litre slow cooker)

While it is not necessary to pour the glaze over the meat, it adds a whole new dimension of flavour and only takes a few extra minutes. Any leftover corned beef is delicious the next day in sandwiches with pickles.

2kg lean corned silverside
3 tablespoons honey
2 tablespoons balsamic vinegar
1 star anise
10 allspice berries or 1½ teaspoons ground allspice
1 onion, halved
1 tablespoon Worcestershire sauce

Glaze
⅓ cup honey
2 teaspoons soy sauce
1 tablespoon balsamic vinegar
1 teaspoon mustard powder
1 tablespoon brown sugar

Place the meat in the slow cooker and pour in enough water to come three-quarters of the way up the side. Add the honey, vinegar, spices, onion and Worcestershire sauce and stir to combine.

Place the lid on the cooker and cook for 5–6 hours on High or 10–12 hours on Low until meat is tender.

Remove the meat from the cooker and place in a baking dish.

Heat the oven to 180°C.

Mix together all the glaze ingredients and pour over the meat. Place in the oven for 15–20 minutes, basting once or twice with the glaze during cooking.

Remove from the oven and leave to rest for at least 20 minutes before slicing.

Serve with mashed potatoes and seasonal vegetables.

LASAGNE

Serves 6
(for a 3.5–4.5 litre slow cooker)

1½ tablespoons cornflour
⅓ cup cold milk
1 egg
2½ cups milk
¼ cup grated parmesan cheese,
   plus 1 tablespoon extra
⅔ cup grated tasty cheese
5 cups Bolognese sauce (see recipe on page 110)
250g instant lasagne sheets

To make the cheese sauce, mix the cornflour with the cold milk to a paste.

Heat the milk to boiling point and thicken with the cornflour paste. Simmer for 2 minutes, stirring constantly, then whisk in the egg. Stir through the parmesan and half the tasty cheese. Add salt and white pepper to taste.

Spread one-third of the Bolognese sauce over the base of the cooker and cover with one-third of lasagne sheets, broken into pieces to fit. Top with half of remaining Bolognese sauce, then one-third of cheese sauce and half of remaining lasagne sheets, then repeat these layers. Finish with a layer of cheese sauce.

Combine the extra parmesan and remaining tasty cheese and sprinkle over the top.

Place lid on cooker and cook for 3 hours on Low.

MEATBALLS WITH SPICY BARBECUE SAUCE

Serves 4
(for a 3.5–4.5 litre slow cooker)

Meatballs

1 onion
½ stalk celery (optional)
600g good quality beef mince
½ cup fresh breadcrumbs
1 egg
2 teaspoons soy sauce
2 teaspoons Worcestershire sauce
2 teaspoons chutney (any sort)
2 teaspoons tomato sauce (ketchup)
¾ teaspoon salt

Spicy Barbecue Sauce

½ cup tomato sauce (ketchup)
1 tablespoon white or cider vinegar
2 teaspoons brown sugar
2 teaspoons honey
2 teaspoons sherry
1 tablespoon sweet chilli sauce
¼ teaspoon mustard powder

Peel and grate the onion and very finely chop the celery. Place in a bowl with rest of ingredients and mix well. Roll into walnut-size balls.

To make the spicy barbecue sauce, place all ingredients in a small saucepan and heat until the sugar is dissolved.

Cover base of the slow cooker with meatballs, leaving a little space between each. Spoon a layer of the sauce over the meatballs. Place remaining meatballs evenly over the top (there will probably only be a few extra for this). Spoon the remaining sauce over the top.

Place lid on cooker and cook for 3½–4 hours on High.

Remove the meatballs with a slotted spoon. Serve meatballs drizzled with a little of the spicy barbecue sauce.

MOROCCAN BEEF

Serves 4–6
(for a 3.5–4.5 litre slow cooker)

750g lean diced beef
1 onion, finely chopped
2 cloves garlic, crushed
2 teaspoons finely grated orange rind
1 teaspoon ground turmeric
1½ teaspoons sweet paprika
2 teaspoons ground cumin
1 teaspoon ground coriander
½ teaspoon garam masala
2 ~~teaspoons ground cinnamon~~ *cushew nuts onto wingapots!*
2 teaspoons chutney (any sort)
2 teaspoons quince or redcurrant jelly
1 tablespoon honey
1¼ cups chicken or beef stock (or 1¼ cups water with
  ¾ teaspoon stock powder)
2 teaspoons cornflour mixed to a paste with 1 tablespoon
  cold water (optional)

Place all the ingredients except the cornflour paste in the slow cooker
and stir to combine. Place the lid on the cooker and cook for 4–5 hours
on High or 8–10 hours on Low until meat is tender.

Remove the lid and, if needed, thicken the sauce by stirring in some or all
of the cornflour paste. Replace the lid and cook for 10 minutes on High.
Add salt and pepper to taste.

Serve over plain boiled or steamed rice or couscous.

OLD-FASHIONED BEEF CURRY

Serves 4–6
(for a 3.5–4.5 litre slow cooker)

800g lean stewing beef, such as chuck, blade
   or gravy beef
2 onions
2 carrots
½ small parsnip
2 teaspoons curry powder
1 tablespoon soy sauce
1 tablespoon Worcestershire sauce
1 tablespoon chutney (any sort)
1 tablespoon apricot jam
1½ cups stock or water
1½ teaspoons salt
1 tablespoon cornflour (optional)

Trim all visible fat from the meat and dice. Peel and dice the onions.
Peel and slice the carrots and parsnip. Place in the slow cooker, along
with the curry powder, soy sauce, Worcestershire sauce, chutney, jam,
stock or water and salt. Stir well to combine.

Place lid on cooker and cook for 4–5 hours on High or 8 hours on Low.

If necessary, mix the cornflour with about 2 tablespoons of cold water
to a paste and use a little or all of it to thicken the dish. Add salt and
pepper to taste.

Osso Buco

Serves 4
(for a 3.5–4.5 litre slow cooker)

1kg shin beef on the bone (about 3 pieces)
1 onion
1 carrot
1 stalk celery
2 cloves garlic
1 teaspoon dried thyme
1 sprig thyme
1 teaspoon salt
2 large tablespoons tomato paste
1 cup white wine
1½ cups diced fresh, canned or bottled tomatoes
1 tablespoon cornflour

Cut the outer fat from the meat. Peel and dice the onion. Peel and slice the carrot. Cut the celery into 1cm slices. Peel and crush the garlic. Place all the vegetables in the slow cooker and place the meat on top.

Sprinkle over the thyme and salt. Spread the tomato paste over the top, then pour in the wine and tomato.

Place lid on cooker and cook for 5 hours on High or 8–9 hours on Low.

Mix the cornflour with about 2 tablespoons of cold water to a paste and use a little or all of it to thicken the sauce. Add salt and pepper to taste.

PINEAPPLE MEATBALLS

Serves 4–6
(for a 4–4.5 litre slow cooker)

Although this sounds very 1970-ish, it is a dish that is always extremely popular with the children of our household — and adults too for that matter. Unless you have a great aversion to pineapple, it is well worth making.

When I make this, I often double the meatball mixture and put half away in the fridge for the next night to make hamburgers.

Meatballs
600g lean beef mince
1 small onion, grated
1 egg
½ cup fresh breadcrumbs
3 teaspoons soy sauce
2 teaspoons Worcestershire sauce
2 teaspoons tomato sauce (ketchup)
2 teaspoons chutney (any sort)
½ teaspoon salt

Sauce
1 red capsicum, deseeded
1 large stalk celery
1 small onion
1 carrot
450g can pineapple pieces in natural juice
1 tablespoon soy sauce
2 tablespoons sugar

2 tablespoons white vinegar

1 teaspoon chicken or vegetable stock powder

2 teaspoons cornflour mixed to a paste with 1 tablespoon
    cold water (optional)

boiled or steamed rice, to serve

To make the meatballs, mix all the ingredients together well and set aside.

To make the sauce, cut the capsicum, celery, onion and carrot into thin strips approximately 4cm long and place in the base of the slow cooker. Stir to combine.

Roll the meat mixture into walnut-sized balls and place on top of the vegetables in the cooker.

Drain the pineapple and reserve the juice. Place 1 cup of the pineapple pieces in a bowl, add the reserved juice and the rest of the ingredients except the cornflour paste and mix well. Pour over the meatballs.

Place the lid on the cooker and cook for 4 hours on High or 7–8 hours on Low.

Turn the cooker to High (if set on Low) and lift the meatballs out with a slotted spoon. Keep warm.

If needed, thicken the sauce with some or all of the cornflour paste, stirring through while still hot. Replace the lid and cook for a further 10 minutes on High. Add salt and pepper to taste.

Serve the meatballs over plain rice and drizzle the sauce over the top.

Hint: *The rest of the pineapple can be served with cereal for breakfast, or if you are especially fond of it, all of the pineapple can be used in the sauce.*

POT ROAST OF BEEF

Serves 4–6
(for a 3.5–4.5 litre slow cooker)

1 small onion
1 carrot
1 small parsnip
1.5kg piece lean topside, all outer fat removed
1 teaspoon dried mixed herbs
½ cup red wine
½ cup tomato sauce
3 teaspoons cornflour

Peel and finely chop the onion. Peel and slice the carrot and parsnip.

Place the meat in the slow cooker, add the vegetables and top with the herbs, ¼ cup of water, the red wine and tomato sauce (in this order).

Place lid on cooker and cook for 4 hours on High or 8 hours on Low or until tender.

Remove the meat and vegetables from the cooker. Mix the cornflour with ¼ cup of cold water to a paste and use a little of it to thicken the gravy. Add salt and pepper to taste.

PULLED BEEF

Serves 6
(for a 3.2–4 litre slow cooker)

1.5–2kg piece of boneless beef (such as topside or blade)
½ cup tomato sauce (ketchup)
1 tablespoon mustard powder
2 tablespoons Worcestershire sauce
3 teaspoons brown sugar
1 teaspoon beef, chicken or vegetable stock powder
1 small onion, grated
¼ teaspoon ground allspice
½ teaspoon dried chilli flakes
¼ cup water
2 scant teaspoons cornflour mixed to a paste with
    1 tablespoon cold water

Remove all visible fat from the meat and place in the slow cooker. In a bowl mix together the rest of the ingredients except the cornflour paste and pour over the top. Place the lid on the cooker and cook for 5–6 hours on High or 11–12 hours on Low until the meat is very tender.

Remove the meat from the slow cooker and shred with forks. Stir the cornflour paste into the liquid in the cooker. Place the lid on the cooker and cook for 10 minutes more on High. Return the shredded meat to the cooker and stir to combine. Add a little hot water or stock if needed to make a tasty moist mixture. Add salt and pepper to taste.

Delicious served hot in crusty bread rolls.

RICH BEEF CASSEROLE

Serves 4–6
(for a 3.5–4.5 litre slow cooker)

2 carrots
1 onion
½ capsicum
750g lean diced beef
½ cup sliced mushrooms (optional)
¼ cup red wine
2 tablespoons tomato sauce (ketchup)
1 tablespoon soy sauce
2 teaspoons Worcestershire sauce
3 teaspoons chutney (any sort)
1 teaspoon salt
3 teaspoons cornflour (optional)

Peel and slice the carrots. Peel and dice the onion. Remove the seeds and membrane from the capsicum and dice. Place in the slow cooker with the beef, mushrooms, if using, wine, sauces, chutney, salt and ½ cup of water.

Place lid on cooker and cook for 4 hours on High or 6 hours on Low.

If necessary, mix cornflour with ¼ cup of cold water to a paste and use a little or all of it to thicken the dish.

Add salt and pepper to taste.

RICH BEEF AND VEGETABLE CASSEROLE

Serves 4–6
(for a 3.2–4.5 litre slow cooker)

750g lean diced beef
1 onion, diced
1 parsnip, sliced
125g mushrooms, sliced
1 green capsicum, deseeded and diced
1 stalk celery, sliced
2 carrots, sliced
1 teaspoon salt
½ cup red wine or port
1 tablespoon tomato paste
1 tablespoon chutney (any sort)
2 teaspoons soy sauce
1 tablespoon Worcestershire sauce
½ cup beef or chicken stock or water
1 tablespoon sweet chilli sauce
2 teaspoons tomato sauce (ketchup)
3 teaspoons cornflour mixed to a paste with 1 tablespoon
    cold water

Place all the ingredients except the cornflour paste in the slow cooker, stir, place the lid on the cooker and cook for 4–5 hours on High or 8–10 hours on Low until meat is tender.

Stir in the cornflour paste, replace the lid and cook for 10 minutes on High to thicken. Add salt and pepper to taste.

Serve with plain boiled or steamed rice or creamy mashed potatoes and seasonal vegetables.

SAUSAGES IN ONION GRAVY

Serves 4–6
(for a 3.2–4.5 litre slow cooker)

1kg extra-lean beef or pork sausages
2 large or 3 medium onions, thinly sliced
1 tablespoon vinegar (any sort)
1½ teaspoons brown sugar
1 tablespoon chutney (any sort)
3 teaspoons Worcestershire sauce
1½ teaspoons mustard powder
½ cup beer (doesn't matter if it's flat)
1½ teaspoons cornflour mixed to a paste with 2 teaspoons
    cold water

Place the sausages and onion in the slow cooker.

Mix together the vinegar, sugar, chutney, Worcestershire sauce, mustard
powder and beer. Pour over the sausages and onion and stir to combine.

Place the lid on the cooker and cook for 3 hours on High or 6 hours on
Low.

Lift out the sausages and thicken the gravy with some or all of the
cornflour paste. Add salt and pepper to taste. Return the sausages to the
sauce, replace the lid and cook for 10 minutes more on High.

Serve with creamy mashed potatoes and seasonal vegetables.

Savoury Beef

Serves 4–6
(for a 3.5–4.5 litre slow cooker)

Savoury beef makes a tasty filling for pies, large or small. To make a quick pie, I keep cooked squares or triangles of puff pastry and place them on top of hot savoury beef straight from the cooker. Leave them there for a few minutes, with the lid off, where they heat through quite rapidly. This dish also makes an excellent base for cottage pie. After cooking, spoon creamy mashed potato over the top and scatter with grated cheese. Replace the lid and leave for a few minutes in the slow cooker until the cheese has melted.

125g lean bacon
1 onion
1 carrot
½ stalk celery
2 teaspoons olive oil
750g good quality beef mince
1½ cups stock, or water with
   2 teaspoons stock powder
1 tablespoon tomato sauce (ketchup)
2 teaspoons Worcestershire sauce
2 teaspoons soy sauce
2 teaspoons sweet chilli sauce
¾ teaspoon salt
1 tablespoon cornflour (optional)
seasonal vegetables, to serve

Remove the rind from the bacon and chop finely. Peel the onion and carrot and chop finely, along with the celery.

Heat the oil in a heavy-based saucepan and cook the bacon and mince until brown. Transfer to the slow cooker.

Pour the stock into the saucepan and bring to the boil, stirring. Pour over the meat. Add the chopped vegetables, then the sauces and salt. Stir to combine.

Place lid on cooker and cook for 4 hours on High or 7–8 hours on Low.

If necessary, mix the cornflour with about 2 tablespoons of cold water to a paste and use a little or all of it to thicken the dish. Add a little extra salt and a little pepper if needed. Serve with seasonal vegetables.

Spiced Beef Strips with Capsicum and Beans

Serves 4

(for a 3.5–4.5 litre slow cooker)

1kg lean beef strips
2 red capsicums
1 onion, cut in half lengthways and thinly sliced
2 cloves garlic, crushed
½ cup diced canned or fresh tomatoes
1 tablespoon wine (red or white)
2 tablespoons Worcestershire sauce
1 tablespoon balsamic vinegar
1½ tablespoons brown sugar
1 tablespoon tomato paste
1 tablespoon sweet chilli sauce
½ teaspoon salt
1 teaspoon sweet paprika
½ teaspoon ground allspice
½ teaspoon ground oregano
3 teaspoons cornflour mixed to a paste with 1 tablespoon
     cold water (optional)
400g can red kidney beans

Place the beef in the slow cooker.

Remove the seeds and cores from the capsicums and cut the flesh into strips the same size as the meat. Add to the beef in the cooker along with the onion and garlic.

Mix together the rest of the ingredients except the cornflour paste and stir into the cooker.

Place the lid on the cooker and cook for 4–5 hours on High or 8–10 hours on Low until the meat is tender.

Thicken the sauce, if needed, with some or all of the cornflour paste. Stir in the beans. Replace the lid and cook for a further 10 minutes on High. Add salt and pepper to taste.

Serve with plain steamed or boiled rice, couscous or creamy mashed potatoes and seasonal vegetables.

SPICY TOMATO MEATBALLS

Serves 4–6
(for a 3.5–4.5 litre slow cooker)

500g can good quality tomato soup
2 teaspoons sweet chilli sauce
2 teaspoons Worcestershire sauce
1 cup water or chicken stock

Meatballs
350g lean beef mince
350g sausage mince
1 slice of bread, crumbed
2 teaspoons soy sauce
2 teaspoons Worcestershire sauce
2 teaspoons smooth-textured chutney (any sort)
¾ teaspoon salt

Mix the tomato soup, sweet chilli sauce, Worcestershire sauce and water or stock together in the slow cooker.

To make the meatballs, mix all the ingredients together in a bowl until well combined. Shape into walnut-sized balls and place in the cooker, ensuring that the meatballs are covered with the liquid. Spoon the sauce over the top, if necessary.

Place the lid on the cooker and cook for 4 hours on High or 6–8 hours on Low. Add salt and pepper to taste before serving over pasta and/or with seasonal vegetables.

STEAK AND KIDNEY PUDDING

Serves 4
(for a 3.2–4.5 litre slow cooker)

If you don't like kidney, you can simply leave it out, or use some mushrooms instead.

Filling
1 tablespoon vegetable oil
500g lean stewing beef, diced
2 lamb's kidneys, cores removed, diced
1 onion, diced
1 tablespoon plain flour
1 cup beef or chicken stock (or 1 cup water with
    ½ teaspoon stock powder)
2 teaspoons Worcestershire sauce
2 teaspoons chutney (any sort)
1 teaspoon apricot jam
¼ teaspoon salt

Pastry
250g plain flour
125g butter, diced
¼ teaspoon salt
1 egg yolk
¼ cup cold water
1 egg white, lightly beaten

Heat the oil in a large saucepan over high heat and sauté the beef and kidney until well coloured. Add the onion and cook for 2 minutes more. Reduce the heat and stir in the flour, then gradually stir in the stock. Add the Worcestershire sauce, chutney, jam and salt and bring to the boil. Stir until thickened. Add salt and pepper to taste. Leave to cool while making the pastry.

Place the flour, butter and salt in the bowl of a food processor and process until the mixture resembles breadcrumbs. Mix together the egg yolk and water and add to the flour mixture with the motor running until the mixture forms a ball.

Grease a 1 litre pudding basin.

Place a saucer upside down or a low wire rack in the slow cooker and pour in boiling water to a depth of 2cm. Place the lid on the cooker.

On a lightly floured surface, roll out two-thirds of the dough to fit the base and side of the pudding basin. Put the pastry in place and brush, right up to the edge, with a little of the eggwhite.

Roll out the remaining pastry to fit the top of the basin and set aside.

Pour the meat mixture into the pastry-lined basin and top with the other piece of pastry. Crimp the edges together to ensure a good seal. Use any scraps of pastry to make pastry leaves for the top.

Cover the basin with foil and crimp tightly around the edges, then tie with kitchen string. This ensures that no moisture gets into the pudding.

Place the basin in the cooker on the inverted saucer. Pour in extra boiling water to come halfway up the side of the basin. Place the lid on the cooker and cook for 5–6 hours on High or 10–12 hours on Low.

Serve from the basin with seasonal vegetables and creamy mashed potatoes.

STEAK AND KIDNEY SPONGE

Serves 6
(for a 3.5–4.5 litre slow cooker)

300g lamb kidneys
1kg oyster blade steak, or similar
2 onions
1 tablespoon Worcestershire sauce
1 tablespoon chutney
2 teaspoons quince jelly*
¼ cup red wine
1¼ teaspoons salt
1 tablespoon cornflour
1¼ cups self-raising flour
¼ teaspoon mustard powder
2 eggs
1 cup milk
60g butter, melted, plus 1 teaspoon extra

Cut the kidneys in half and remove the hard core. Cut into 1cm dice. Remove any visible fat from the steak and cut into 2cm dice. Peel and dice the onions. Place all in the slow cooker.

Add the Worcestershire sauce, chutney, quince jelly, wine and 1 teaspoon of salt to the cooker. Stir to combine.

Place lid on cooker and cook for 4–5 hours on High or 7–8 hours on Low, or until the meat is tender.

Mix the cornflour with about 2 tablespoons of cold water to a paste and use a little or all of it to thicken the mixture. Add salt and pepper to taste. Turn cooker setting to High and replace lid.

Place flour, mustard powder and remaining salt in a bowl and make a well in centre. Separate the eggs. Whisk the yolks and milk together until well combined and pour into the dry ingredients, along with the melted butter. Mix together with a metal spoon.

Whisk the egg whites until stiff peaks form, then fold into the flour mixture. Pour evenly over the steak and kidney mixture. Spray a piece of baking paper, slightly larger than the cooker, with cooking oil and place greased-side down over cooker.

Replace lid and cook for 45 minutes on High.

Rub over surface of the sponge with the extra butter and sprinkle with a little freshly ground black pepper.

*   *Redcurrant or cranberry jelly, or even plum or apricot jam can be used in place of the quince jelly.*

STEAK AND STOUT

Serves 4
(for a 3.5–4.5 litre slow cooker)

2 onions
1 clove garlic
1 cup stout
750g lean diced beef
1½ teaspoons salt
3 teaspoons cornflour (optional)

Peel and chop the onions. Peel and crush the garlic. Place in the slow cooker with the stout, beef and salt. Stir to combine.

Place lid on cooker and cook for 5–6 hours on High.

If necessary, mix the cornflour with ¼ cup of cold water to a paste and use a little or all of it to thicken the dish. Add salt and pepper to taste.

Note: *This tasty mixture also makes a wonderful filling for a pie.*

STROGANOFF

Serves 6
(for a 3.5–4.5 litre slow cooker)

1kg blade steak (or similar)
2 onions
2 cloves garlic
350g mushrooms
3 large tablespoons tomato paste
1 tablespoon Worcestershire sauce
2 teaspoons salt
1 tablespoon cornflour (optional)
⅓ cup sour cream
hot buttered noodles, to serve

Remove any visible fat from the steak and cut into 5cm x 8mm strips. Peel and dice the onions. Peel and crush the garlic. Wipe and slice the mushrooms.

Place the onion and garlic in the base of the slow cooker, top with the meat, then the mushroom.

Mix together the tomato paste, Worcestershire sauce, salt and 1 cup of water and pour into the cooker.

Place lid on cooker and cook for 5 hours on High or 8 hours on Low.

If necessary, mix the cornflour with about 2 tablespoons of cold water to a paste and stir in a little or all of it to thicken the dish. Allow to cook for 5 minutes more, then mix in the sour cream. Add salt and pepper to taste. Serve with hot buttered noodles.

STUFFED CAPSICUMS

Serves 4–6
(for a 3.5–4.5 litre slow cooker)

For this recipe, the extra visual appeal to the dish is using different colour capsicums, if you can get them, otherwise just use three of any colour available.

    1 red capsicum
    1 green capsicum
    1 yellow capsicum
    1 onion
    1 cup fresh breadcrumbs
    600g good quality beef mince
    1 teaspoon paprika
    2 teaspoons Worcestershire sauce
    2 teaspoons soy sauce
    3 teaspoons chutney or relish (any sort)
    ½ teaspoon salt
    ¼ teaspoon dried oregano or thyme
    1 cup diced fresh, canned or bottled tomatoes
    2 tablespoons tomato paste
    1 clove garlic
    2 teaspoons sweet chilli sauce

Cut all the capsicums in half, lengthways, then remove the stalks, seeds and membrane. Set aside.

Peel and chop the onion very finely. Place onion and breadcrumbs into a bowl with the mince, paprika, Worcestershire sauce, soy sauce, chutney or relish, salt and herbs. Mix until well combined.

Mix together the diced tomato, tomato paste, garlic and sweet chilli sauce. Spread over the base of the slow cooker.

Fill the prepared capsicum halves with the mince mixture and place on top of the tomato mixture.

Place lid on cooker and cook for 4 hours on High or 8 hours on Low.

SWEET AND SOUR BEEF

Serves 4
(for a 3.5–4.5 litre slow cooker)

3 carrots
1 onion
1 red capsicum
600g diced beef
2 teaspoons soy sauce
2 teaspoons Worcestershire sauce
2 teaspoons chutney
½ cup brown sugar
½ cup cider vinegar
4 pineapple rings, diced,
    or 250g canned pineapple pieces
½ cup pineapple juice
1 teaspoon salt
3 teaspoons cornflour

Peel and slice the carrots. Peel and dice the onion. Remove the stalk, seeds and membrane from the capsicum and chop into 2.5cm pieces. Place in the slow cooker with ½ cup of water and the remaining ingredients, except the cornflour.

Place lid on cooker and cook for 4–5 hours on High or 8–9 hours on Low.

Mix the cornflour with ¼ cup of cold water to a paste and use a little or all of it to thicken the dish to the desired consistency. Add salt and pepper to taste.

TEX MEX BEEF

Serves 4
(for a 3.5–4 litre slow cooker)

800g beef cheeks (or stewing beef such as chuck, blade,
    shin or gravy beef)
4 cloves garlic, crushed
2 onions, diced
1 tablespoon chutney (any sort)
4 teaspoons ground cumin
½ teaspoon dried oregano
2 teaspoons ground coriander
½ teaspoon ground cinnamon
¼ teaspoon ground cloves
3 teaspoons brown sugar
1 tablespoon tomato sauce (ketchup)
1 tablespoon sweet chilli sauce or 1 long red chilli,
    chopped, or ½ teaspoon dried chilli flakes
2 teaspoons soy sauce
3 teaspoons Worcestershire sauce
¼ cup red wine
½ cup beef stock or water
2 tablespoons tomato paste
1 teaspoon salt
3 teaspoons cornflour mixed to a paste with 1 tablespoon
    cold water (optional)
20g dark chocolate, chopped

Remove all visible fat from the meat and cut into 1.25cm dice. Place in the slow cooker with the rest of the ingredients except the cornflour paste and chocolate and stir to combine.

Place the lid on the cooker and cook for 4 hours on High or 7–8 hours on Low until meat is tender.

If needed, stir in the cornflour paste, replace the lid and cook for 10 minutes more on High. Stir in the chocolate until melted. Add salt and pepper to taste.

Serve with polenta or rice or nachos and a green salad.

Tilly's Indian Sweet Curry Beef

Serves 6
(for a 3.5–4.5 litre slow cooker)

This curry recipe came back from India with the surgeon grandfather of our elderly friend Tilly. It is ideally suited to long, slow cooking. Reduce the curry powder if you like less heat, though it is not as fiery as you might think at first glance.

2 carrots
1 onion
1 stalk celery
2 apples
1kg lean stewing beef, such as chuck, gravy beef or blade
1 tablespoon sultanas
1 tablespoon relish or chutney (any sort)
1 tablespoon tomato sauce (ketchup)
1 tablespoon Worcestershire sauce
1 tablespoon golden syrup
2 tablespoons brown sugar
1½ tablespoons curry powder
2 teaspoons salt
½ cup stock or water
3 teaspoons cornflour (optional)
steamed rice, to serve

Peel the carrots and onion and cut into 1cm dice. Cut the celery into 1cm slices. Peel, core and grate the apples. Place in the slow cooker.

Remove any visible fat from the meat and cut into 2cm dice. Place on top of vegetables. Add the sultanas, relish or chutney, tomato sauce, Worcestershire sauce, golden syrup, brown sugar, curry powder, salt and stock or water. Stir gently to combine.

Place lid on cooker and cook for 4–5 hours on High or 8–9 hours on Low.

If necessary, mix the cornflour with about 2 tablespoons of cold water to a paste and use a little or all of it to thicken the curry. Add salt and pepper to taste. Serve with steamed rice.

TOMATO SPIRALLI BEEF

Serves 6
(for a 3.5–4.5 litre slow cooker)

2 onions

1 red capsicum

2 cloves garlic

2 teaspoons olive oil

500g good quality beef mince

¾ cup diced fresh, canned or bottled tomatoes

½ cup chopped semi-dried tomato

3 large tablespoons tomato paste

1 tablespoon tomato sauce (ketchup)

1 teaspoon redcurrant or quince jelly
   (even sugar will do)

½ teaspoon salt

2–3 cups cooked spiralli pasta

⅓ cup grated parmesan cheese

½ cup grated tasty cheese

green salad, to serve

garlic bread, to serve

Peel and dice the onion. Remove the stalk, seeds and membrane from the capsicum and dice finely. Peel and crush the garlic.

Heat the oil in a frying pan and cook the mince until browned. Transfer to the slow cooker. Add the onion, capsicum, garlic, diced tomato, semi-dried tomato, tomato paste, tomato sauce, redcurrant or quince jelly, salt and 1¼ cups of water. Stir to combine.

Place lid on cooker and cook for 4 hours on High or 8 hours on Low.

Heat the cooked pasta, then stir into the contents of the cooker, together with the grated parmesan. Add salt and pepper to taste.

Scatter the tasty cheese evenly over the top. Replace the lid and leave for a few minutes until the cheese melts.

Serve with green salad and garlic bread.

VINDALOO WITH MINTED CUCUMBER YOGHURT

Serves 4
(for a 3.2–3.5 litre slow cooker)

Don't be tempted to skip the minted cucumber yoghurt with this recipe as it complements the rich, spiced meat to perfection.

Vindaloo

900g lean diced beef
4 cloves garlic, crushed
1½ tablespoons grated green ginger root
1 long red chilli, thinly sliced
2 teaspoons ground cumin
1 teaspoon ground turmeric
1 teaspoon mustard powder
1½ teaspoons ground cinnamon
½ teaspoon ground allspice
¾ teaspoon salt
½ teaspoon ground cardamom
2 teaspoons brown sugar
½ cup chicken, beef or vegetable stock (or ½ cup water
    with ¼ teaspoon stock powder)
¼ cup white or cider vinegar
3 teaspoons tomato sauce (ketchup)
2 teaspoons cornflour mixed to a paste with 1 tablespoon
    cold water (optional)

Minted Cucumber Yoghurt

½ Lebanese cucumber
1½ cups Greek-style or plain yoghurt
¼ teaspoon salt
2 teaspoons lemon juice
1½ tablespoons chopped mint

To make the vindaloo, place all the ingredients except the cornflour paste in the slow cooker. Place the lid on the cooker and cook for 4–5 hours on High or 8–9 hours on Low until meat is tender.

Turn the cooker to High (if set on Low) and thicken, if needed, with some or all of the cornflour paste. Replace the lid and cook for a further 10 minutes on High. Add salt and pepper to taste.

To make the minted cucumber yoghurt, remove the seeds from the cucumber and grate the flesh into a clean tea towel. Gather the tea towel up around the grated flesh and squeeze to remove the moisture from the cucumber, then mix with the rest of the ingredients.

Serve the vindaloo with the minted cucumber yoghurt and with plain boiled or steamed rice.

WAKEFIELD STEAK

Serves 4–6
(for a 3.5–4.5 litre slow cooker)

800g lean diced beef
1 onion, diced
1 carrot, diced
1 teaspoon ground ginger
1 teaspoon curry powder
1 teaspoon mustard powder
1 teaspoon ground allspice
2 tablespoons sultanas
1½ tablespoons tomato paste
2 teaspoons chutney (any sort)
1½ tablespoons Worcestershire sauce
1 tablespoon white, cider or balsamic vinegar
2 teaspoons quince or redcurrant jelly or apricot jam
1 cup chicken or beef stock or water
¾ teaspoon salt
3 teaspoons cornflour mixed to a paste with 1 tablespoon
   cold water (optional)

Combine all the ingredients except the cornflour paste in the slow cooker.

Place the lid on the cooker and cook for 4–5 hours on High or 8–9 hours on Low until meat is tender.

Remove the lid and, if needed, thicken the sauce by stirring in some or all of the cornflour paste. Replace the lid and cook for 10 minutes on High.

Add salt and pepper to taste. Serve with plain steamed or boiled rice and/or seasonal vegetables.

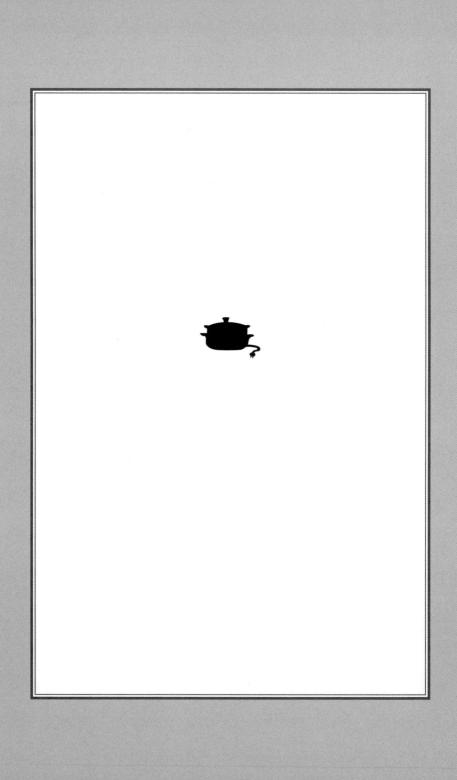

LAMB

APRICOT AND ROSEMARY LAMB WITH REDCURRANT JUS

Serves 6
(for a 3.5–4.5 litre slow cooker)

1.5–2kg leg of lamb, tunnel-boned*
1 onion
⅓ cup dried apricots
1 cup fresh breadcrumbs
2 teaspoons chutney
2 teaspoons chopped fresh rosemary leaves
½ teaspoon dried rosemary
½ teaspoon grated lemon rind
½ teaspoon salt
2 teaspoons oil (optional)

Redcurrant Jus
2 teaspoons redcurrant jelly
2 teaspoons tomato paste
1 teaspoon chicken or vegetable stock powder
2 teaspoons cornflour (optional)

Remove any visible fat from the leg of lamb. Peel and grate the onion. Chop the dried apricots. Place in a bowl with the breadcrumbs, chutney, fresh and dried rosemary, lemon rind and salt. Mix well, then stuff into the cavity of the lamb leg.

If you wish, heat oil in a heavy-based frying pan and brown the lamb lightly on all sides, before placing in the slow cooker.

Place lid on cooker and cook for 4 hours on High or 8 hours on Low.

Remove the lamb from the cooker, reserving the juices, and place on a board. Cover with foil and leave to rest while making the redcurrant jus.

To make the jus, place a strainer over a medium saucepan and strain the juices from the cooker. Add the redcurrant jelly, tomato paste and stock powder and bring to the boil. Boil until there is approximately 1 cup of liquid remaining.

If necessary, mix the cornflour with 1 tablespoon of cold water to a paste and use a little or all of it to thicken the jus. Add salt and pepper to taste.

*   *Ask your butcher to remove the bone from the lamb for you.*

BRAISED LAMB SHANKS WITH LEMON COUSCOUS

Serves 4
(for a 3.5–4.5 litre slow cooker)

3 carrots
1 onion
1.5kg lamb shanks (4 or 5)
1 clove garlic
250g tomatoes, chopped
1 cup tomato sauce (ketchup)
½ cup medium dry or dry sherry
1 heaped tablespoon tomato paste
2 teaspoons chutney (any sort)
2 teaspoons quince jelly (optional)
2 teaspoons vegetable stock powder
1 teaspoon preserved lemon or grated lemon rind
1 tablespoon cornflour (optional)

Lemon Couscous
1 cup couscous
1 teaspoon grated lemon rind
½ teaspoon vegetable stock powder
1 cup boiling water
1½ tablespoons chopped parsley

Peel the carrots and cut into quarters. Peel and dice the onion. Place in the slow cooker and put the lamb shanks on top.

Peel and crush the garlic and add to the cooker with the remaining ingredients, except the cornflour, adding 1 cup of water last. Stir gently.

Place lid on cooker and cook for 4 hours on High or 8–9 hours on Low.

Add salt and pepper to taste. If necessary, mix the cornflour with about ¼ cup of cold water to a paste and use a little or all of it to thicken the pan juices. Stir through the braise and cook for a further 5 minutes.

To make the lemon couscous, combine the couscous, lemon rind and stock powder in a bowl. Pour the boiling water evenly over the couscous mixture. Cover and leave to stand for 5 minutes. Fluff up the couscous with a fork.

To serve, fold the parsley through the couscous, or sprinkle over the dish.

FRUITY LAMB TAGINE

Serves 4–6
(for a 3.5 litre slow cooker)

750g lean diced lamb

60g pitted prunes

60g sultanas

60g diced dried apricots

2 teaspoons ground cumin

2 teaspoons ground coriander

1 teaspoon ground ginger

1 teaspoon ground allspice

1 tablespoon chutney (any sort)

3 teaspoons redcurrant jelly

2 teaspoons curry powder

1 teaspoon salt

½–1 teaspoon dried chilli flakes or 1 tablespoon sweet chilli
   sauce

1 cup chicken stock

3 teaspoons cornflour mixed to a paste with
   1½ tablespoons cold water (optional)

400g can chickpeas, drained and rinsed

Place all the ingredients except the cornflour paste and chickpeas in the slow cooker. Place the lid on the cooker and cook for 4 hours on High or 7–8 hours on Low.

If needed, mix in some or all of the cornflour paste to thicken, stirring while adding it. Then mix in the chickpeas. Add salt and pepper to taste.

Replace the lid on the cooker and cook for 5–10 minutes more on High.

Serve with couscous.

INDIAN SPICED ROAST LAMB

Serves 4–6
(for a 4.5–5.5 litre slow cooker)

Ask your butcher to remove the lamb bone for you.

> 1 leg of lamb, bone and visible fat removed
> 1 clove garlic, crushed
> 2 teaspoons finely grated green ginger root
> ½ teaspoon ground turmeric
> 1 teaspoon ground cumin
> 1 teaspoon ground coriander
> ½ teaspoon garam masala
> ½ teaspoon dried chilli flakes (optional)
> ½ teaspoon brown sugar
> 1 teaspoon salt
> 2 teaspoons lemon juice
> 1 tablespoon soy sauce
> 3 teaspoons cornflour mixed to a paste with 2 tablespoons
> cold water (optional)

Place the lamb in the slow cooker. Mix the rest of the ingredients together except the cornflour paste and rub all over the surface of the lamb. Place the lid on the cooker and cook for 5–6 hours on High or 10–12 hours on Low until meat is tender.

Remove the lamb from the cooker, cover with foil and leave to rest for 10 minutes before slicing. Meanwhile, if needed, mix some or all of the cornflour paste into the pan juices to thicken slightly. Add salt and pepper to taste. Cook with the lid on for 10 minutes more on High.

Slice the meat and serve with the sauce and seasonal vegetables.

IRISH STEW

Serves 4

(for a 3.5–4.5 litre slow cooker)

The first time I made this in the slow cooker, our Irish friend Mervyn happened to come to visit us. After an ample serving of the stew, he said, 'It tastes like it came straight from my Aunt Connie's stew pot, but I'm so blootered I'll have to have a pan crock!' Little did he know the aptness of his words, prepared as the stew was in the crockpot. Translated it means: 'I'm so full I'll need to have a little lie down.'

700g potatoes
2 onions
500g lean diced lamb
1 teaspoon salt
3 teaspoons cornflour (optional)

Peel the potatoes and cut into 3cm chunks. Peel and dice the onion. Place in the slow cooker. Place the lamb on top. Sprinkle with the salt and pour ¾ cup of water over the mixture.

Place lid on cooker and cook for 5 hours on High or 8–9 hours on Low.

If necessary, mix the cornflour with about 2 tablespoons of cold water to a paste and use a little or all of it to thicken the stew. Add salt and pepper to taste.

Lamb with Apricots and Rosemary

Serves 6
(for a 3.5–4.5 litre slow cooker)

1 onion
½ red capsicum
½ cup semi-dried tomatoes
½ cup sliced dried apricots
¼ cup chopped chorizo sausage
2 teaspoons quince or redcurrant jelly or apricot jam
2 teaspoons Worcestershire sauce
2 teaspoons soy sauce
1 tablespoon tomato paste
1 cup stock (any sort)
750g lean diced lamb
1 tablespoon chopped rosemary
2 teaspoons salt
2 teaspoons cornflour (optional)

Peel and dice the onion. Remove the stalk, seeds and membrane from the capsicum and dice. Chop the semi-dried tomatoes. Place in the slow cooker with the dried apricots, chorizo, jelly, Worcestershire sauce, soy sauce, tomato paste, stock, lamb, rosemary and salt. Stir well to combine.

Place lid on cooker and cook for 4–5 hours on High or 7–8 hours on Low.

If necessary, mix the cornflour with about 1 tablespoon of cold water to a paste and use a little or all of it to thicken the dish. Add salt and pepper to taste.

LAMB KORMA

Serves 4–6
(for a 3.2–4.5 litre slow cooker)

750g lean diced lamb
2 onions, diced
3 cloves garlic, crushed
2 teaspoons grated green ginger root
2 long red chillies, deseeded and diced
1 teaspoon ground turmeric
1 teaspoon mustard powder
1 teaspoon ground cumin
½ teaspoon ground coriander
½ teaspoon ground cardamom
¼ teaspoon ground cloves
400g can diced tomatoes
¾ cup coconut milk
1½ teaspoons chicken or vegetable stock powder
3 teaspoons cornflour mixed to a paste with 1 tablespoon
    cold water, optional

Place all the ingredients except cornflour paste in the slow cooker and stir to combine.

Place the lid on the cooker and cook for 4–5 hours on High or 8–9 hours on Low until meat is tender. Add salt and pepper to taste.

Serve over plain boiled or steamed rice.

LAMB AND QUINCE HOTPOT

Serves 6
(for a 3.5–4.5 litre slow cooker)

800g lean lamb
800g quinces
2 onions
½ cup apple juice
½ cup water
1 tablespoon Worcestershire sauce
1 tablespoon sweet chilli sauce
1 tablespoon well-flavoured chutney,
    such as green tomato
2 teaspoons tomato paste
1 teaspoon ground cumin
1 teaspoon salt
3 teaspoons cornflour (optional)

Remove any visible fat from the lamb and dice. Peel and core the quinces and cut into 1.25cm dice. Peel and finely dice the onion. Place all in the cooker.

Add the remaining ingredients, except the cornflour, and stir to combine.

Place lid on cooker and cook for 3½ hours on High or 7 hours on Low.

If necessary, mix the cornflour with about 2 tablespoons of cold water to a paste and use a little or all of it to thicken the dish. Add salt and pepper to taste.

LAMB ROGAN JOSH

Serves 4–6
(for a 3.2–4.5 litre slow cooker)

750g lean diced lamb

3 cloves garlic, crushed

2 onions, diced

2 teaspoons grated green ginger root

¼ teaspoon ground cloves

3 teaspoons ground coriander

1 tablespoon ground cumin

1 teaspoon ground cardamom

1 teaspoon ground turmeric

3 teaspoons garam masala

400g can diced tomatoes

1 teaspoon chicken or vegetable stock powder

2 teaspoons cornflour

1 tablespoon tomato paste

2 teaspoons golden syrup

2 teaspoons chutney (any sort)

2 teaspoons Worcestershire sauce

½ teaspoon salt

2 teaspoons tomato sauce (ketchup)

2 teaspoons lemon juice

1 cup plain yoghurt

Place all the ingredients except the yoghurt in the slow cooker and mix well.

Place the lid on the cooker and cook for 4–5 hours on High or 8–10 hours on Low until meat is tender.

Mix in the yoghurt, replace the lid and cook for 10 minutes more on High to heat through. Add salt and pepper to taste.

Serve with plain boiled or steamed rice.

LAMB AND SWEET POTATO WITH SPINACH AND CHEESY RICE CRUST

Serves 6–8
(for a 3.5–4.5 litre slow cooker)

600g sweet potatoes
1 onion
1kg lean lamb
2 teaspoons redcurrant jelly
juice of 1 lemon
½ cup stock or water
1½ teaspoons salt
1 tablespoon tomato sauce (ketchup)
3 teaspoons sweet chilli sauce
1 tablespoon cornflour

Spinach and Cheesy Rice Crust
1 cup cold cooked rice
1½ cups self-raising flour
½ cup milk
2 eggs
2 teaspoons Worcestershire sauce
60g butter, melted
1 cup shredded spinach or silverbeet
1 tablespoon chopped parsley
¾ cup grated tasty cheese
1 teaspoon salt

Peel the sweet potato and cut into 1cm dice. Peel and dice the onion. Remove any visible fat from the lamb and dice. Place in the slow cooker with the redcurrant jelly, lemon juice, stock or water, salt, tomato sauce and sweet chilli sauce. Stir to combine.

Place lid on cooker and cook for 4–5 hours on High or 8–9 hours on Low.

Mix the cornflour with about 2 tablespoons of cold water to a paste and use a little or all of it to thicken the mixture. Add salt and pepper to taste. Replace lid and turn cooker setting to High.

To make the spinach and cheesy rice crust, place the rice, flour and milk in a bowl but do not stir. Separate the eggs. Whisk the egg yolks and add to the rice mixture, then add the Worcestershire sauce and melted butter and mix together very well. Add the spinach or silverbeet, parsley, cheese and salt. Mix well.

Whisk the eggwhites until stiff peaks form, then fold into the rice mixture until well combined.

Spoon the rice mixture evenly over the lamb mixture.

Replace lid and cook for 1 hour on High.

LANCASHIRE HOTPOT

Serves 6
(for a 4–5 litre slow cooker)

700g potatoes
1kg lean diced lamb
2 onions, diced
300g lean bacon, rind removed, diced
1 cup chicken or vegetable stock (or 1 cup water with
    ¾ teaspoon stock powder)
2 tablespoons chopped parsley, approximately

Peel the potatoes and cut into 1.5cm cubes. Place in the slow cooker with the rest of the ingredients and stir to combine well.

Place the lid on the cooker and cook for 4–5 hours on High or 8–10 hours on Low until meat is tender.

Add salt and pepper to taste.

Sprinkle each serve with the chopped parsley. I love this served with buttered fresh crusty bread.

LEG OF LAMB CREOLE

Serves 6
(for a 4.5–5.5 litre slow cooker)

Ask your butcher to remove the lamb bone for you.

1 leg of lamb, bone and visible fat removed
1 onion, diced
1 carrot, sliced
1 clove garlic, crushed
½ cup red wine or claret
1½ tablespoons Worcestershire sauce
1½ tablespoons vinegar (any sort)
1 teaspoon redcurrant jelly or brown sugar
2 teaspoons sweet chilli sauce

Gravy
½ teaspoon salt or chicken stock powder
3 teaspoons cornflour mixed to a paste with 2 tablespoons
    cold water (optional)

Place the lamb in the slow cooker. Add the onion, carrot and garlic.

Combine the rest of the ingredients in a bowl and pour over the lamb.

Place the lid on the cooker and cook for 5–6 hours on High or 9–10 hours on Low until the lamb is tender.

Remove the lamb to a platter, cover with foil and leave to rest for
15 minutes.

To make the gravy, add the salt or stock powder to the cooker. If needed, stir in the cornflour to thicken slightly. Replace the lid and while the lamb is resting cook for 10 minutes on High to heat and thicken the gravy. Add salt and pepper to taste.

Serve with seasonal vegetables.

MIDDLE EASTERN LAMB STEW

Serves 4
(for a 3.5–4.5 litre slow cooker)

This dish, with its pungent citrus and spice undertones, should be served with couscous or steamed rice and most definitely accompanied by a side dish of a little natural yoghurt sprinkled with chopped mint. To lighten the flavours a little, half a cup of natural yoghurt can also be mixed in at the end of cooking time.

750g lean lamb
1 onion
2 cloves garlic
1 tablespoon honey
1 teaspoon turmeric
1 teaspoon ground cumin
½ teaspoon ground coriander
½ cup stock (any sort)
1 teaspoon salt
1 teaspoon grated green ginger root
1 teaspoon orange rind
juice of 1 lemon
1 teaspoon brown sugar
1 teaspoon very finely diced preserved lemon rind
2 teaspoons cornflour (optional)
1 cup natural yoghurt, to serve,
      plus ½ cup extra (optional)
3 teaspoons finely chopped mint

Remove any visible fat from the lamb and dice. Peel and dice the onion. Peel and crush the garlic. Place all in the slow cooker and add the honey, turmeric, cumin, coriander, stock, salt, ginger, orange rind, lemon juice, brown sugar and preserved lemon rind and stir to mix well.

Place lid on cooker and cook for 3½–4 hours on High or 7–8 hours on Low.

If necessary, mix the cornflour with about 1 tablespoon of cold water to a paste and use a little or all of it to thicken the stew. Stir in the extra yoghurt, if desired. Add salt and pepper to taste.

Serve with the yoghurt sprinkled with the chopped mint to the side.

Moussaka

Serves 6
(for a 3.5–4.5 litre slow cooker)

600g eggplants
2 teaspoons olive oil
600g lean lamb mince
1 large onion
4 cloves garlic
2 teaspoons Worcestershire sauce
2 teaspoons chutney (any sort)
1 teaspoon salt
2 large tablespoons tomato paste
1½ cups diced fresh, canned or bottled tomatoes
1 tablespoon cornflour
⅔ cup grated tasty cheese, plus ½ cup extra
½ cup grated parmesan cheese

Cheese Sauce
1½ tablespoons cornflour
2⅓ cups milk
1 egg
½ cup grated tasty cheese

Remove the ends from the eggplants and cut into 1cm slices. Cook in two batches in the microwave for about 5–6 minutes on High. Dry on paper towel to soak up any excess liquid. Press lightly to make sure the eggplant is as dry as possible.

Heat the oil in a saucepan and brown the lamb mince, stirring from time to time to break it up well.

Peel and finely dice the onion. Peel and crush the garlic. Add to the lamb and cook for a further minute. Add the Worcestershire sauce, chutney, salt, tomato paste, tomato and ½ cup of water. Bring to the boil and cook for about 4 minutes. Mix the cornflour with about 2 tablespoons of cold water to a paste and use it to thicken the mixture.

To make the cheese sauce, mix the cornflour with ⅓ cup of the milk to a paste. Heat the remaining milk to boiling point and thicken with the cornflour paste, stirring constantly with a wire whisk. Remove from the heat and whisk in the egg and cheese.

Spray the slow cooker with cooking oil. Spread a little of the lamb mixture over the base, then add a layer of eggplant slices. Top with half the remaining lamb, ⅓ cup tasty cheese and half the remaining eggplant. Finish with the remaining lamb, ⅓ cup tasty cheese and the remaining eggplant. Pour over the cheese sauce. Scatter over the parmesan combined with the extra tasty cheese.

Place lid on cooker and cook for 2 hours on Low. Leave to stand for 30 minutes, if possible, before serving.

Moroccan Lamb

Serves 4
(for a 3.5–4.5 litre slow cooker)

2 tablespoons olive oil
500g lamb mince
1 large or 2 small onions
4 cloves garlic
2 teaspoons ground cumin
2 teaspoons ground coriander
¼ teaspoon ground cardamom
1 tablespoon chopped dried apricots
1½ tablespoons chopped dried figs
2 tablespoons slivered almonds
2 teaspoons lemon juice
1 cup stock or water
2 teaspoons honey
2 teaspoons chutney (any sort)
1 teaspoon salt
1 tablespoon sweet chilli sauce
2 tablespoons chopped parsley
2 teaspoons cornflour (optional)
couscous, to serve

Heat the oil in a heavy-based saucepan and lightly brown the lamb mince, stirring from time to time to break it up. Peel and dice the onion. Peel and crush the garlic. Add to the mince and cook for a further minute. Add the cumin, coriander and cardamom and cook for another minute.

Add the apricot, fig, almonds, lemon juice, stock or water, honey, chutney, salt and sweet chilli sauce. Stir to combine. Pour mixture into the slow cooker.

Place lid on cooker and cook for 2 hours on High or 3½ hours on Low.

If necessary, mix the cornflour with about 1 tablespoon of cold water to a paste and use it to thicken the dish. Add salt and pepper to taste.

Mix the parsley through the lamb at the end of cooking time. Serve with couscous.

Persian Lamb and Rhubarb Stew

Serves 6
(for a 3.5–4.5 litre slow cooker)

The combination of rhubarb with lamb and the addition of herbs and spices make this stew really, really sumptuous. The rhubarb does not dominate, but rather adds a subtle, sharp fruitiness to the dish.

1kg lean diced lamb
500g rhubarb stalks, diced
1 onion, diced
3 cloves garlic, crushed
2 teaspoons ground allspice
1 teaspoon ground cumin
½ teaspoon ground coriander
½ teaspoon ground cinnamon
¼ teaspoon ground cardamom
3 teaspoons chutney (any sort)
1 tablespoon tomato sauce (ketchup)
5 teaspoons brown sugar
1 tablespoon quince or redcurrant jelly (or extra brown sugar)
2 teaspoons chicken or vegetable stock powder
½ cup water
½ cup chopped parsley
¼ cup chopped mint
3 teaspoons cornflour mixed to a paste with 1 tablespoon cold water (optional)

Combine all the ingredients except the parsley, mint and cornflour paste in the slow cooker and stir.

Place the lid on the cooker and cook for 4–5 hours on High or 8–10 hours on Low until meat is tender.

Stir in half the parsley and all the mint, replace the lid and cook on High for 5 minutes more. Thicken with some or all of the cornflour paste, if needed, and add salt and pepper to taste.

I like this stew best served over couscous. Sprinkle each serving with the remaining chopped parsley.

SLOW ROASTED SHOULDER OF LAMB WITH BRAISED VEGETABLES

Serves 6
(for a 4.5–5.5 litre slow cooker)

Ask your butcher to bone out the lamb shoulder and remove any visible fat.

- 1 parsnip
- 2 carrots
- 1 potato
- 2 onions
- 2 teaspoons fish sauce
- 2 teaspoons Worcestershire sauce
- 1 tablespoon tomato sauce (ketchup)
- ½ cup water
- 2 teaspoons instant coffee powder or granules
- 1 shoulder of lamb, bone and visible fat removed
- 2 cloves garlic, crushed
- ½ teaspoon salt
- ¼ teaspoon freshly ground black pepper
- 2 x 10cm sprigs rosemary
- 2 teaspoons cornflour mixed to a paste with 1 tablespoon cold water (optional)

Peel the vegetables and cut into 1cm dice. Place in the slow cooker.

Mix together the sauces, water and coffee, pour over the vegetables and stir to combine. Place the lamb on top and spread on the crushed garlic. Sprinkle with the salt and pepper. Top with the sprigs of rosemary.

Place the lid on the cooker and cook for 5–6 hours on High or 10–12 hours on Low until the meat is very tender.

Remove the meat from the cooker and cover with foil. Set aside to rest for 15–20 minutes.

If needed, mix some or all of the cornflour paste into the cooker to thicken the gravy just slightly. Add salt and pepper to taste.

Cut the meat into 1cm slices and place on the vegetables and gravy that have been spooned onto each plate. Drizzle with a little extra gravy.

Serve with creamy mashed potatoes and seasonal vegetables.

TSIMMES

Serves 6
(for a 4.5 litre slow cooker)

This unusual dish is a pleasant mix of sweet and sour and fruity, a perfect complement to the lamb.

1 apple
2 carrots
2 parsnips
850g sweet potato
1 onion, diced
1kg lean diced lamb
¾ cup pitted prunes
½ teaspoon ground cinnamon
½ teaspoon ground allspice
¾ cup orange juice
1 bay leaf
1 teaspoon grated green ginger root
1 tablespoon tomato sauce (ketchup)
1 teaspoon chicken stock powder
1½ teaspoons marmalade
1 tablespoon honey
3 teaspoons cornflour mixed to a paste with 1 tablespoon
    cold water

Peel, core and dice the apple. Peel the carrots and parsnips and cut into 8mm slices. Peel the sweet potato and cut into 1cm cubes. Place the vegetables in the slow cooker with the lamb.

Add the rest of the ingredients except the cornflour paste and stir to combine.

Place the lid on the cooker and cook for 5–6 hours on High or 10–11 hours on Low until meat is tender.

Turn the cooker to High (if set on Low) and stir in some or all of the cornflour paste to thicken. Add salt and pepper to taste, replace the lid and cook for 10 minutes more.

Serve with seasonal vegetables or over couscous.

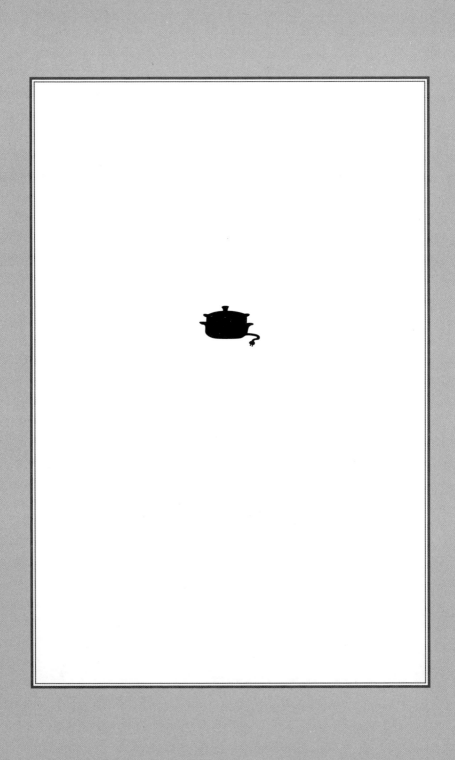

PORK

BAKED HAM WITH MAPLE, MUSTARD AND MARMALADE GLAZE

Serves 4–6
(for a 4.5 litre slow cooker)

Ham cooked in the slow cooker is absolutely delicious and tender. It is one of the few dishes where the fat is left on the meat. The spiced glaze in this recipe gives a final delectable touch for the mere extra step of placing it in the oven for a few minutes to crisp the outside.

I used my 4.5 litre capacity slow cooker to cook a 2.2kg leg of ham. For a larger ham you will need a correspondingly larger cooker.

      Up to 2.2kg leg ham
      ½ cup maple syrup
      3 teaspoons marmalade
      3 teaspoons balsamic vinegar
      3 teaspoons sherry
      3 teaspoons whole grain mustard
      6 whole cloves
      1 piece star anise

Remove the outer skin from the ham.* Score the fat underneath to form a diamond pattern, being careful not to cut right through to the flesh underneath, then place the ham in the slow cooker. Mix together the rest of the ingredients until well combined, then pour over the meat. Cook for 5–6 hours on High or 10–12 hours on Low.

Remove the ham from the cooker and place in a baking dish. Heat the oven to 200°C.

Strain the sauce from the cooker into a saucepan and bring to a rapid boil. Boil until reduced to about ¾ cup. Spoon over the ham.

Bake the ham for 10 minutes, then spoon the glaze from the bottom of the dish over the ham and cook for a further 5–10 minutes until golden.

Serve hot with seasonal vegetables or cold with salads or as a sandwich filling.

* *To remove the skin from the ham, make a small cut on the outer rim and prise the skin back. If you have any problems doing this, simply use a sharp knife to slice off the thin layer of skin.*

BARBECUE RIBS

Serves 4
(for a 3.5–4.5 litre slow cooker)

This recipe is very handy not only for a family, but also if you are having guests for dinner or a barbecue. The ribs can be cooked to a delicious tenderness all day in the slow cooker, then placed under a grill or on a barbecue hotplate for a few minutes to crisp up before serving.

This amount is enough for four, but it can easily be doubled to serve a crowd.

1kg pork ribs
3 cloves garlic, crushed
¼ cup tomato sauce (ketchup)
¼ cup barbecue sauce
1 tablespoon Worcestershire sauce
1 tablespoon honey
¾ teaspoon salt
1 teaspoon mustard powder
½ teaspoon dried chilli flakes (optional)

Place the ribs in the slow cooker. Mix the rest of the ingredients together, add to the cooker and stir through well.

Place the lid on the cooker and cook for 4–5 hours on High or 8–9 hours on Low until the pork is tender.

CASSOULET

Serves 4–6

(for a 3.5–4.5 litre slow cooker)

800g lean diced pork
500g extra lean pork sausages
125g lean bacon, rind removed, diced
400g can diced tomatoes
2 tablespoons tomato paste
2 tablespoons chopped sage
1 bay leaf
15 pickling onions, peeled or 3 onions, quartered
3 teaspoons Worcestershire sauce
3 teaspoons sweet chilli sauce
2 teaspoons sweet paprika
3 teaspoons redcurrant jelly (or brown sugar)
½ cup water
2 teaspoons chicken or vegetable stock powder
3 teaspoons cornflour mixed to a paste with 1 tablespoon
    cold water (optional)
400g can lima or similar beans, drained and rinsed

Place the pork in the slow cooker. Cut the sausages into 6cm lengths with a sharp knife and place in the cooker with the bacon, tomatoes, tomato paste, sage, bay leaf, onions, sauces, paprika, redcurrant jelly (or sugar), water and stock powder. Stir to combine. Place the lid on the cooker and cook for 4–5 hours on High or 8–9 hours on Low until meat is tender.

If needed, stir in some or all of the cornflour paste to thicken.

Mix the beans into the cassoulet, replace the lid and cook for 10 minutes more on High to heat through. Add salt and pepper to taste.

CHILLI PORK WITH ORANGE

Serves 4–6
(for a 3.5–4.5 litre slow cooker)

700g lean diced pork
1 onion, diced
1 strip of orange rind
½ cup orange juice
2 teaspoons grated orange rind
1 red capsicum, deseeded and diced
1 tablespoon sweet chilli sauce
3 teaspoons tomato sauce (ketchup)
2 teaspoons soy sauce
1 teaspoon chicken stock powder
1 teaspoon quince or redcurrant jelly or apricot jam
½ cup chicken stock or water
1½ teaspoons white vinegar
½ teaspoon salt

Put all the ingredients in the slow cooker. Place the lid on the cooker and cook for 4 hours on High or 7–8 hours on Low until meat is tender. Add salt and pepper to taste.

Serve with plain boiled or steamed rice.

CREAMY PORK AND RED CAPSICUMS

Serves 4–6
(for a 3.5–4.5 litre slow cooker)

500g red capsicums
1 onion
3 cloves garlic
250g tomatoes
800g lean diced pork
1 teaspoon chicken or vegetable stock powder
1½ teaspoons salt
1 tablespoon chutney (any sort)
½ cup stock
1 teaspoon sugar
1 tablespoon tomato paste
1 tablespoon paprika
1 tablespoon cornflour (optional)
⅔ cup sour cream
¼ cup finely chopped parsley
mashed potatoes and seasonal vegetables, to serve

Remove stalks, seeds and membranes from the capsicums and cut into 1cm dice. Peel and dice the onion. Peel and crush the garlic. Dice the tomatoes. Place in the slow cooker and add the pork, stock powder, salt, chutney, stock, sugar, tomato paste and paprika.

Place lid on cooker and cook for 4 hours on High or 7–8 hours on Low. If necessary, mix the cornflour with about 2 tablespoons of cold water to a paste and use a little or all of it to thicken the mixture.

Stir in sour cream and add salt and pepper to taste. Sprinkle with parsley and serve with mashed potatoes and seasonal vegetables.

CURRIED SAUSAGES

Serves 6
(for a 3.5–4.5 litre slow cooker)

2 onions
1 carrot
1 stalk celery
1 small zucchini (optional)
700g cooked sausages
½ cup diced fresh, canned or bottled tomato
2 teaspoons soy sauce
2 teaspoons tomato sauce (ketchup)
2 teaspoons plum jam (or similar, but avoid
    jams with pips)
2 teaspoons chutney (any sort)
2 teaspoons curry powder
1 teaspoon salt
1½ cups water
1 tablespoon cornflour (optional)
steamed rice or baked jacket potatoes, to serve

Peel the onions and carrot, and finely dice along with the celery and zucchini, if using. Place in the slow cooker.

Slice the sausages into 1cm lengths and add to the cooker with the tomato, soy sauce, tomato sauce, jam, chutney, curry powder, salt and water.

Place lid on cooker and cook for 3½ hours on High or 7 hours on Low.

If necessary, mix the cornflour with about 2 tablespoons of cold water to a paste and use a little or all of it to thicken the dish. Add salt and pepper to taste.

Serve over steamed rice or baked jacket potatoes.

FRAGRANT PORK CURRY

Serves 6
(for a 3.5–4.5 litre slow cooker)

2 onions
3 cloves garlic
1kg lean diced pork
1 tablespoon ground cumin
1 tablespoon ground coriander
1 tablespoon ground turmeric
½ teaspoon ground cardamom
1 star anise
1 cup diced tomato
1 tablespoon Worcestershire sauce
3 teaspoons sweet chilli sauce
3 teaspoons plum sauce
3 teaspoons soy sauce
1 tablespoon chutney (any sort)
3 teaspoons peanut butter (optional)
1 teaspoon salt
½ cup coconut cream
3 teaspoons cornflour

Peel and dice the onions. Peel and crush the garlic. Place in the
slow cooker with the pork, cumin, coriander, turmeric, cardamom,
star anise, tomato, Worcestershire sauce, sweet chilli sauce, plum
sauce, soy sauce, chutney, peanut butter, if using, and salt. Stir to
combine.

Place lid on cooker and cook for 5–6 hours on High or 10–11 hours on Low.

Stir in the coconut cream. If necessary, mix the cornflour with about 2 tablespoons of cold water to a paste and use a little or all of it to thicken the curry. Add salt and pepper to taste.

FRUITY PORK WITH CORIANDER

Serves 4–6
(for a 3.5–4.5 litre slow cooker)

750g lean diced pork
180g dried apricots, diced
60g raisins
2 onions, diced
2 carrots, thinly sliced
1 stalk celery, sliced
2 tablespoons chopped red capsicum
1 teaspoon grated green ginger root
1 tablespoon lemon juice
1½ teaspoons brown sugar
2 teaspoons chutney (any sort)
1½ teaspoons chicken or vegetable stock powder
3 teaspoons sweet chilli sauce
1½ teaspoons Dijon mustard
1 cup dry or medium-dry cider
¼ cup water
2 teaspoons cornflour mixed to a paste with 1 tablespoon
    cold water (optional)
2 tablespoons chopped coriander (optional)

Place the pork, dried apricots, raisins, onion, carrot, celery, capsicum, ginger, lemon juice, sugar, chutney, stock powder, sweet chilli sauce, mustard, cider and water in the slow cooker.

Place the lid on the cooker and cook for 4–5 hours on High or 8–9 hours on Low.

If needed, thicken by stirring in some or all of the cornflour paste. Replace the lid on the cooker and cook for 10 minutes more on High. Stir in the coriander, if using. Add salt and pepper to taste.

Serve with plain boiled or steamed rice.

Italian Meatballs

Serves 4
(for a 3.5–4.5 litre slow cooker)

Meatballs

2 eggs

½ onion

350g lean pork mince

150g beef sausage mince

½ cup fresh breadcrumbs

2 tablespoons flour

2 tablespoons ricotta

2 teaspoons plum sauce

1 tablespoon chopped parsley

1 tablespoon chopped basil

1 teaspoon salt

Sauce

½ onion

400g diced canned or bottled tomato

2 tablespoons red wine

2 tablespoons tomato sauce (ketchup)

2 teaspoons Worcestershire sauce

2 teaspoons plum sauce

2 teaspoons paprika

2 teaspoons brown sugar

1 teaspoon salt

To make the meatballs, whisk the eggs and very finely dice or grate the onion. Add the remaining meatball ingredients. Mix well and roll into walnut-size balls.

To make the sauce, dice the onion and place in a separate bowl with the remaining ingredients.

Spoon 3 tablespoons of the sauce in the base of the slow cooker. Place a layer of meatballs on top, leaving a small space between them. Drizzle a little of the sauce over, add another layer of meatballs and cover evenly with the rest of the sauce.

Place lid on cooker and cook for 4 hours on High or 7–8 hours on Low.

LENTIL STEW WITH ITALIAN SAUSAGES

Serves 4
(for a 3.2–3.5 litre slow cooker)

750g extra lean Italian sausages (available at most
supermarkets)
1 cup dried red lentils
2 onions, diced
3 cloves garlic, crushed
400g can diced tomatoes
3 tablespoons chopped basil
¼ cup red wine
2 cups chicken stock (or 2 cups water with 1½ teaspoons
stock powder)
1 teaspoon brown sugar
2 teaspoons sugar
½ teaspoon salt
3 teaspoons chutney (any sort)
crusty bread or couscous, to serve

Cut the sausages into 5cm lengths and place in the slow cooker with the
lentils, onion, garlic, tomatoes, 1 tablespoon of the basil, the wine, stock,
sugars, salt and chutney.

Place the lid on the cooker and cook for 3–4 hours on High or 7 hours
on Low.

Stir the remaining basil into the stew. Add salt and pepper to taste.

Serve with fresh crusty bread or couscous.

MEAT ROLL WITH SPINACH AND BACON STUFFING

Serves 6
(for a 3.5–4.5 litre slow cooker)

125g chorizo sausage

1 small onion

1 clove garlic

1 egg

500g beef mince

300g lean pork mince

1 cup fresh breadcrumbs

2 teaspoons tomato sauce (ketchup)

2 teaspoons sweet chilli sauce

1 tablespoon plain flour

1 teaspoon salt

½ cup diced canned or bottled tomatoes

1 tablespoon tomato paste

1 teaspoon salt

1 teaspoon sugar

Spinach and Bacon Stuffing

¼ cup pitted kalamata olives

¼ cup semi-dried tomatoes

3 tablespoons pine nuts

120g lean rindless bacon

60g baby spinach leaves

1 egg, lightly whisked

1 tablespoon plain flour

5 tablespoons grated parmesan cheese

Remove skin from the chorizo and chop very finely. Peel and grate the onion. Peel and crush the garlic. Whisk the egg until well broken up. Place all in a bowl with the beef and pork mince, breadcrumbs, tomato sauce, chilli sauce, flour and salt and combine well. Set aside while preparing the stuffing.

To make the spinach and bacon stuffing, chop the olives, semi-dried tomatoes, pine nuts and bacon, and place in a bowl. Pour boiling water over the spinach leaves in a separate bowl and leave to stand for 1 minute. Drain. When cool enough to handle, squeeze out all moisture from spinach and chop finely. Add to the bacon mixture with the egg, flour and parmesan. If you wish, add ½ teaspoon of salt.

Spread a piece of plastic wrap approximately 50cm long on a board or bench. Place the meat mixture onto it and pat out to a rectangle about 25cm x 15cm. Spread the stuffing evenly over the meat, leaving a 1cm rim around the edges. Roll up from the narrow edge by lifting the edge of the plastic wrap to start the rolling and guide the rest of the way. Seal ends by pressing together firmly. Carefully lift the roll into the slow cooker, removing the plastic wrap.

Mix together the tomato, tomato paste, salt and sugar and spread over the top of the meat roll.

Place lid on cooker and cook for 4 hours on High or 7–8 hours on Low.

Slice the meat roll in the cooker, or remove with care and slice to serve.

OLD-FASHIONED PORK PIE

Serves 4–6
(for a 4.5 litre or larger slow cooker)

I put this recipe together after a lively discussion on ABC Radio Tasmania on the subject of pork pies. A listener rang in and related that pork pies were traditionally made for fox hunters to take out on the hunt. The hard pastry, generally just used to enclose the meat, was thrown away and only the pork filling eaten. Whether or not this is the case, I do know the pastry on some pork pies I have tasted is indeed very hard. This seemed a great pity as the pastry is actually very tasty, so I decided to try making a pork pie in the slow cooker, while at the same time baking one in the oven by way of comparison. The slow cooker version was much nicer. The pastry is softer and the herbs in the filling are more pronounced, so the pie was infinitely more delicious.

Making a pork pie is well worth the effort. It is best to prepare the filling first as, if the pastry gets cold, it will not roll out properly.

Keep in mind that a pork pie is to be eaten cold, never hot.

Filling
450g lean pork
60g lean bacon, rind removed, diced
2 teaspoons finely grated onion
1 teaspoon chopped sage
1 teaspoon chopped thyme
½ teaspoon salt
3 scant teaspoons plain flour
1½ cups chicken stock (see page 406 but make with 4 cups
    water not 5 cups) or 1½ cups of bought chicken stock
    plus 3 teaspoons of gelatine*

Rich Hot Water Pastry

250g plain flour
¼ teaspoon salt
2½ tablespoons milk
2½ tablespoons water
120g lard, roughly chopped
1 egg yolk
a little lightly beaten eggwhite

For the filling, cut the pork into 1cm dice and mix with the bacon, onion, sage, thyme, salt, flour and 2 tablespoons of the stock. Set aside while making the pastry.

Place an upturned saucer or small rack in the base of the slow cooker and pour in 1 cup of boiling water. Place the lid on the cooker and turn to High.

To make the pastry, place the flour and salt in a bowl and make a well in the centre. Combine the milk, water and lard in a saucepan and heat gently until the lard has melted, then increase the heat and bring to the boil. Pour the milk mixture into the well and mix through the flour together with the egg yolk to make a soft dough.

Grease a 16cm round cake tin, line the base with baking paper and grease again.

Cut one-third from the pastry and set aside. Roll out the remaining pastry on a lightly floured surface until large enough to line the base and side of the tin. Fit in place. Roll out the other piece of pastry large enough to sit over the top.

Spoon the filling evenly into the pastry-lined tin. Brush the edge of the pastry with a little water. Cover with the pastry that has been rolled out for the top. Crimp the edges together well. Cut a 2.5cm round out of the middle and cover with a piece of foil 3cm larger than the top of the tin. Crimp around the edges and tie under the rim with kitchen string to ensure a good seal.

Place the tin in the slow cooker and pour more boiling water around it to come halfway up the side of the tin. Place the lid on the slow cooker and cook for 5–6 hours on High.

Remove the tin from the cooker and leave the pie to cool to lukewarm.

Meanwhile, heat the remaining stock in a saucepan to boiling point and remove from the heat. If using bought chicken stock sprinkle over the gelatine and whisk to dissolve. Cool to lukewarm. If the jelly starts to set, simply reheat gently to lukewarm. Pour the stock mixture carefully, a little at a time, into the hole in the centre of the pie. Refrigerate the pie until the filling is set, preferably overnight.

The next day, run a knife around the edge and turn the pie out of the tin.

This pie is delicious served with a really good pickle, such as green tomato or zucchini pickle or piccalilli.

*   *Instead of using chicken stock (and gelatine), you can make your own stock for the pie by using the pork bones and the knuckle from a leg of pork. Dice the meat from the bone for the pie, then simply put the bones and knuckle with herbs, salt, an onion and about 3 cups of water in a slow cooker or in a saucepan. Cook for 4 hours on High or 8 hours on Low. If you are using a saucepan on the stovetop, use 4 cups water and cook for 2 hours, then strain off the liquid. Leave until cold and then lift off the fat (this can be kept in the fridge and used later as lard for roasting potatoes). The liquid will be gelatinous when cold, so reheat it to lukewarm and use it as the stock for pouring into the cooled pie. It will set beautifully.*

PORK WITH LEMON, LEEK AND MUSTARD SAUCE

Serves 4
(for a 3.2–4.5 litre slow cooker)

1kg lean diced pork
2 leeks, white part only, thinly sliced
1 small onion, diced
2 teaspoons soy sauce
3 rounded teaspoons whole grain mustard
2 teaspoons quince jelly or 1½ teaspoons sugar
1 teaspoon finely grated lemon rind
juice of 1 large lemon
3 teaspoons dry white wine
½ cup chicken stock or water
¾ teaspoon salt
3 teaspoons cornflour mixed to a paste with 1 tablespoon
    cold water (optional)
⅓ cup cream
1 egg yolk
white pepper, to taste

Place all the ingredients except the cornflour paste, cream and egg yolk in the slow cooker and stir to combine. Cover with the lid and cook for 4–5 hours on High or 8–9 hours on Low until meat is tender.

If needed, thicken with some or all of the cornflour paste.

Whisk together the cream and egg yolk and mix through the sauce. Add salt and white pepper to taste.

Serve over plain boiled or steamed rice with seasonal vegetables or a salad.

PORK AND POLENTA PIE

Serves 6
(for a 3.5–4.5 litre slow cooker)

1 onion
2 cloves garlic
1 red capsicum
1 tablespoon olive oil
500g lean pork mince
1 tablespoon Worcestershire sauce
1 tablespoon sweet chilli sauce
2 teaspoons zucchini pickle
    (or other well-flavoured pickle)
1½ teaspoons paprika
1½ teaspoons salt
1 tablespoon polenta
1 cup fresh or frozen corn kernels
1¾ cups diced fresh, canned or bottled tomatoes
3 tablespoons tomato paste
2 teaspoons cornflour
½ cup grated tasty cheese

Polenta Topping
1 egg
1 cup milk
60g ricotta
1½ cups self-raising flour
½ cup polenta
1 tablespoon grated parmesan cheese
¾ teaspoon salt
30g melted butter

Peel and finely dice the onion. Peel and crush the garlic. Remove the stalk, seeds and membrane from the capsicum and dice.

Heat the oil in a heavy-based saucepan and lightly brown the mince. Add the onion, garlic and capsicum and cook for a further minute. Transfer mixture to the slow cooker. Add the Worcestershire sauce, sweet chilli sauce, zucchini pickle, 1 teaspoon paprika, salt, polenta, corn, tomato and tomato paste. Stir to combine.

Place lid on cooker and cook for 2 hours on High.

Mix the cornflour with about 1 tablespoon of cold water to a paste and use a little or all of it to thicken the mixture. Add salt and pepper to taste. Replace the lid.

To make the polenta topping, whisk the egg, milk and ricotta together until well combined. Mix in the flour, polenta, parmesan, salt and melted butter. Stir until very smooth, then spoon evenly over the meat mixture. Sprinkle with the tasty cheese and remaining paprika.

Replace lid and cook for 1½ hours on High, or until the topping is set.

PORK IN SPICY VEGETABLE SAUCE

Serves 4–6
(for a 3.5–4.5 litre slow cooker)

1 onion
1 red capsicum
400g sweet potato
1 carrot
1 small parsnip
2 cloves garlic
1 small apple
750g lean diced pork
¼ cup tomato sauce (ketchup)
1 tablespoon cider vinegar
2 tablespoons Worcestershire sauce
1 tablespoon brown sugar
1 teaspoon ground ginger
¼ teaspoon ground allspice
1 tablespoon cornflour (optional)

Peel the onion and dice finely. Remove the stalk, seeds and membrane
from the capsicum and dice. Peel the sweet potato, carrot and parsnip
and cut into 1cm dice. Peel and crush the garlic. Peel, core and finely
dice the apple. Remove all visible fat from the pork. Place all in the
slow cooker with the tomato sauce, vinegar, Worcestershire sauce,
sugar, ginger and allspice.

Place lid on cooker and cook for 4–5 hours on High or 7–8 hours on
Low. If necessary, mix the cornflour with about 2 tablespoons of cold
water to a paste and use a little or all of it to thicken the dish. Add salt
and pepper to taste.

PULLED PORK

Serves 6–8
(for a 4.5–5 litre oval slow cooker)

Pulled pork is delicious served hot, and equally or more so the next day in a warm bread roll or in sandwiches.

    1.5–2kg leg of pork
    ½ cup tomato sauce (ketchup)
    2 teaspoons brown sugar
    ½ cup barbecue sauce
    2 teaspoons honey
    2 teaspoons marmalade
    1 tablespoon red wine vinegar
    2 tablespoons Dijon mustard
    1½ tablespoons sweet chilli sauce
    2 tablespoons Worcestershire sauce
    1 tablespoon rum (any sort)
    3 cloves garlic, crushed
    1 teaspoon salt or chicken stock powder
    ½ teaspoon coffee powder or granules

Remove all visible fat from the pork.

Place all the ingredients in the slow cooker. Cover with the lid and cook for 4–5 hours on High or 8–10 hours on Low until the pork is very tender. Lift out and remove any bones.

Shred the meat with two forks and return to the cooker to cook for 20 minutes more on High. Add salt and pepper to taste.

Serve in warm fresh bread rolls, as a filling in wraps.

ROAST PORK WITH CIDER SAUCE

Serves 6–8

(for a 4.5–6 litre slow cooker)

If you would like to have crackling with your pork, simply remove the rind, place it on two paper towels and sprinkle with a little salt. Cover with two more paper towels and place in the microwave on High for 5 minutes. Now remove and cut the backing fat from the rind. Return the rind to the microwave and continue to cook on High until crisp.

> 3kg leg of pork, approximately
> 200g sweet potato
> 2 carrots
> 1 onion
> 1 parsnip
> 1 clove garlic, crushed
> ½ cup dry or medium-dry cider
> ⅓ cup tomato sauce (ketchup)
> 2 teaspoons quince or redcurrant jelly (or brown sugar)
> ½ teaspoon salt
> 3 teaspoons cornflour mixed to a paste with 1 tablespoon
>   cold water

Remove the rind and all visible fat from the pork.

Peel the vegetables, cut into 1cm dice and place in the slow cooker with the garlic, then place the prepared pork on top.

Mix together the cider and tomato sauce and pour over the pork. Spread the quince or redcurrant jelly over the top and sprinkle with the salt.

Place the lid on the cooker and cook for 5–6 hours on High or 9–11 hours on Low until the pork is very tender.

Remove the pork from the cooker, cover with foil and leave to rest for 20 minutes.

Stir the cornflour paste into the juices in the cooker, replace the lid and cook for 10–15 minutes more on High. Add salt and white pepper to taste.

Slice the pork and serve with the gravy from the slow cooker and seasonal vegetables.

ROAST PORK WITH PRUNES AND APRICOT JUS

Serves 4–6
(for a 3.5–4.5 litre slow cooker)

1.5kg pork roast
1 small onion
8 prunes
1 cup fresh breadcrumbs
1 tablespoon chopped fresh sage
1 egg
½ teaspoon salt
pinch of dried sage (optional)
½ cup apricot nectar
1 teaspoon stock powder (any sort)
2 teaspoons lemon juice
2 teaspoons tomato sauce (ketchup)
3 teaspoons sweet chilli sauce
2 teaspoons Dijon mustard
2 teaspoons cornflour (optional)

Remove all fat from the pork and cut a pocket part way through the centre.

Peel and grate the onion. Remove stones from prunes and chop. Combine with the breadcrumbs, sage, egg, salt and dried sage, if using. Stuff into the pocket in the pork and tie up the roast with string to enclose the filling.

Spray the slow cooker with cooking oil or grease lightly with butter. Place the roast in the cooker. Combine the apricot nectar, stock powder, lemon juice, tomato sauce, sweet chilli sauce and mustard. Pour over the pork.

Place lid on cooker and cook for 5 hours on High or 9–10 hours on Low.

Remove pork from cooker, retaining the juices, and leave to rest.

To make the jus, strain the juices from the cooker into a small saucepan. Bring to the boil and reduce until about 1 cup remains.

If necessary, mix the cornflour with about 1 tablespoon of cold water to a paste and use a little or all of it to thicken the jus. Add salt and pepper to taste.

STEAMED PORK BUNS

Makes 6 dumplings
(for a 4–4.5 litre slow cooker)

You will need a wire rack to fit in the base of your slow cooker for this recipe.

For the pastry
1½ cups plain flour
2 teaspoons baking powder
¼ teaspoon salt
30g lard
½ cup warm water
1 teaspoon white vinegar

For the filling
250g pork mince
2 tablespoons bacon, finely diced
1cm piece fresh green ginger root, finely grated
1 clove garlic, crushed
1 spring onion, finely chopped
1 cup finely shredded cabbage
2 teaspoons soy sauce
1 teaspoon barbecue or Hoi Sin sauce
1 teaspoon tomato or apricot chutney
1½ teaspoons oyster sauce
1 egg, lightly beaten
3 teaspoons cornflour
¼ teaspoon salt, optional

First make the pastry. Mix together the flour, baking powder and salt, then rub in the lard with the fingertips until the mixture resembles breadcrumbs. Pour in the combined water and vinegar and mix to make a soft dough, adding a few drops of extra water if necessary. Cover and leave to stand while making the filling.

To make the filling, mix all the ingredients together until well combined.

Pour ½ cup of hot water into the slow cooker and turn on to High. Place a wire rack in the base of the cooker and cut a piece of baking paper to fit over the top of the rack. Place the lid on the cooker and leave to heat while preparing the dumplings.

Divide the dough into 6 even pieces. On a lightly floured surface, roll each piece out to a 14cm diameter circle. Divide the mixture into 6 portions and shape into a ball. Place one ball of filling into the centre of each round of pastry. Brush around edges with a little water and gather up the pastry to form a small parcel around the meat. Press edges together to seal well, then turn over to form neat dumplings with the seam on the underside.

When all the dumplings are prepared, place on the baking paper in the slow cooker. Place lid on cooker and cook on High for 3 hours.

SWEET AND SOUR PORK

Serves 4–6
(for a 3.5–4.5 litre slow cooker)

1kg lean diced pork

2 onions

2 carrots

1 red capsicum

1 green capsicum

420g can pineapple rings in natural juice, drained and juice
  reserved

1 tablespoon soy sauce

1 tablespoon tomato sauce (ketchup)

3 teaspoons sweet chilli sauce

1 tablespoon dry or medium-dry sherry

½ cup brown sugar

½ cup white or cider vinegar

1 teaspoon salt

3 teaspoons cornflour mixed to a paste with 1½ tablespoons
  cold water (optional)

Place the pork in the slow cooker.

Peel the onions and carrots and cut them into thin strips. Remove the
seeds and cores from the capsicums and cut into strips. Cut the pineapple
into strips also. Place all the stips in the slow cooker with the sauces,
sherry, sugar, vinegar, salt and ½ cup of the reserved pineapple juice.

Place the lid on the cooker and cook for 4 hours on High or 8 hours on Low.

If needed, stir in some or all of the cornflour paste to thicken. Add salt
and white pepper to taste. Serve over plain steamed or boiled rice.

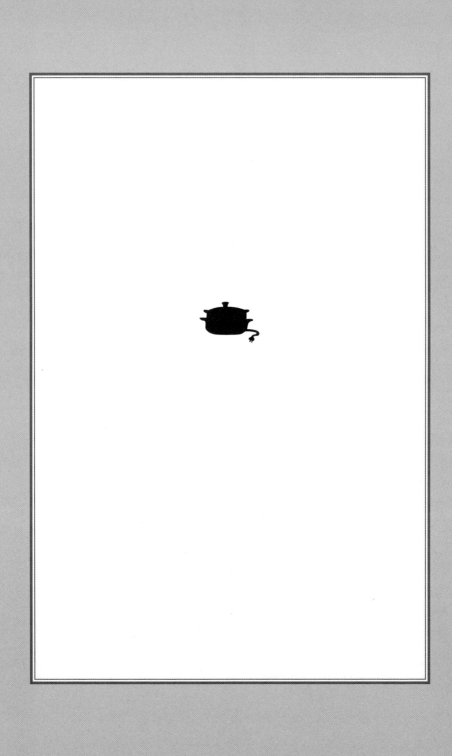

FISH AND
OTHER SEAFOOD

AROMATIC FISH CURRY

Serves 4
(for a 3.5–4.5 litre slow cooker)

600g firm-fleshed fish fillets
1 small onion
2 tablespoons very finely diced leek
1 tablespoon very finely diced lemongrass
1 teaspoon ground cumin
1 teaspoon ground coriander
½ teaspoon garam masala
½ teaspoon ground cardamom
1 teaspoon ground turmeric
3 teaspoons sweet chilli sauce
2 teaspoons chutney (any sort)
¾ cup coconut milk
½ teaspoon salt
2 teaspoons cornflour
1½ tablespoons chopped coriander

Cut the fish into 2.5cm dice and place in the slow cooker. Peel and very finely dice the onion and add to the cooker with the leek, lemongrass, cumin, coriander, garam masala, cardamom, turmeric, sweet chilli sauce, chutney, ¼ cup of coconut milk and salt.

Place lid on cooker and cook for 2–2½ hours on Low.

Mix the remaining coconut milk with the cornflour until smooth. Place in a small saucepan and bring to the boil, stirring until it thickens. Stir into the curry in the cooker. Scatter the curry with the coriander and serve on steamed rice.

FLATHEAD WITH SPICED POTATO CREAM

Serves 4–6
(for a 3.5–4.5 litre slow cooker)

The spice mixture seeps into the potatoes and leek, resulting in a delicious spiced cream that in no way overpowers the delicate flavour of the fish.

350g potatoes, coarsely grated
70g butter, melted
1 leek, white part only, very thinly sliced
600g flathead fillets, with skin
1½ teaspoons mustard powder
1½ teaspoons sweet paprika
½ teaspoon vegetable stock powder
2 teaspoons brown sugar
2 tablespoons lime juice
2 tablespoons cream
white pepper, to taste

Quickly mix together the grated potatoes and melted butter to stop the potatoes browning. Mix in the leek.

Grease the base of the slow cooker and cover with the potato mixture. Place the flathead fillets on top, skin side down.

Mix together the mustard powder, paprika, stock powder, sugar and lime juice and spoon over the fish. Place the lid on the cooker and cook on Low for 2½–3 hours, or until the fish is cooked. Remove the fish from the cooker and keep warm.

Mix the cream into the potato mixture, cover the cooker with the lid and cook for 5 minutes on High. Add salt and white pepper to taste. Serve portions of the fish on the spiced potato cream.

GUMBO

Serves 4–6
(for a 4–4.5 litre slow cooker)

This tasty seafood stew is delicious served with fresh crusty bread or as a marinara sauce over pasta, topped with a little shaved parmesan.

> 300g white fish fillets (such as ling, flathead, whiting or
>   monkfish)
> 1 calamari hood, thinly sliced (or extra 100g white fish fillet)
> 1 onion, diced
> 4 cloves garlic, crushed
> 1 red capsicum, deseeded and diced
> 3 rounded tablespoons tomato paste
> 1 tablespoon tomato sauce (ketchup)
> 2 teaspoons Worcestershire sauce
> 3 teaspoons sweet chilli sauce
> 3 teaspoons chutney (any sort)
> 1½ tablespoons chopped fresh basil
> ½ teaspoon salt
> ½ teaspoon brown sugar
> 1 teaspoon vegetable, chicken or fish stock powder
> 3 teaspoons chopped thyme
> 1 cup diced canned or fresh tomatoes
> 1 tablespoon chopped parsley
> 300g uncooked medium-sized prawns, peeled and deveined
> 250g scallops, cleaned
> pasta, to serve (any sort)
> ½ cup shaved or grated parmesan cheese, to serve
>   (optional)

Cut the fish into 2cm cubes and place in the slow cooker with the calamari, onion, garlic, capsicum, tomato paste, sauces, chutney, basil, salt, sugar, stock powder, thyme and tomatoes. Stir to combine, cover with the lid and cook for 3 hours on Low.

Stir in the parsley, prawns and scallops and cook for 10 minutes more on Low until just cooked through. Add salt and pepper to taste.

Serve over pasta with a little shaved or grated parmesan, if liked.

MIDDLE EASTERN SPICED FISH

Serves 4
(for a 3.5 litre slow cooker)

250g tomatoes
600g fish fillets (such as trevalla, monkfish or ling)
1½ teaspoons ground turmeric
2 teaspoons ground cumin
1½ teaspoons ground coriander
½ teaspoon dried chilli flakes
½ teaspoon ground cardamom
½ teaspoon finely grated lemon rind
½ teaspoon brown sugar
¼ teaspoon salt
½ teaspoon finely grated green ginger root
1 tablespoon lemon or lime juice
¼ cup coconut cream

Cut the tomatoes into 6mm slices and place evenly over the base of the slow cooker. Cut the fish into 5cm pieces and place in a bowl. Add the spices, lemon rind, sugar, salt, ginger and lemon or lime juice. Mix well so that the fish is evenly and thoroughly coated. Spoon the entire contents of the bowl evenly over the tomatoes.

Place the lid on the cooker and cook for 2½–3 hours on Low. Stir in the coconut cream, replace the lid and cook for a further 5 minutes.

Serve with couscous made by thoroughly mixing together in a bowl:
1½ cups of couscous, ½ teaspoon of finely grated lemon rind, ¼ teaspoon of chicken or vegetable stock powder and 1½ cups of boiling water. Leave to stand for 5 minutes, then fluff up with a fork and serve.

OCEAN TROUT FILLETS WITH SPICY ASIAN GLAZE

Serves 4
(for a 3.5–4.5 litre slow cooker)

600g ocean trout fillets
1 spring onion, white part only
1 clove garlic
1 teaspoon grated green ginger
2 tablespoons sherry
1 tablespoon soy sauce
2 teaspoons honey
1 teaspoon cornflour

Cut the fish into 10cm x 5cm pieces. Place in the slow cooker. Slice the spring onion and scatter over the fish.

Peel and crush the garlic. Place in a bowl with the ginger, sherry, soy sauce and honey and mix to combine. Pour over the fish.

Place lid on cooker and cook for 2–2½ hours on Low.

Remove fish to a serving dish.

Mix the cornflour with about 1 tablespoon of cold water to a paste. Pour the juices in the cooker into a small saucepan. Bring to the boil and thicken with the cornflour paste to make a glaze. Cook for a further minute. Add a little salt, if needed. Spoon a little of the glaze over each portion of fish.

SALMON CUTLETS WITH DRIED FRUIT AND LIME

Serves 4
(for a 3.5–4.5 litre slow cooker)

2 teaspoons very finely diced lemongrass
1 teaspoon olive oil
juice of 1 lime
1 teaspoon finely grated lime rind
4 salmon cutlets
1 small onion
¾ cup chopped dried apricots
¼ cup chopped raisins
2 teaspoons seeded mustard
1 teaspoon redcurrant or quince jelly
¼ cup white wine
¼ cup apricot nectar
2 teaspoons cornflour

Place 1 teaspoon of lemongrass, oil, lime juice and rind in base of slow cooker. Place the salmon cutlets on top.

Peel and very finely dice the onion. Place in a bowl with the remaining lemongrass, dried apricots, raisins, mustard and reducurrant or quince jelly. Spread evenly over the fish.

Mix together the white wine and apricot nectar and pour over the fish.

Place lid on cooker and cook for 2–2½ hours on Low.

Meanwhile, mix the cornflour with about 2 tablespoons of cold water to a paste.

Remove fish from cooker.

Immediately thicken the mixture in the cooker with a little or all of the cornflour paste. Add salt and pepper to taste, if required.

Place a small amount of the fruit mixture on each serving plate, top with a salmon cutlet and drizzle with a little of the jus from the cooker.

SALMON, LEEK AND ASPARAGUS COBBLER

Serves 6
(for a 3.5–4.5 litre slow cooker)

150g asparagus stalks

2 leeks, white part only, sliced (or 2 small onions, thinly
    sliced)

700g salmon fillets, cut into 2cm cubes

¾ cup chicken or fish stock (or ¾ cup water with
    ½ teaspoon stock powder)

juice of 1 lemon

½ teaspoon finely grated lemon rind

½ teaspoon Dijon mustard

¼ teaspoon salt

½ cup cream

2 teaspoons cornflour

2 egg yolks

½ cup grated tasty cheese

white pepper, to taste

Cobbler Topping

1 cup self-raising flour

45g butter, melted

1 egg, lightly beaten

1 tablespoon grated parmesan cheese

3 teaspoons snipped chives

3 teaspoons chopped parsley

⅓ cup milk

Peel any tough outer layer of asparagus stalks and cut the stalks into 1cm pieces.

Place the leek and asparagus in the base of the slow cooker and place the salmon on top.

Mix together the stock, lemon juice and rind, mustard and salt and pour over the salmon.

Place the lid on the cooker and cook for 2 hours on Low.

Turn the cooker to High. In a bowl, whisk together the cream and cornflour until just combined, then whisk in the egg yolks. Stir into the mixture in the slow cooker, together with the grated cheese. Add salt and white pepper to taste. Place the lid on the cooker.

To make the cobbler topping, mix the flour, butter, egg, parmesan, chives, parsley and milk in a bowl and drop dessertspoonfuls over the salmon mixture. Cover with the lid and cook for 25 minutes on High.

Serve with fresh seasonal vegetables or a green salad.

SEAFOOD LAKSA

Serves 4–6

(for a 4–4.5 litre slow cooker)

400g white fish fillets (such as ling or whiting)

200g calamari, cleaned

1 onion, finely diced

3cm piece of green ginger root, peeled and finely grated

4 cloves garlic, crushed

2 teaspoons finely chopped lemongrass, white part only, or
  ½ teaspoon finely grated lemon rind

2 teaspoons ground cumin

1½ teaspoons ground coriander

1 teaspoon ground turmeric

3 teaspoons fish sauce

3 teaspoons brown sugar

1 teaspoon smooth peanut butter (optional)

2 tablespoons lemon or lime juice

1½ teaspoons chicken or vegetable stock powder

400ml can coconut milk

200g uncooked medium-sized prawns, peeled and
  deveined with tail intact

400g fresh egg noodles

3 tablespoons chopped coriander leaves

1 long red chilli, deseeded and finely chopped, to serve
  (optional)

Cut the fish into 3cm pieces and slice the calamari thinly. Place in the slow cooker with the onion, ginger, garlic, lemongrass, spices, fish sauce, sugar, peanut butter, if using, lemon juice, stock powder and coconut milk and stir to combine. Cover with the lid and cook for 3 hours on Low.

Stir in the prawns and egg noodles and cook for 5–10 minutes.

Stir in half the coriander. Add salt and pepper to taste.

Serve bowls of laksa sprinkled with the remaining coriander and the chilli, if liked.

SPANISH-STYLE STUFFED SQUID WITH CREAMY POTATO CASSEROLE

Serves 4
(for a 3.5–4.5 litre slow cooker)

The slow cooker is an ideal way to cook squid – the extended cooking time tenderises and moistens it, making it succulent and delicious. In this recipe, the stuffed squid is cooked on a bed of diced potato to form a delicious potato casserole as the squid is gently slow-cooked.

100g chorizo sausage

90g leek (white part only)

2 tomatoes

1 clove garlic

2 teaspoons olive oil

¼ cup diced bacon

1 egg

½ teaspoon finely diced preserved lemon rind,
    or 1 teaspoon finely grated lemon rind

¼ cup finely shredded basil leaves

1 cup fresh breadcrumbs

4 medium squid tubes, cleaned

750g potatoes

¼ cup chicken or fish stock

30g butter, cut into small pieces

juice of ½ lemon

3 teaspoons cornflour

1 tablespoon sour cream

1 teaspoon mayonnaise (optional)

1½ tablespoons chopped parsley

254

Dice the chorizo very finely. Wash the leek well and dice finely, along with the tomatoes. Peel and crush the garlic.

Heat the oil and sauté the chorizo, bacon and leek for 5 minutes, then add the tomato and garlic and sauté for a further 3 minutes. Lightly whisk the egg. Add to the sautéed mixture with the preserved lemon, basil and breadcrumbs. Mix well.

Use the mixture to stuff the squid tubes, leaving a little space at each end of the tube. Set aside while preparing the potatoes.

Turn the slow cooker setting to High. Peel the potatoes and cut into 1cm dice. Place in base of cooker with the stock and butter. Stir to combine. Place the filled squid tubes on the potato mixture and drizzle over the lemon juice.

Place lid on cooker, turn setting to Low and cook for 3 hours.

Remove squid tubes to a dish. Mix the cornflour with about 2 tablespoons of cold water and use a little or all of it to thicken the potato mixture. Mix in the sour cream, mayonnaise, if using, and parsley.

Slice the squid and serve with the creamy potato casserole on the side.

WHOLE OCEAN TROUT WITH APRICOT AND ALMOND STUFFING

Serves 4–6
(for a 3.5–4.5 litre slow cooker)

1 small onion
1 tablespoon finely chopped fennel
2 tablespoons chopped dried apricots
2 tablespoons finely chopped almonds
2 tablespoons lime juice
1 teaspoon finely grated lime rind
1 tablespoon chopped parsley
½ teaspoon salt
1 egg
1 ocean trout or similar firm-fleshed fish,
    cleaned and scaled

To make the stuffing, peel and very finely dice the onion. Place in a bowl with the fennel, apricot, almonds, lime juice and rind, parsley and salt. Lightly whisk the egg and combine with the other stuffing ingredients. Stuff the fish with this mixture.

In the slow cooker, place a piece of baking paper large enough to cover the base and most of the way up the sides. Place the fish on this.

Place lid on cooker and cook for 2½ hours on Low.

Note: *Choose a fish that will fit in your cooker — it may be necessary to remove the head and tail.*

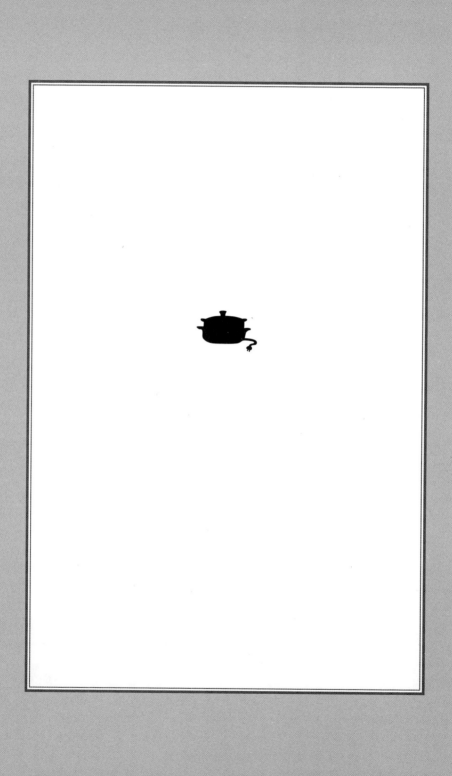

VEGETABLES
AND MOSTLY
VEGETARIAN

BOMBAY POTATOES

Serves 4
(for a 3.2–3.5 litre slow cooker)

It is best to use a waxier-type potato for this recipe, or at least one that does not go to mush during cooking. Ask your vegetable supplier if in doubt.

Although the recipe specifies peeling the potatoes, you can use washed potatoes, in which case they need not be peeled.

> 1kg potatoes
> 1 onion, diced
> 2 teaspoons garam masala
> 2 teaspoons ground cumin
> 2 teaspoons ground coriander
> 1 teaspoon sweet paprika
> 1 teaspoon salt
> 3 teaspoons chutney (any sort)
> 3 teaspoons sweet chilli sauce
> 1 tablespoon tomato sauce (ketchup)
> 400g can diced tomatoes

Peel the potatoes and cut into 2cm dice. Place in the slow cooker with the rest of the ingredients and stir to combine, making sure that the potatoes are coated with the sauce.

Cover with the lid and cook for 3½–4 hours on High or 7–8 hours on Low. Add salt and pepper to taste.

BRUSSELS SPROUTS WITH HONEY AND BACON

Serves 4

(for a 3.5–4.5 litre slow cooker)

400g Brussels sprouts
3 tablespoons chicken stock
1 teaspoon seeded mustard
1 teaspoon honey
1 small onion
125g rindless bacon
2 teaspoons oil

Cut the bases from the Brussels sprouts, remove any tough outer leaves and cut in half. Mix the stock with honey and mustard. Drizzle a small amount in base of slow cooker and add sprouts, cut-side up.

Peel and finely dice the onion. Dice the bacon. Heat the oil in a small saucepan and sauté the onion and bacon until the onion is transparent. Scatter over the sprouts. Drizzle with the rest of the stock, honey and mustard mixture.

Place lid on cooker and cook on High for 1½ hours, or until sprouts are tender.

CABBAGE SAVOURY

Serves 4
(for a 3.5–4.5 litre slow cooker)

4 cups shredded cabbage, firmly packed
2 onions
2 carrots
1½ stalks celery
180g bacon, rind removed
1 tablespoon cider vinegar
1 teaspoon sugar
½ teaspoon salt

Place cabbage in the slow cooker.

Peel the onions and carrots and finely dice. Dice the celery and bacon. Add to the cooker with the vinegar, sugar and salt. Mix well.

Place lid on cooker and cook for 2–3 hours on High.

Stir and add salt and pepper to taste.

CANNELLONI WITH SPINACH AND FETTA

Serves 4–6
(for a 3.5–4.5 litre slow cooker)

250g frozen spinach or fresh baby silverbeet leaves
1 small onion
375g fetta cheese, crumbled
1½ cups grated tasty cheese
¾ cup grated parmesan cheese
2 teaspoons chopped parsley
3 eggs
250g instant cannelloni shells
3 cups diced canned or bottled tomatoes or passata
2 tablespoons tomato paste
1 teaspoon sugar
½ teaspoon salt

Cook the spinach or silverbeet in 3 tablespoons water for 3 minutes. Drain well and leave to cool, then squeeze to remove all liquid. Chop finely.

Peel and grate the onion. Combine the spinach and onion with the fetta, 1 cup of tasty cheese, ½ cup of parmesan and the parsley. Whisk the eggs and mix through. Fill the cannelloni shells with this mixture.*

Mix together the tomato, tomato paste, sugar and salt. Spread a thin layer in the base of the slow cooker, and then put a layer of the cannelloni shells. Spread half the remaining tomato mixture, then the rest of the shells and top with the last of the tomato mixture. Combine the remaining tasty cheese and parmesan and scatter over the top.

Place lid on cooker and cook for 1½–2 hours on High.

* *It is much easier to fill the cannelloni shells using a piping bag. Disposable piping bags are available at most supermarkets.*

Note: *Use a mixture of half fetta, half ricotta if a little less saltiness is preferred. Personally, I like the sharp saltiness of the fetta.*

CAPONATA

Serves 4–6
(for a 3.2–4.5 litre slow cooker)

This delicious, tasty dish is ideal for vegetarians or as a side dish. Serve with fresh crusty bread or garlic bread.

500g eggplant
2 onions
1 stalk celery
20 black olives
400g can diced tomatoes
5 teaspoons capers in brine, drained
2 tablespoons pine nuts (optional)
1 tablespoon tomato paste
¼ cup sugar
⅓ cup white vinegar
1 tablespoon sweet chilli sauce
1 teaspoon salt (optional)

Cut the eggplant into 1.5cm cubes and place in the slow cooker.

Dice the onions and slice the celery into 1cm lengths. Add to the slow cooker with the rest of the ingredients and stir to mix.

Place the lid on the cooker and cook for 4 hours on High or 7–8 hours on Low. Add salt and pepper to taste.

CIDER BRAISED ONIONS

Serves 4–6 as a side dish
(for a 3.2–3.5 litre slow cooker)

If pickling onions are hard to access, simply use the smallest ones you can find.

>   750g pickling onions, peeled
>   ½ cup dry or medium-dry cider
>   ¾ teaspoon Dijon mustard
>   1 teaspoon sugar
>   ½ teaspoon salt

Place the onions in the slow cooker. Mix the rest of the ingredients together and pour over the onions.

Place the lid on the cooker and cook for 3 hours on High or 6 hours on Low.

COURTNEY'S LENTIL AND VEGETABLE RAGOUT

Serves 6 as a main course, 10 as a side dish
(for a 4.5–5 litre slow cooker)

A hearty and healthy meal for vegetarians or a side dish to feed many.

125g dried red lentils
2 onions, diced
350g sweet potato, diced
400g eggplant, cut into 1cm cubes
200g zucchini, cut into 1cm cubes
2 carrots, diced
400g can diced tomatoes
3 teaspoons tomato paste
3 cups vegetable stock (or 3 cups water with 2 teaspoons
    stock powder)
3 teaspoons sweet chilli sauce
1½ tablespoons tomato sauce (ketchup)
400g can chickpeas, drained and rinsed
400g can three bean mix or kidney beans, drained and
    rinsed
1 teaspoon quince jelly or brown sugar
couscous or steamed or boiled rice, to serve

Place all the ingredients in the slow cooker and stir to combine. Place
the lid on the cooker and cook for 4 hours on High or 7–8 hours on Low.
Add salt and pepper to taste.

Serve on couscous or rice.

DHAL

Serves 4–6
(for a 3.5–4.5 litre slow cooker)

1 onion
1 clove garlic
2 tomatoes
180g red lentils
2 teaspoons ground cumin
2 teaspoons ground coriander
1 teaspoon ground turmeric
3 cups stock (any sort) or water
1 teaspoon salt
3 teaspoons sweet chilli sauce
3 teaspoons tomato chutney
½ cup coconut cream

Peel and dice the onion. Peel and crush the garlic. Dice the tomatoes.
Place in the slow cooker with the lentils, cumin, coriander, turmeric,
stock or water and salt. Stir to combine.

Place lid on cooker and cook for 6 hours on Low.

Stir through the sweet chilli sauce, chutney and coconut cream.
Add salt and pepper to taste.

HERBED PUMPKIN CASSEROLE

Serves 4
(for a 3.2–3.5 litre slow cooker)

750g pumpkin (such as Kent, Jap or butternut)
1 apple, peeled, cored and diced (such as Golden Delicious
or Granny Smith)
125g lean bacon, rind removed, diced
1 onion, diced
juice of ½ orange
1½ cups chicken or vegetable stock (or 1½ cups water with
1 teaspoon stock powder)
1 tablespoon chopped parsley, plus 1 tablespoon extra
1 teaspoon chopped thyme
3 teaspoons cornflour mixed to a paste with
1½ tablespoons cold water

Peel the pumpkin, remove and discard any seeds and cut into 2.5cm
cubes. Place in the slow cooker with the apple, bacon, onion, orange
juice, stock, parsley and thyme. Stir to mix well. Place the lid on the
cooker and cook for 3 hours on High or 6 hours on Low.

If the casserole needs thickening, mix in some or all of the cornflour
paste. Stir in the extra parsley and add salt and pepper to taste.

HOMEMADE BAKED BEANS

Serves 6
(for a 3.5–4.5 litre slow cooker)

This is a recipe developed by our 16-year-old daughter, Courtney, which she has adapted here for the slow cooker. It's extremely easy to prepare, nutritious and so delicious that you will never again return to the canned variety.

> 500g dried haricot or navy beans
> 2 onions
> 3½ cups tomato purée
> 3 tablespoons tomato paste
> 1½ tablespoons mild-flavoured honey
> 3 teaspoons vegetable stock powder

Cover the beans with cold water (at least 3 cm). Leave to soak overnight. The next day, drain off the liquid. Cook for 15 minutes in boiling water. Drain.

Peel and finely dice the onion and place in the slow cooker with the beans, 1 cup of water, tomato purée, tomato paste, honey and stock powder.

Place lid on cooker and cook for 4 hours on High or 7 hours on Low.

Note: *For variation, add a smoked ham hock to the cooker along with the rest of the ingredients for a lovely rich, meaty sauce. Extend the cooking time on Low to 8 hours if you do this. When ready to serve, remove the hock from the cooker, take the meat from the bone and return it to the baked bean mixture.*

HONEY CARROTS WITH CITRUS AND PARSLEY

Serves 4–6
(for a 3.5–4.5 litre slow cooker)

750g carrots
½ teaspoon grated orange rind
½ cup orange juice
2 teaspoons lemon juice
½ teaspoon salt
1 tablespoon honey
2 teaspoons butter
1–2 tablespoons finely chopped parsley

Peel the carrots and cut into thin strips. Place in the slow cooker with the orange rind, orange juice, lemon juice and salt. Drizzle over the honey.

Place lid on cooker and cook for 3 hours on High, or until carrot is just tender (check after 2½ hours).

Remove carrot from cooking liquid with a slotted spoon and place in a serving dish. Cut the butter into 4–6 pieces and stir through the carrot to coat. Add salt and pepper to taste, then stir through the parsley.

HOT POTATO SALAD

Serves 6

(for a 3.5–4.5 litre slow cooker)

1kg potatoes
1 onion
2 cloves garlic
180g lean bacon
1 teaspoon salt
½ cup chicken stock
1 tablespoon cornflour
½ cup cold milk
1 cup cream
2 teaspoons Dijon or seeded mustard
2 teaspoons cider vinegar
1 cup grated tasty cheese
2 tablespoons finely chopped parsley

Peel the potatoes and cut into 1.25cm dice. Peel and finely dice the onion. Peel and crush the garlic. Remove rind from bacon and dice. Place in the slow cooker and add the salt and chicken stock.

Place lid on cooker and cook for 3 hours on High or 6 hours on Low.

When cooking time is almost complete, mix the cornflour with the milk to a paste. Heat the cream until boiling and thicken with the cornflour paste. Mix in the mustard, vinegar and cheese. Stir until cheese is melted.

Remove lid from cooker and stir in the cheese sauce. Mix well.

Serve topped with chopped parsley.

Hungarian Potatoes

Serves 4–6 as a side dish
(for a 3.5–4.5 litre slow cooker)

This is a good, hearty side dish or even a main course vegetarian meal.

750g potatoes
1 onion
1 stalk celery
1 red capsicum
1 leek, white part only (optional)
2 cloves garlic, crushed
2 teaspoons paprika
3 teaspoons Worcestershire sauce
2 teaspoons olive oil
1¼ cups diced tomatoes (fresh, canned or bottled)
3 teaspoons tomato paste
3 teaspoons chutney (any sort)
1 teaspoon brown sugar
3 teaspoons chopped sage or thyme
1 teaspoon salt
2 rounded tablespoons sour cream
chopped parsley, to serve (optional)

Peel the potatoes and cut into 1.25cm cubes. Dice the onion and slice the celery. Deseed and dice the capsicum and slice the leek, if using. Place all the vegetables in the slow cooker with the rest of the ingredients except the sour cream and stir to combine.

Cover with the lid and cook for 4 hours on High or 7–8 hours on Low.

Stir in the sour cream, then add salt and pepper to taste.

Serve sprinkled with chopped parsley, if liked.

Leeky Thyme Potatoes

Serves 4–6
(for a 3.5–4.5 litre slow cooker)

1.5kg potatoes (such as Kennebecs or Bintjes)

2 large leeks, white part only

½ teaspoon salt

2 tablespoons chopped thyme

1 cup chicken or vegetable stock (or 1 cup water with
 ¾ teaspoon stock powder)

30g butter, melted

1½ teaspoons cornflour mixed to a paste with 1 tablespoon
 cold water (optional)

2 tablespoons cream (optional)

Peel and thinly slice the potatoes.

Wash and slice the leeks.

Place a layer of a third of the potato slices in the slow cooker, sprinkle with some of the salt, top with a layer of half the leeks and half the thyme. Repeat layering, then finish with the remaining potato slices. Pour in the stock and press down slightly so that as much potato as possible is covered with the liquid.

Brush the top layer of potato with the melted butter.

Place the lid on the cooker and cook for 4 hours on High or 8 hours on Low.

Remove the lid and stir in some or all of the cornflour paste to thicken, if needed. Stir in the cream, if using. Add salt and pepper to taste.

MEDITERRANEAN POTATOES WITH OLIVES

Serves 4–6

(for a 3.5–4.5 litre slow cooker)

2 onions

2 cloves garlic

750g potatoes

1 large red capsicum

1 cup pitted kalamata olives

1¾ cups diced tomatoes (fresh, canned or bottled)

3 tablespoons tomato paste

3 teaspoons chutney

1½ teaspoons salt

1 teaspoon sugar

3 teaspoons cornflour (optional)

Peel and dice the onions. Peel and crush the garlic. Peel and cut the potatoes into 1cm dice. Place in the slow cooker with the remaining ingredients and stir to combine.

Place lid on cooker and cook for 4–4½ hours on High or 8–9 hours on Low.

If necessary, mix the cornflour with about ¼ cup of cold water to a paste and use a little or all of it to thicken the dish. Add salt and pepper to taste.

MEDLEY OF VEGETABLES IN CHEESE AND PARSLEY SAUCE

Serves 4–6
(for a 3.5–4.5 litre slow cooker)

1kg mixed fresh vegetables, such as parsnips, carrots,
   sweet potato, celery
1 cup stock (or 1 cup water with 2 teaspoons stock
   powder)
1½ tablespoons cornflour
1⅓ cups milk
1 cup grated tasty cheese
2 teaspoons Dijon mustard
3 tablespoons chopped parsley

Peel all the vegetables and cut into 1cm dice. Place in the slow cooker with the stock.

Place lid on cooker and cook for 3 hours on High or 6 hours on Low.

Near the end of cooking time, mix the cornflour with ½ cup of the milk to a paste. Heat the remaining milk until boiling and quickly whisk in the cornflour paste. Stir in the cheese and mustard.

When the vegetables are cooked, stir the cheese sauce through, together with the chopped parsley.

MIDDLE EASTERN RICE

Serves 4–6
(for a 3.2–3.5 litre slow cooker)

2 cups long-grain rice

½ cup pine nuts

½ cup currants

4 cups chicken stock (or 4 cups water with 3 teaspoons
   stock powder)

½ teaspoon ground turmeric

2 tablespoons chopped parsley

4 silverbeet leaves or 2 cups baby English spinach leaves,
   shredded

Place the rice, pine nuts, currants, stock and turmeric in the slow cooker and stir to combine. Place the lid on the cooker and cook for 1½–2 hours on High or 3 hours on Low.

Stir in the parsley and silverbeet or spinach. Replace the lid on the cooker and cook for 10 minutes more. Add salt and pepper to taste.

MINTED BABY POTATOES

Serves 4–6

1kg small potatoes (such as Pink Eyes)
2 tablespoons softened butter, plus 1 tablespoon extra
½ teaspoon salt
3 tablespoons finely chopped mint

Scrub the potatoes very well, or peel them if you prefer, and place in the slow cooker with the softened butter and salt.

Place lid on cooker and cook for 2–3 hours on High or 4 hours on Low.

Drain off any liquid from the cooker and add the extra butter and mint. Stir carefully to combine. Add salt and pepper to taste.

MUSHROOM AND BACON RISOTTO

Serves 4
(for a 3.5–4.5 litre slow cooker)

By conventional cooking methods arborio rice would be used. However, this goes too gluggy in the slow cooker so long-grain rice is used here. You may need to use a little extra stock at the end.

> 1 onion, finely diced
> 250g mushrooms, sliced
> 2 cloves garlic, crushed
> 200g lean bacon, rind removed, diced
> 1 cup long-grain rice
> juice of ½ large lemon
> 2½ cups chicken or vegetable stock (or 2½ cups water with
>   1 teaspoon stock powder)
> 3 teaspoons chopped thyme
> ½ cup chopped semi-dried tomatoes
> ½ teaspoon salt (optional)
> ½ cup pouring or thickened cream
> ½ cup grated or shaved parmesan cheese
> 45g butter, diced
> 1–2 tablespoons chopped parsley, to serve

Place the onion, mushrooms, garlic, bacon, rice, lemon juice, stock, thyme, tomatoes and salt in the slow cooker and stir to combine.

Place the lid on the cooker and cook for 2 hours on High or 4 hours on Low.

Stir in the cream, parmesan and butter. Add salt and pepper to taste.

Sprinkle with the chopped parsley to serve.

NAPOLITANA SAUCE

Serves 6
(for a 3.2–4.5 litre slow cooker)

This dish is ideal for serving with pasta. Any leftovers can be added to a gravy or soup or as a sauce to top a pizza.

> 1 large onion, diced
> 1 large red capsicum, deseeded and diced
> 4 cloves garlic, crushed
> 1 teaspoon apricot jam or brown sugar
> 1 tablespoon chopped fresh rosemary or basil
> 1 teaspoon vegetable stock powder
> 2 x 400g cans diced tomatoes
> 3 teaspoons soy sauce
> 3 teaspoons Worcestershire sauce
> 1 tablespoon tomato sauce (ketchup)
> 3 teaspoons chutney (any sort)
> 1 tablespoon sweet chilli sauce
> 3 teaspoons cornflour mixed to a paste with 2 tablespoons
>   cold water (optional)
> cooked pasta, to serve (any sort)
> grated parmesan cheese, to serve

Place all the ingredients except the cornflour paste in the slow cooker, cover with the lid and cook for 4 hours on High or 8 hours on Low.

Thicken slightly, if needed, by stirring in the cornflour paste. Add salt and pepper to taste.

Serve over pasta and top with the grated parmesan.

PAPRIKA POTATOES

Serves 6
(for a 3.5–4.5 litre slow cooker)

1.5kg potatoes
1 onion
2 cloves garlic
3 teaspoons paprika
1½ teaspoons seeded mustard
1 tablespoon tomato sauce (ketchup)
1 cup stock
1 teaspoon lemon juice
1 teaspoon Worcestershire sauce
½ teaspoon salt
3 tablespoons sour cream
3 teaspoons cornflour (optional)

Peel the potatoes and cut into 1.5cm dice. Peel and dice the onion, and peel and crush the garlic. Add to the slow cooker with the paprika, mustard, tomato sauce, stock, lemon juice, Worcestershire sauce and salt.

Place lid on cooker and cook for 3 hours on High or 6 hours on Low.

Turn off the heat and stir through the sour cream.

If necessary, mix the cornflour with about ¼ cup of cold water to a paste and use a little or all of it to thicken the dish. Add salt and pepper to taste.

PARSNIP AND PARMESAN MASH

Serves 4–6
(for a 3.5–4.5 litre slow cooker)

1kg parsnips
¼ cup stock (any sort) or water
60g butter
¾ teaspoon salt
1½ teaspoons lemon juice
2 tablespoons cream
2 teaspoons grated parmesan cheese

Peel the parsnips and cut into thin strips. If the inner core of any parsnip is tough or stringy, discard it and use an extra parsnip to make up the lost weight.

Place in the slow cooker with the stock or water, half of the butter and the salt.

Place lid on cooker and cook for 3 hours on High or 5 hours on Low, or until parsnip is very soft.

Add the remaining butter and purée until smooth. Whisk in the lemon juice, cream and parmesan. Add salt and pepper to taste.

PEPERONATA

Serves 4–6
(for a 3.5–4.5 litre slow cooker)

This is not a true peperonata, but it has come to be our home version, evolving over the years to make this tasty dish. It can be used as a vegetarian meal in its own right, or serves well as a side dish, or even as the tomato topping for a pizza.

750g red capsicums
300g tomatoes
300g zucchini
2 onions
4 cloves garlic
⅓ cup tomato paste
1 tablespoons sweet chilli sauce
1 tablespoon chutney (any sort)
1 teaspoon sugar
1 teaspoon salt
3–4 teaspoons cornflour (optional)

Remove the stalk, seeds and membrane from the capsicums and cut into 1.25cm dice. Chop the tomatoes into 1.25cm dice. Trim the zucchini and cut into 1.25cm dice. Peel and finely dice the onions. Peel and crush the garlic.

Place vegetables in the slow cooker and add the tomato paste, sweet chilli sauce, chutney, sugar and salt. Stir to combine.

Place lid on cooker and cook for 4 hours on High or 7–8 hours on Low.

Add salt and pepper to taste. If necessary, mix the cornflour with about 2 tablespoons of cold water to a paste and use a little or all of it to thicken the dish.

PEPPERED RICE WITH PEAS

Serves 4–6

(for a 3.2–4.5 litre slow cooker)

1 red capsicum
1 green capsicum
1½ cups long-grain rice
1 onion, diced
½ teaspoon salt
3 cups vegetable or chicken stock (or 3 cups water with
    2 teaspoons stock powder)
1 cup fresh or frozen peas
2 tablespoons chopped parsley
30g butter, diced

Remove the seeds and cores from the capsicums and dice. Place in the slow cooker with the rice, onion, salt and stock. Stir to combine.

Place the lid on the cooker and cook for 2 hours on High or 3–3½ hours on Low.

Near the end of the cooking time, pour boiling water over the peas in a heatproof bowl, then strain off the liquid. Add the peas to the slow cooker with the parsley and stir to combine. Cook for 20 minutes more. Stir in the butter. Add salt and pepper to taste.

PILAF

Serves 4–5

(for a 3.5–4.5 litre slow cooker)

2 onions

4 cloves garlic

2 cups long grain rice

5 cups warm chicken stock (or 5 cups water with
1 tablespoon stock powder)

2 teaspoons dried basil

Peel and finely dice the onions. Peel and crush the garlic.

Place all ingredients in the slow cooker and stir to combine.

Place lid on cooker and cook for 2 hours on High or 3½–4 hours on Low.

Add salt and pepper to taste.

POLENTA

Serves 6
(for a 3.5–4.5 litre slow cooker)

1½ cups polenta
2½ cups milk
2½ cups water
1½ teaspoons salt
½ cup cream
1 cup grated parmesan cheese

Place the polenta in the slow cooker.

Place the milk, water and salt in a saucepan and bring to the boil. Pour over the polenta.

Place lid on cooker and cook for 1¼ hours on High or 2½ hours on Low.

Stir in the cream and parmesan. Add salt to taste.

Note: *You may need to add a little extra cream, milk or water to bring the dish to the consistency you require.*

POTATOES BOULANGÈRE WITH BACON

Serves 4
(for a 3.5–4.5 litre slow cooker)

600g potatoes
2 onions
125g bacon, rind removed
2 tablespoons chopped parsley
½ teaspoon salt, approximately (optional)
1 cup chicken stock (or 1 cup water with ½ teaspoon stock
   powder)

Peel the potatoes and onions and cut into thin slices (about 6mm).
Dice the bacon.

Layer in the slow cooker as follows:
   one-third of the potato slices;
   half the onion;
   a light sprinkling of salt, if using;
   one-third of the bacon;
   one-third of the parsley;
   one-third of the potato slices;
   the remaining onion;
   a light sprinkling of salt, if using;
   one-third of the bacon;
   one-third of the parsley;
   the remaining potato slices;
   a light sprinkling of salt, if using;
   the remaining bacon;
   the remaining parsley.

Pour the stock over the top. Cover the cooker with the lid and cook for 3 hours on High or 5–6 hours on Low approximately until the potato is cooked through. Add salt and pepper to taste.

Potato and Cauliflower Curry

Serves 4–6
(for a 3.2–3.5 litre slow cooker)

600g potatoes
450g cauliflower
3 cloves garlic, crushed
2 onions, diced
2 tomatoes, diced
3 teaspoons mustard powder
3 teaspoons ground cumin
½ teaspoon garam masala
½ teaspoon brown sugar
1 teaspoon vegetable stock powder
½ teaspoon salt
1 tablespoon sweet chilli sauce
¼ cup dry or medium-dry apple cider
¾ cup water
1 tablespoon tomato sauce (ketchup)
65ml coconut milk
2 teaspoons cornflour mixed to a paste with 1 tablespoon
    cold water (optional)
¼ cup chopped coriander (optional)
boiled or steamed rice or couscous, to serve

Peel the potatoes and cut into 2cm cubes. Place in the base of the slow cooker.

Cut the cauliflower into florets (not too small) and place over the potatoes, together with the garlic, onion and tomato.

Mix together the mustard powder, cumin, garam masala, sugar, stock powder, salt, sweet chilli sauce, cider, water, tomato sauce and coconut milk and pour over the vegetables.

Place the lid on the cooker and cook for 3–4 hours on High or 7 hours on Low.

If needed, thicken with some or all of the cornflour paste. Mix in the coriander, if using, and add salt and pepper to taste.

Serve over plain rice or couscous.

PUMPKIN RISOTTO

Serves 4–6
(for a 3.5–4.5 litre slow cooker)

1 large onion
1 clove garlic
1 cup long-grain rice
2½ cups chicken stock, or (2½ cups water with
    3 teaspoons stock powder)
1 cup puréed cooked pumpkin
¾ cup grated parmesan cheese
½ cup milk
½ cup cream
2 teaspoons lemon juice

Peel and finely dice the onion. Peel and crush the garlic. Place in the slow cooker with the rice and stock and mix well.

Place lid on cooker and cook for 2½–3 hours on High or 4–5 hours on Low.

Stir and fold in the pumpkin, parmesan, milk, cream and lemon juice until well combined. Add salt and pepper to taste.

PUMPKIN TIMBALES WITH PARSLEY BUTTER

Serves 6
(for a 3.5–4.5 litre slow cooker)

½ cup milk
60g grated tasty cheese
30g grated parmesan cheese
2 eggs
¼ cup self-raising flour
½ cup cooked mashed pumpkin, cooled
½ cup creamed corn
¼ teaspoon salt
2 tomatoes
60g butter
1½ tablespoons finely chopped parsley

Heat the milk in a saucepan until boiling, then stir in the cheeses until melted.

In a bowl, whisk together the eggs, flour, pumpkin, corn and salt, then fold in the cheese mixture until well combined.

Grease six 200ml metal dariole moulds.

Cut the tomatoes into 8mm thick slices. Place a piece of tomato in the base of each mould (cutting to size if necessary).

Spoon the pumpkin mixture into each mould to two-thirds full. Place a slice of tomato on top. Place the moulds in the slow cooker and pour in boiling water to come halfway up the sides of the moulds.

Place the lid on the cooker and cook for 2½ hours on High or 5 hours on Low.

Remove the timbales with oven mitts and leave to stand in the moulds for 5 minutes, then turn out onto serving plates.

Melt the butter and add the parsley, then drizzle a little over each timbale before serving.

RANCHER'S EGGS

Serves 4
(for a 3.2–3.5 litre slow cooker)

This delicious Mexican-style breakfast dish is very easy to prepare – and when put on the night before, requires only a few minutes in the morning to cook the eggs. It is generally served over corn tortillas but I often serve it over thick slices of lightly toasted sourdough bread.

600g canned diced tomatoes
1 onion, finely diced
½ red capsicum, deseeded and diced
2 cloves garlic, crushed
1 teaspoon ground cumin
¾ teaspoon ground oregano
3 teaspoons sweet chilli sauce
1 teaspoon vegetable or chicken stock powder
½ teaspoon brown sugar
¾ teaspoon salt
2 teaspoons cornflour mixed to a paste with 1 tablespoon
    cold water (optional)
4–6 eggs
corn tortillas, to serve
grated tasty cheese, to serve
refried beans, to serve (optional)

Place all the ingredients except the cornflour paste and eggs in the slow cooker, stir well to combine.

Cover with the lid and cook for 4 hours on High or 8–9 hours on Low. Add salt and pepper to taste.

If needed, thicken with some or all of the cornflour paste – you need to be able to make hollows in the mixture in which to sit the eggs. Break in the eggs, turn the cooker to High, cover with the lid and cook for a few minutes until the eggs are cooked to your liking.

Serve over tortillas sprinkled with cheese. Some people like to serve the eggs with refried beans, which are available at supermarkets.

Note: *To feed a crowd, use a larger cooker and double the recipe. The number of eggs that will fit in your cooker will determine the number of people you can feed.*

RATATOUILLE

Serves 6
(for a 3.2–3.5 litre slow cooker)

2 onions
1 small eggplant
300g zucchini
1 red (or green) capsicum, deseeded
120g mushrooms
3 cloves garlic, crushed
400g can diced tomatoes
2 teaspoons sweet paprika
3 teaspoons sweet chilli sauce
2 teaspoons Worcestershire sauce
3 teaspoons chutney (any sort)
1 tablespoon tomato paste
1½ teaspoons brown sugar
1½ teaspoons salt
2–3 sprigs rosemary
pasta, couscous or polenta, to serve
crusty bread, to serve

Dice the onion and cut the eggplant, zucchini and capsicum into 1cm cubes. Slice the mushrooms. Place the vegetables in the slow cooker with the rest of the ingredients and stir to combine. Cover with the lid and cook for 3 hours on High or 6 hours on Low. Add salt and pepper to taste.

Serve as a vegetarian dish with pasta, couscous or polenta and fresh crusty bread.

Note: *This is also good used as a pizza topping, topped with slices of mozzarella and torn basil leaves.*

RED CABBAGE AND BACON BRAISE

Serves 4

(for a 3.5–4.5 litre slow cooker)

1 onion
1 apple
150g diced bacon
5 cups finely shredded red cabbage
1 teaspoon sugar
½ teaspoon salt
1 teaspoon caraway seeds
1 tablespoon cider vinegar
30g butter

Peel and finely dice the onion. Peel, core and dice the apple. Place in the slow cooker with the bacon and cabbage. Add the sugar, salt, caraway seeds, vinegar and 1 tablespoon of water. Mix well.

Cut the butter into small pieces and dot over the top of the cabbage mixture.

Place lid on cooker and cook for 2 hours on High.

Add salt and pepper to taste.

RED CABBAGE WITH ORANGE AND CARAWAY SEEDS

Serves 4–6 as a side dish
(for a 3.2–3.5 litre slow cooker)

½ red cabbage (about 1.25kg), finely shredded

1 onion, diced

2 teaspoons grated orange rind

juice of 1 orange

1 tablespoon balsamic vinegar

3 teaspoons brown sugar

1 teaspoon golden syrup

1 teaspoon caraway seeds

1 teaspoon salt or chicken stock powder

3 teaspoons cornflour mixed to a paste with
    1½ tablespoons cold water (optional)

Place all the ingredients except the cornflour paste in the slow cooker and stir to combine. Cover with the lid and cook for 3 hours on High or 6 hours on Low.

Thicken, if needed, with some or all of the cornflour paste and add salt and pepper to taste.

ROASTED RED CAPSICUM AND EGGPLANT LASAGNE

Serves 6
(for a 4.5–5 litre slow cooker)

700g red capsicums
500g eggplant
200g zucchini
1 onion
2 teaspoons salt
200g pumpkin
300g sweet potato
1 tablespoon chopped rosemary
2 x 400g cans diced tomatoes
3 teaspoons cornflour
2 cloves garlic, crushed
½ teaspoon brown sugar
1 teaspoon salt, extra
3 teaspoons chutney (any sort)
3 teaspoons sweet chilli sauce
400g fresh lasagne sheets
½ cup grated parmesan cheese
crusty bread or garlic bread and green salad, to serve

Cut the capsicums in half and remove the seeds and cores. Place under a hot grill, skin side up, until the skin blackens. Wrap in plastic wrap and leave to cool for a few minutes, by which time the skin will peel off easily.

Meanwhile, cut the eggplant, zucchini and onion into 8mm slices and place in a colander with the salt and mix well. Leave to stand for 30 minutes, then rinse and pat dry with paper towel.

Peel the pumpkin and sweet potato and cut into 6mm slices. Mix together.

Mix together the rosemary, tomatoes, cornflour, garlic, sugar, extra salt, chutney and sweet chilli sauce.

Place a layer of the sauce mixture in the base of the slow cooker, then add a layer of lasagne sheets and continue to layer as follows:

>eggplant, zucchini and onion mixture;
>pumpkin and sweet potato mixture;
>sauce mixture;
>lasagne sheets;
>eggplant, zucchini and onion mixture;
>pumpkin and sweet potato mixture;
>sauce mixture;
>lasagne sheets;
>sauce mixture.

Place the lid on the cooker and cook for 3½–4 hours on High or 7–8 hours on Low. Remove the lid from the cooker and sprinkle the parmesan on top. Cover with the lid and cook on High until the cheese has melted (about 5–10 minutes).

Serve with fresh crusty bread or garlic bread and green salad.

ROOT VEGETABLE PURÉE

Serves 4–6 as a side dish
(for a 3.2–3.5 litre slow cooker)

The combination of root vegetables in this dish is really delicious. However, you can vary it to include any other root vegetables.

180g carrots
500g parsnips
80g swede or turnip
300g sweet potato
¾ cup chicken or vegetable stock (or ¾ cup water with
    ½ teaspoon stock powder)
½ teaspoon salt
50g butter, diced

Peel the vegetables and cut into 3cm cubes. Place in the slow cooker with the stock and salt. Cover with the lid and cook for 4 hours on High or 7–8 hours on Low.

Mash the mixture until very smooth or purée with a stick blender. Whisk in the butter. Add salt and pepper to taste.

Note: *For a really rich and even more delicious dish, add ½ cup grated tasty cheese and 2 tablespoons cream at the end of cooking time.*

SPANISH POTATOES WITH CHORIZO AND BLACK OLIVES

Serves 4–6
(for a 3.5–4.5 litre slow cooker)

This dish makes a delicious sauce for pasta. Top each serve with shaved parmesan.

You can leave the chorizo out if preferred.

700g potatoes
1 large red capsicum
1 onion, diced
2 cloves garlic, crushed
½ teaspoon salt
1 teaspoon sugar
½ cup shredded basil leaves
2 teaspoons sweet paprika
3 teaspoons tomato paste
1 tablespoon tomato sauce (ketchup)
2 chorizos (about 250g), sliced
½ cup black olives

Peel the potatoes and cut into 1cm cubes. Remove the seeds and core from the capsicum and cut into 1cm pieces.

Place the potato and capsicum in the slow cooker with the rest of the ingredients and stir to combine. Cover with the lid and cook for 4 hours on High or 7–8 hours on Low. Add salt and pepper to taste.

SPICED LENTILS

Serves 4–6

(for a 3.5–4.5 litre slow cooker)

This dish has been a specialty of our daughter Courtney since she first invented it when she was 12 years old. It remains a household favourite and is ideal as a vegetarian main course. She has adapted the recipe here for the slow cooker.

1 cup green lentils
3 cups water
2 teaspoons coriander seeds
2 teaspoons cumin seeds
½ teaspoon whole cloves
1 teaspoon ground turmeric
½ teaspoon cayenne pepper
1 teaspoon sugar
1½ teaspoons salt
1 cup crushed fresh, canned
   or bottled tomatoes
1 large tablespoon tomato paste
1 onion
1 carrot
4 cloves garlic

Combine the lentils and water in a bowl and leave to soak overnight.

The next day, pour the lentils and water mixture into the slow cooker.

In a mortar and pestle or spice grinder, grind to a powder the coriander and cumin seeds and cloves. Add to the cooker with the turmeric, cayenne pepper, sugar, salt, tomato and tomato paste.

Peel the onion and carrot and dice finely. Peel and crush the garlic. Add to the cooker and stir to combine.

Place lid on cooker and cook for 8–9 hours on Low. Add salt and pepper to taste.

SPICED PUMPKIN PURÉE

Serves 6
(for a 3.2–3.5 litre slow cooker)

This delicious dish I find is best cooked on Low. It is an excellent side dish for meats or chicken.

1kg pumpkin
2 cloves garlic, crushed
½ cup dried red lentils
1 teaspoon ground coriander
2 teaspoons ground cumin
½ teaspoon mustard powder
½ teaspoon garam masala
1 tablespoon sweet chilli sauce
¾ cup coconut milk
¾ cup water
¾ teaspoon salt

Peel the pumpkin, remove and discard the seeds, then cut the flesh into 2.5cm cubes. Place in the slow cooker with the rest of the ingredients and stir to combine.

Place the lid on the cooker and cook for 4 hours on High or 7 hours on Low. Add salt and pepper to taste.

SPICY CAULIFLOWER, POTATO AND PEA CURRY

Serves 6
(for a 3.5–4.5 litre slow cooker)

1 onion

3 cloves garlic

750g potatoes

375g cauliflower florets

juice of 1 lime or lemon

½ teaspoon finely grated lime or lemon rind

3 teaspoons zucchini pickle
(or other well-flavoured pickle)

2 teaspoons ground cumin

1 teaspoon ground coriander

1 teaspoon curry powder

1 cup coconut milk

½ cup coconut cream

1½ cups fresh or frozen peas

2 long red chillies (optional)

3 teaspoons tomato chutney

3 teaspoons seeded mustard

1 tablespoon tomato sauce (ketchup)

2 teaspoons golden syrup

1 tablespoon cornflour (optional)

2 tablespoons natural yoghurt

finely chopped mint, to serve

Peel and finely dice the onion. Peel and crush the garlic. Peel the potatoes and cut into 1cm dice. Place all in the slow cooker with the cauliflower, lime or lemon juice and rind, zucchini pickle, cumin, coriander, curry powder and coconut milk.

Place lid on cooker and cook for 4 hours on High.

Stir in the coconut cream, then add the peas. Finely dice the chillies, if using, and stir through. Replace lid and cook for a further 30 minutes.

Stir in the chutney, mustard, tomato sauce and golden syrup. If necessary, mix the cornflour with about 2 tablespoons of cold water to a paste and use a little or all of it to thicken the curry. Stir in the yoghurt. Add salt and pepper to taste.

Serve sprinkled with a little chopped mint.

SPICY PUMPKIN CURRY

Serves 4–6
(for a 3.5–4.5 litre slow cooker)

When cooked, this curry will contain a pumpkin purée, as well as defined pieces of pumpkin.

750g pumpkin
1 onion
2 cloves garlic
1 cup chicken or vegetable stock
    or (1 cup water with 2 teaspoons stock powder)
1 teaspoon ground coriander
2 teaspoons ground cumin
½ teaspoon ground fenugreek
½ teaspoon ground fennel
½ teaspoon ground turmeric
½ teaspoon dried mint
2 teaspoons chutney (any sort)
1 tablespoon tomato paste
1 teaspoon salt
½ cup coconut cream
2 teaspoons cornflour (optional)

Peel the pumpkin and cut into 2cm pieces. Peel and chop the onion. Peel and crush the garlic. Place in the slow cooker with the stock, coriander, cumin, fenugreek, fennel, turmeric, mint, chutney, tomato paste and salt. Mix well.

Place lid on cooker and cook for 3 hours on High or 5½ hours on Low.

Stir in the coconut cream. Add salt and pepper to taste.

If necessary, mix the cornflour with about 1½ tablespoons of cold water to a paste and use a little or all of it to thicken the curry.

STUFFED TOMATOES

Serves 4
(for a 3.5–4.5 litre slow cooker)

500g firm tomatoes (about 4 tomatoes)
2 tablespoons water

Filling
1 small onion, grated
1½ tablespoons chopped parsley
100g bacon, rind removed, diced
2 teaspoons Worcestershire sauce
1 egg, lightly beaten
½ cup breadcrumbs
90g parmesan cheese, grated

Cut the tomatoes in half and scoop out the pulp and seeds.

Mix together the filling ingredients and fill the cavities in the tomatoes.

Pour the water into the base of the slow cooker and arrange the stuffed tomatoes on top.

Place the lid on the cooker and cook for 2 hours on High or 3½–4 hours on Low.

SWEDE AND POTATO MASH

Serves 6
(for a 3.5–4.5 litre slow cooker)

750g swedes
500g potatoes
1 small onion
60g lean rindless bacon
1 teaspoon salt
¼ cup chicken stock or water
2 large tablepoons sour cream
chopped parsley, to serve

Peel the swedes, potatoes and onion, then cut into 1.25cm dice. Dice the bacon. Place in the slow cooker with the salt and stock.

Place lid on cooker and cook for 5 hours on High or 8 hours on Low.

Purée the mixture until very smooth. Stir in the sour cream. Add salt and pepper to taste. Serve topped with a little chopped parsley.

SWEET POTATO AND ROSEMARY PURÉE

Serves 4–6
(for a 3.5–4.5 litre slow cooker)

1kg peeled sweet potato
1 clove garlic
¾ cup chicken stock
juice of ½ orange
2 teaspoons lemon juice
2 teaspoons butter
1½ teaspoons salt
1½ tablespoons sour cream
1 tablespoon cream (optional)
2 teaspoons very finely chopped
    fresh rosemary leaves
toasted pine nuts, to serve (optional)

Cut the sweet potato into 3cm pieces and place in the slow cooker. Peel and crush the garlic and add to the potato, along with the chicken stock, orange juice, lemon juice, butter and salt. Stir to combine.

Place lid on cooker and cook for 4 hours on High or 8 hours on Low, or until the sweet potato is very soft.

Purée the mixture. Stir through the sour cream, cream, if using, and rosemary. Add salt and white pepper to taste. Serve scattered with toasted pine nuts, if using.

TURKISH RISOTTO

Serves 4—6
(for a 3.5–4.5 litre slow cooker)

This dish is quite moist — a delicious accompaniment to a curry or casserole-style dish.

> 1½ cups long-grain rice
> 4 cups vegetable or chicken stock (or 4 cups water with
>   2½ teaspoons of stock powder)
> ½ cup chopped dried apricots
> ¼ cup currants
> ⅓ cup slivered almonds
> ½ teaspoon salt
> 1 teaspoon ground turmeric
> 1 onion, finely diced
> 1 stalk celery, finely diced
> 3 tablespoons chopped parsley

Place all the ingredients except the parsley in the slow cooker and stir to combine.

Place the lid on the cooker and cook for 2½–3 hours on High until the rice is tender.

Fluff up the rice with a fork while at the same time mixing through the chopped parsley. Add salt and pepper to taste.

VEGETARIAN CURRY WITH TOFU

Serves 4–6
(for a 3.5–4.5 litre slow cooker)

1 onion
1kg vegetables, such as pumpkin, sweet potato, carrot,
    parsnip, potato, kohlrabi, cauliflower
1 clove garlic
1 long red chilli (optional)
2 teaspoons ground cumin
1 teaspoon ground coriander
1 teaspoon ground turmeric
½ teaspoon ground cardamom
½ teaspoon garam masala
1 star anise
2 teaspoons stock powder
1 teaspoon finely grated green ginger root
¾ cup diced fresh, canned or bottled tomato
2 tablespoons tomato paste
2 tablespoons sweet chilli sauce
350g tofu, cut into 1.5cm cubes
1 tablespoon cornflour
½ cup coconut cream

Peel the onion and vegetables (as appropriate) and cut into 1.5cm dice.
Break cauliflower, if using, into florets. Peel and crush the garlic.
Remove stalk end, seeds and membrane from the chilli, if using, and
chop finely. Place all in the slow cooker.

Add the cumin, coriander, turmeric, cardamom, garam masala, star anise, stock powder or salt, ginger, tomato, tomato paste, sweet chilli sauce and ½ cup water. Mix well.

Add the tofu and stir through carefully.

Place lid on cooker and cook for 4 hours on High or 7–8 hours on Low.

Mix the cornflour with about 3 tablespoons of cold water to a paste and use a little or all of it to thicken the mixture. Stir in the coconut cream. Add salt and pepper to taste.

VEGETABLE CASSEROLE

Serves 6
(for a 3.5–4.5 litre slow cooker)

750g sweet potato

120g carrots

2 onions

100g parsnip

150g tomatoes, diced

1 red capsicum, deseeded and diced

2 tablespoons tomato paste

juice of ½ small lemon

¾ teaspoon salt

3 teaspoons tomato sauce (ketchup)

3 teaspoons sweet chilli sauce

1 cup vegetable stock (or 1 cup water with 1 teaspoon
     stock powder)

3 teaspoons cornflour mixed to a paste with 1 tablespoon
     cold water

Peel the sweet potato, carrots, onions and parsnip and cut into 1cm cubes. Place in the slow cooker with the tomato, capsicum, tomato paste, lemon juice, salt, sauces and stock. Stir to combine. Cover with the lid and cook for 4 hours on High or 7–8 hours on Low. Turn the cooker to High (if set on Low) and stir in all the cornflour paste to thicken, if needed. Add salt and pepper to taste.

VEGETABLE KORMA

Serves 4
(for a 3.2–4.5 litre slow cooker)

300g potatoes
200g sweet potato
100g pumpkin (such as Kent, Jap or butternut)
200g parsnips
2 onions
3 cloves garlic, crushed
3 teaspoons grated green ginger root
400ml can coconut milk
1½ tablespoons sweet chilli sauce
3 teaspoons ground cumin
1 teaspoon garam masala
1 teaspoon mustard powder
1½ teaspoons ground coriander
1 teaspoon salt
1½ tablespoons tomato paste
couscous and naan, to serve
Greek-style yoghurt, to serve

Peel the vegetables and cut into 1.5cm pieces. Place in the slow cooker with the rest of the ingredients and mix well.

Place the lid on the cooker and cook for 4–5 hours on High or 8–9 hours on Low. Add salt and pepper to taste.

Serve as a side dish or main vegetarian meal with couscous and naan and a little Greek-style yoghurt on the side.

VEGETABLES FOR A ROAST

Serves 4
(for a 3.5–5 litre slow cooker)

This method of cooking vegetables makes a roast possible, even for the busiest of days. The vegetables are gently cooked all day long, then, a few minutes before serving, are quickly browned in a little oil on the stovetop. It reduces messy washing-up significantly and the vegetables are wonderfully flavoured. You can use different vegetables if you prefer, for example turnips, sweet potato, or golden beets.

      2 carrots
      2 parsnips
      4 small onions
      4 cloves garlic
      1kg pumpkin (such as Kent, Jap or butternut)
      3 tablespoons water

Peel the vegetables, cut the carrots into chunks, not too thick (no more than 2.5cm), and place in the base of the slow cooker. Cut the parsnips into similar-sized pieces and place on top, then scatter the onions and garlic cloves around the cooker. Cut the pumpkin into large chunks or wedges and place on top. Pour in the water. Place the lid on the cooker and cook for 4 hours on High or 7–8 hours on Low.

A few minutes before serving, pour some oil to a depth of 8mm in a frying pan. Heat to 180°C approximately. Remove the vegetables from the cooker and cook in the oil on one side until browned, then turn over and brown on the other side. They are now ready to serve with your roast meat.

Note: *Use the liquid that remains in the base of the slow cooker to make a gravy if you need it, or add to a soup another time. (If using later, store in the fridge or freezer in an airtight container.)*

VEGETABLES IN SPICY PEANUT SAUCE

Serves 4–6

(for a 3.5–4.5 litre slow cooker)

Excellent as a vegetarian meal or as a side dish.

500g washed potatoes
2 onions
400g sweet potato
1 parsnip, 250g approximately
2 teaspoons curry powder
1½ teaspoons ground cumin
1 teaspoon ground coriander
1 teaspoon salt
juice of ½ lemon
1 tablespoon soy sauce
3 teaspoons sweet chilli sauce
4 rounded tablespoons peanut butter (crunchy or smooth)
400ml can coconut milk
steamed or boiled rice or couscous and pappadums, to
    serve

Cut the potatoes into 1cm cubes and place in the slow cooker. Peel and cut the onions, sweet potato and parsnip into 1cm cubes and add to the cooker, together with the spices, salt, lemon juice, sauces, peanut butter and coconut milk. Stir to combine.

Place the lid on the cooker and cook for 3 hours on High or 5–6 hours on Low. Add salt and pepper to taste.

Serve with plain rice or couscous and pappadums.

VEGETARIAN LASAGNE WITH EGGPLANT AND CAPSICUM

Serves 4–6
(for a 3.5–4.5 litre slow cooker)

400g eggplant
1 tablespoon salt, plus 1½ teaspoons extra
500g red capsicums
3 teaspoons cornflour
150g mushrooms
1 onion
3 cloves garlic
810g diced canned or bottled tomatoes
3 large tablespoons tomato paste
1 tablespoon chutney (any sort)
3 teaspoons Worcestershire sauce
2 teaspoons soy sauce
3 teaspoons chilli sauce
1½ teaspoons sugar
250g packet instant lasagne sheets
½ cup shredded basil leaves

Cheese Sauce
350g ricotta
3 teaspoons cornflour
3 eggs
1 teaspoon salt
½ cup grated tasty cheese
1 cup grated fresh parmesan

Cut the eggplant into 6mm slices. Place in a colander, sprinkle with the salt and mix well. Leave to stand for 30 minutes, then rinse and pat dry.

Mix the cornflour with about 2 tablespoons of cold water to a paste and set aside.

To prepare the tomato sauce, remove the stalks, seeds and membrane from the capsicums and cut into 2cm dice. Place in a heatproof dish, cover with plastic wrap and microwave for 5 minutes on high. Drain off the liquid.

Wipe and dice the mushrooms. Peel and dice the onion. Peel and crush the garlic. Place in a medium saucepan with the tomato, tomato paste, chutney, Worcestershire sauce, soy sauce, chilli sauce, sugar and extra salt. Cook over medium-high heat, stirring often until sauce is reduced to two-thirds its original volume. Thicken with the cornflour paste.

To make the cheese sauce, whisk together the ricotta, cornflour, eggs and salt, then add the tasty cheese and half the parmesan.

Turn the slow cooker setting to High and spray with cooking oil or grease with butter. Spread 3 tablespoons of the tomato sauce over the base.

Top with one-third of the eggplant, then one-third of the lasagne sheets, broken into pieces to fit cooker, and spread with a little more tomato sauce. Then cover with half the remaining eggplant, then half the capsicum, half the basil, a small amount of tomato sauce and a small amount of the cheese sauce. Top with half the remaining lasagne sheets, spread with tomato sauce, and then layer with the remaining eggplant, capsicum and basil. Top with the rest of the tomato sauce, a layer of cheese sauce, then the last of the lasagne sheets, cheese sauce and parmesan.

Place lid on cooker and cook for 2 hours on High.

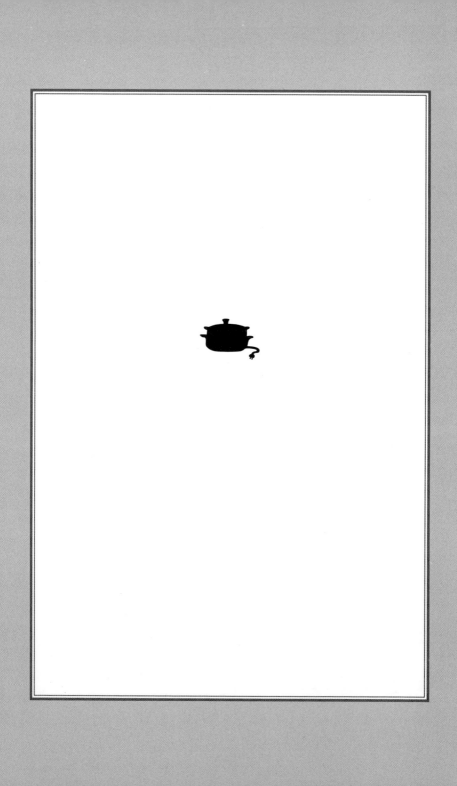

DESSERTS

APPLE AND CINNAMON SPONGE PUDDING

Serves 4–6

(for a 3.5–4.5 litre slow cooker)

1kg apples
juice of 1 lemon
½ cup sugar, plus 2 teaspoons extra
2 teaspoons butter
½–1 teaspoon ground cinnamon
ice-cream, cream or yoghurt, to serve

Sponge Topping
1 egg
¾ cup sugar
½ cup milk
1½ cups self-raising flour
1 teaspoon grated lemon rind
2 tablespoons lemon juice
60g butter, melted

Peel and core the apples and cut into eighths. Place in the slow cooker with the lemon juice, ½ cup of sugar and ¼ cup of water.

Place lid on cooker and cook for 2–3 hours on High or 4–5 hours on Low.*

Turn cooker setting to High while preparing the sponge topping. Whisk the egg and sugar together, then whisk in the milk, flour, lemon rind, lemon juice and melted butter (all at once). Pour evenly over the apple in the cooker.

Replace lid and cook for about 45 minutes to 1 hour on High, or until well risen and cooked through.

Remove lid from cooker and rub the butter over the surface of the sponge, then sprinkle with the extra sugar and cinnamon. Serve with ice-cream, cream or yoghurt.

* _Alternatively, you can cook the apples on the stovetop, but will need to add about ¹/₄ cup extra water. When cooked, place in the slow cooker while still hot and proceed with the recipe._

APPLE DUMPLINGS IN BUTTERSCOTCH SAUCE

Serves 4
(for a 3.5–4.5 litre slow cooker)

2 apples
1 cup self-raising flour
1 teaspoon sugar
3 teaspoons butter
1 teaspoon finely grated lemon rind
1 egg yolk
1 cup brown sugar, lightly packed
1 tablespoon butter
1 tablespoon golden syrup
ice-cream, cream or yoghurt, to serve

Peel and core the apples and cut into quarters, lengthways. Lightly grease the inside of the slow cooker with butter or spray with cooking oil.

Mix the flour, sugar and a pinch of salt in a bowl. Cut the butter into small pieces and rub into the flour mixture with your fingertips until the mixture resembles fine breadcrumbs. Mix in the lemon rind. Lightly whisk the egg yolk and mix in with about ¼ cup of cold water, or just enough to make a soft dough.

Divide the dough into eight equal pieces and flatten each of them out a little. Take each piece of apple and mould a piece of dough around it. Place the 'dumplings' in the slow cooker.

Place the brown sugar, butter, golden syrup and 1½ cups of water in a small saucepan and bring to the boil. Pour over the dumplings. Place lid on cooker and cook for 1–1½ hours on High. Serve dumplings with ice-cream, cream or yoghurt.

APPLE GOLDEN SYRUP DUMPLINGS

Serves 4
(for a 3.5–4.5 litre slow cooker)

1 tablespoon butter
½ cup sugar
2 tablespoons golden syrup
cream, ice-cream or yoghurt, to serve

Dumplings
1 cup self-raising flour
3 level teaspoons butter
2 tablespoons coarsely grated apple
milk, to combine

Place butter, sugar, golden syrup and 1½ cups of water in the slow cooker. Place lid on cooker and cook for approximately 40 minutes on High or until boiling.*

When syrup is almost boiling, make the dumplings.

Place the flour in a bowl and rub in the butter with your fingertips. Stir in the grated apple, then mix to a soft dough with milk. Roll into walnut-size balls.

Take a sheet of baking paper slightly larger than the cooker and spray one side with cooking spray or grease with a little butter.

When the syrup is boiling, place dumplings in the syrup. Place baking paper greased-side down on top of cooker and replace lid.

Cook for 25 minutes on High.

Serve with cream, ice-cream or yoghurt.

*   *Alternatively, preheat the slow cooker on High. Put the water, butter, sugar and golden syrup in a saucepan and bring to the boil, then pour the syrup mixture into the cooker. Place lid on cooker while you prepare the dumplings.*

Apple Self-Saucing Pudding

Serves 4–6

(for a 3.5 litre slow cooker only)

4 cooking apples, such as Granny Smith
1 tablespoon butter
2 rounded tablespoons self-raising flour
¾ cup sugar
2 teaspoons lemon juice

Peel and core the apples, then cut in half lengthways.

Grease the inside of the slow cooker with a little butter or spray with cooking oil.

Place the apple cut-side up in the cooker.

Rub the butter into the flour with your fingertips. Mix in the sugar, ¾ cups of cold water and lemon juice (the mixture will look very unusual). Pour mixture evenly over the apple.

Place lid on cooker and cook for 2 hours on High or 4 hours on Low.

APRICOT CREAM PUDDING

Serves 4
(for a 3.5 litre slow cooker)

825g can apricot halves in natural juice (or equivalent in
    preserved apricot halves), drained
2 eggs
½ cup sugar
¼ cup milk
¼ cup sour cream
3 teaspoons lemon or orange juice
½ cup self-raising flour
½ teaspoon finely grated lemon or orange rind
90g butter, melted
icing sugar, sifted, to dust
vanilla ice-cream or sweetened whipped cream, to serve

Grease the slow cooker.

Arrange the apricot halves, cut side down, over the base of the cooker.

Whisk together the eggs and sugar in a bowl until light and creamy, then
fold in the milk, sour cream, lemon or orange juice, flour, rind and butter.
Pour over the apricots.

Place the lid on the cooker and cook for 2 hours on High.

Dust with a little icing sugar and serve with ice-cream or whipped cream.

Apricot Gingerbread Pudding

Serves 4–6

(for a 4.5 litre slow cooker only)

1 large can apricot halves, or 1 bottle preserved apricots
1¾ cups self-raising flour
½ teaspoon bicarbonate of soda
½ teaspoon ground cinnamon
2 teaspoons ground ginger
1 egg
½ cup milk
3 teaspoons lemon juice
90g butter
60g brown sugar
½ cup golden syrup
ice-cream, crème fraîche or mascarpone, to serve

Drain the apricots, reserving ½ cup of the juice. Place the apricots and reserved juice in the base of slow cooker.

Place the flour, bicarbonate of soda, cinnamon and ginger in a bowl. Whisk in the egg with the milk and lemon juice. Melt the butter, brown sugar and golden syrup together in a small saucepan. Cool slightly and then mix into the bowl with the other ingredients. Pour mixture over the apricots.

Place lid on cooker and cook for 2 hours on High.

Serve with ice-cream, crème fraîche or mascarpone mixed with a little cream.

AUTUMN FRUITS COBBLER

Serves 6
(for a 4.5 litre slower cooker only)

8 cooking apples
2 large stalks rhubarb
1 tablespoon cornflour
1 tablespoon lemon juice
3 cups fresh, frozen or bottled blackberries
¼ cup sugar, plus extra to taste
1 egg
1 teaspoon finely grated lemon rind
1 tablespoon lemon juice
½ cup milk
1½ cups self-raising flour
125g butter, melted
crème fraîche, ice-cream or yoghurt, to serve

Peel and core the apples and cut into chunks. Trim the rhubarb and strip
off any tough outer skin.

Mix the cornflour with about ¼ cup of cold water to a paste. Set aside.

Place the apple and rhubarb in a saucepan with the lemon juice
and ¼ cup of water. Bring to the boil, then simmer until the apple
is tender but not mushy. Add the blackberries, stir and cook for
1 minute, then add the extra sugar to taste. Bring back to the boil
and thicken with the cornflour paste. Pour mixture into the slow cooker
and turn setting down to Low.

Whisk the egg and sugar until creamy, then add the lemon rind, lemon juice, milk, flour and butter (all at once), and whisk until smooth. Place tablespoons of the mixture evenly over the fruit.

Place lid on cooker and cook for 2–3 hours on Low.

Serve with crème fraîche, ice-cream or yoghurt.

Note: *Any fruit can be used in place of those suggested in this recipe. In summer, try using gooseberries or mulberries for instance, in which case you may need to increase the amount of cornflour paste used to thicken the mixture, otherwise it will soak into the cobbler topping a little too much and make it soggy.*

BANANA SELF-SAUCING PUDDING

Serves 4–6

(for a 3.5 litre slow cooker only)

This pudding makes its own rich caramel sauce, in this case lightened by the pleasant addition of a hint of lime and a dash of lemon.

125g butter

¾ cup sugar

1 egg

½ teaspoon ground cinnamon

½ teaspoon bicarbonate of soda

1½ cups self-raising flour

2 tablespoons lime juice

2 teaspoons grated lime rind

1 cup mashed ripe banana

1 teaspoon vanilla essence

Sauce

¾ cup brown sugar, firmly packed

1 teaspoon butter

3 tablespoons golden syrup

2 teaspoons lemon juice

Whisk the butter and sugar together until fluffy, then whisk in the egg. Mix in all the dry ingredients, lime juice and rind, mashed banana and vanilla essence to a smooth batter.

Pour mixture into the slow cooker and smooth out.

Place the brown sugar, butter, golden syrup, lemon juice and 1 cup of water in a saucepan. Bring to the boil, stirring, and pour evenly over the pudding batter.

Place lid on cooker and cook for 2–2¼ hours on High.

BERRIED APPLE PUDDING

Serves 4
(for a 4.5 litre or larger slow cooker)

Pastry

250g plain flour
¼ teaspoon salt
pinch baking powder
60g butter, diced
60g tasty cheese, diced
1 egg, lightly whisked
⅓ cup cold water
1 eggwhite, lightly beaten

Filling

900g cooking apples (such as Granny Smiths)
½ cup sugar
1 tablespoon cornflour
¾ cup berries (such as blueberries, strawberries,
    raspberries or blackberries)

In the base of the slow cooker, place an upturned saucer or low wire rack. Pour in boiling water to a depth of 2cm and turn the cooker to High. Place the lid on the cooker.

To make the pastry, place the flour, salt, baking powder, butter and cheese in the bowl of a food processor and process until the mixture resembles breadcrumbs. With the motor running, pour in the combined egg and water until the mixture comes together to form a ball.

Grease a 1 litre capacity pudding basin.

On a lightly floured surface, roll out two-thirds of the pastry to form a circle large enough to fit the base and side of the basin and put the pastry in place. Brush, right up to the edge, with a little of the eggwhite.

To make the filling, peel, core and cut the apples into 1cm dice and place in a bowl. Mix in the sugar, cornflour and lastly the berries. Spoon into the pastry-lined basin.

Roll the remaining pastry out to form a circle slightly larger than the top of the basin and put in place. Crimp the edges together.

Grease a piece of foil 8cm larger than the top of the basin and place, greased side down, over the basin. Crimp the edges around the rim to seal completely and tie with kitchen string to secure.

Place the pudding on the inverted saucer or wire rack in the cooker and pour in more boiling water until it comes halfway up the side of the basin.

Place the lid on the cooker and cook for 4 hours on High.

Remove the pudding from the cooker and serve with ice-cream or custard.

BERRY MERINGUE PUDDING

Serves 6
(for a 3.5–4.5 litre slow cooker)

800g fresh or frozen berries (any sort)
½ cup sugar, approximately
3 teaspoons cornflour mixed to a paste with
   1½ tablespoons cold water
2 eggwhites
1¼ cups caster sugar
1 teaspoon white or cider vinegar
sweetened whipped cream or vanilla ice-cream, to serve

Turn the slow cooker to Low to preheat for about 5 minutes.

Place the berries in a saucepan and bring to the boil. Sweeten with the sugar to taste, then add the cornflour paste, stirring constantly. Pour the berry mixture into the cooker.

Beat the eggwhites with the caster sugar and vinegar in a bowl until firm peaks form. Place heaped tablespoons of the meringue mixture over the berries.

Place the lid on the cooker and cook for 30 minutes on Low until the topping is set.

Serve with whipped cream or ice-cream.

Black Forest Self-Saucing Pudding

Serves 6
(for a 3.5–4.5 litre slow cooker)

This pudding has a sponge topping with a delicious chocolate cherry brandy sauce.

> 1½ cups canned or bottled pitted cherries,*
> with ½ cup juice reserved
> 1 tablespoon kirsch or brandy
> 1 cup self-raising flour
> ½ cup sugar
> 2½ tablespoons cocoa,
> plus 2 tablespoons extra
> ⅔ cup milk
> 1 teaspoon vanilla essence
> 1 egg
> 100g butter, melted
> 1 cup brown sugar, firmly packed
> 1¾ cups boiling water

Greast the inside of the slow cooker with a little butter or spray with cooking oil.

Combine the cherries, reserved juice and kirsch or brandy and place in base of cooker.

Place the flour, sugar and cocoa in a bowl and mix well. Whisk together the milk, vanilla and egg. Add to the flour mixture along with the melted butter and mix until well combined. Spoon this batter over the cherries and smooth out evenly.

To make the sauce, mix together the brown sugar and extra cocoa. Sprinkle evenly over the cake batter. Gently pour the boiling water over the top.

Place lid on cooker and cook for 2½ hours on High.

*　　*Sour cherries are best for this recipe, but if you are unable to get them then sweet black cherries make a good substitute.*

BLUEBERRY AND ORANGE PUDDING WITH BLUEBERRY SAUCE

Serves 6–8

(for a 3.5–4.5 litre slow cooker)

1 egg

½ cup sugar

½ cup milk

1¼ cups self-raising flour

60g butter, melted

1½ teaspoons grated orange rind

¾ cup fresh or frozen blueberries

cream, ice-cream or yoghurt, to serve

Blueberry Sauce

2 teaspoons cornflour

2 cups fresh or frozen blueberries

1 tablespoon orange juice

1 tablespoon lemon juice

½ cup sugar

Grease a 4-cup capacity metal pudding basin. Line the base of the pudding basin with a circular piece of baking paper to fit in place. Then grease the baking paper with butter or spray with cooking oil.

Whisk the egg and sugar together, then mix in the milk, flour and butter all together. Mix in the orange rind. Fold in the blueberries, then spoon the mixture evenly into the pudding basin. Cover with two layers of foil and tie string around the basin just under the rim to secure the foil and ensure a good seal.

Place pudding basin in cooker, then add boiling water until it reaches two-thirds of the way up the sides of the basin.

Place lid on cooker and cook for 3 hours on High.

To make the blueberry sauce, mix the cornflour with about 1½ tablespoons of cold water to a paste. Place the blueberries, orange and lemon juice and sugar into a small saucepan. Bring to the boil, stirring, then thicken with the cornflour paste.

Remove pudding basin from cooker and leave to stand for 5 minutes. Run a knife around the inside of the basin and invert the pudding onto a plate.

Serve slices of pudding drizzled with ¼ cup or more of the blueberry sauce, plus ice-cream, cream or yoghurt.

BOOZY BAKED APPLES

Serves 4
(for a 3.5–4.5 litre slow cooker)

4–5 cooking apples (such as Granny Smiths)
1 teaspoon ground cinnamon
2 tablespoons sugar
250g seedless red or green grapes
¾ cup white wine (such as chardonnay or riesling)
1 teaspoon rosewater
3 teaspoons honey
1½ teaspoons butter, diced

Peel and core the apples, then cut a ring around the 'equator' of each apple to a depth of approximately 6mm. This helps to keep the apples in shape. Place in the slow cooker.

Mix the cinnamon and sugar together and sprinkle into the cavities of the apples. Fill the remaining space with the whole grapes. Scatter the rest of the grapes around the apples and pour over the combined white wine and rosewater. Distribute the honey over the top of the apple centres, then dot the pieces of butter on top.

Place the lid on the cooker and cook for 2½–3 hours on High or 5–6 hours on Low until the apples are tender.

Serve with mascarpone, sweetened whipped cream or vanilla ice-cream.

CARAMEL APPLE STRUDEL ROLL

Serves 6
(for a 3.5–4.5 litre slow cooker)

90g butter
1½ cups self-raising flour
1 teaspoon lemon juice
½ cup water

Apple Filling
3 apples
½ cup sultanas
¼ cup sugar
1 teaspoon finely grated lemon rind
½ teaspoon ground cinnamon

Caramel Sauce
1½ cups brown sugar
90g butter
2 tablespoons lemon juice
1 cup water

Grease the inside of the slow cooker with a little butter or spray with cooking oil.

To make the pastry, cut the butter into small dice and rub into the flour with a pinch of salt until mixture resembles breadcrumbs. Make a well in the centre and add the lemon juice and half the water. Gradually work into the flour mixture with a metal spoon, adding extra water, if necessary, to make a soft dough. Set aside.

To make the filling, core and coarsely grate the apples and combine with the sultanas, sugar, lemon rind and cinnamon.

Turn the dough out onto a lightly floured board and roll out to a rectangle, approximately 30cm x 20cm.

Spread over the pastry, leaving a 1cm strip clear around the edge. Brush one half of the edge with a little water. Roll up from the long edge, seal the ends and place in the cooker.

To make the caramel sauce, combine all ingredients in a small saucepan. Bring to the boil and pour over the apple strudel roll.

Place lid on cooker and cook on High for 2–2½ hours.

CARAMELISED APPLE PUDDING

Serves 4–6
(for a 3.5–4.5 litre slow cooker)

90g butter
90g brown sugar
500g cooking apples (such as Granny Smiths)

Cake Batter
1 egg
¾ cup sugar
grated rind of 1 lemon
½ cup milk
¼ cup lemon juice
1 cup self-raising flour
½ cup plain flour
60g butter, melted

Melt the butter and sugar together and pour into the cooker. Peel and core the apples and cut into quarters. Place decoratively over the butter and sugar (this will mean layering them up a bit).

To make the cake batter, whisk the egg and sugar together with the lemon rind in a bowl, then whisk in the rest of the ingredients all at once. Pour evenly into the cooker.

Place the lid on the cooker and cook for 3½ hours on Low or until the batter is cooked.

Turn off the cooker, leave to stand for 5 minutes, then invert the pudding onto a serving platter.

Serve with sweetened whipped cream, custard or vanilla ice-cream.

CHERRY AND BUTTERMILK SPONGE PUDDING

Serves 6
(for a 3.5–4.5 litre slow cooker)

You can use fresh or frozen cherries in this recipe, in which case the stones should be removed and the cherries cooked with ¼ cup water and sweetened to taste.

If buttermilk is difficult to find, substitute ¾ cup skim milk mixed with ¼ cup lemon juice (don't worry if it curdles when combined).

825g can pitted sour cherries
3 teaspoons sugar, approximately
2–3 teaspoons cornflour mixed to a paste with 1 tablespoon
  cold water

Buttermilk Sponge
1 egg
¾ cup sugar
1 cup buttermilk
1½ cups self-raising flour
60g butter, melted

Place the cherries with their juice in a saucepan and bring to the boil. Add the sugar to taste and thicken with some or all of the cornflour paste. Pour into the slow cooker.

To make the buttermilk sponge, whisk the egg and sugar together in a bowl until well combined, then all at once fold in the buttermilk, flour and melted butter with a metal spoon or whisk.

Spoon the buttermilk sponge batter evenly over the cherries.

Place the lid on the cooker and cook for 2 hours on Low until the buttermilk sponge is cooked.

Serve with custard and/or vanilla ice-cream.

CHOCOLATE AND ORANGE LIQUEUR POT PUDDINGS (WITH OPTIONAL BLOOD ORANGE ICE-CREAM)

Serves 4
(for a 3.2–4.5 litre slow cooker)

If you don't wish to make the ice-cream, this pudding can be served with sweetened whipped cream or purchased ice-cream. It is also very nice served with ganache, made by boiling 300ml cream, then removing from the heat and stirring in 300g chopped dark chocolate until it has melted. Add a little orange liqueur if liked.

150g dark chocolate, broken into pieces
90g butter, diced
1 tablespoon orange liqueur
3 eggs
1 egg yolk
90g sugar
grated rind of 1 orange
50g plain flour, sifted

Blood Orange Ice-cream (optional)*
600ml pouring or thickened cream
3 egg yolks
120g icing sugar
grated rind of 2 blood oranges
juice of 3 blood oranges

Grease four 200–250ml metal dariole moulds.

Place the chocolate and butter in a heatproof bowl over a saucepan of simmering water (do not let the base of the bowl touch the water). Stir occasionally until melted. Stir in the liqueur. Allow to cool slightly.

Meanwhile beat the eggs, egg yolk, sugar and orange rind together in a bowl until thick and creamy. Gradually beat in the chocolate mixture. Fold in the flour.

Pour the pudding mixture into the prepared moulds and place in the slow cooker. Pour boiling water around the moulds until it reaches halfway up the sides.

Tear off a piece of foil large enough to cover all the puddings and grease one side. Place, greased side down, over the puddings, folding in the edges.

Place the lid on the cooker and cook for 1¼ hours on High.

Using oven mitts, remove the puddings from the cooker. Leave to stand for 5 minutes, then turn out onto serving plates.

To make the ice-cream, whip the cream to soft peaks in a bowl. In a separate bowl, beat the egg yolks and icing sugar until thick, then fold in the cream and orange rind and juice. Pour into a bowl and place in the freezer. When half frozen, beat with electric beaters until smooth, then return to the freezer to freeze completely. Alternatively, churn the ice-cream in an ice-cream machine after the first mixing.

Remove the ice-cream from the freezer a few minutes before serving with the puddings.

* *Although the blood orange ice-cream is not made in a slow cooker, it is well worth making as it is the perfect complement to the pot puddings. If you want to make the ice-cream, this will need to be done several hours ahead of time or the day before. Although blood oranges are specified here, Seville oranges could also be used, or Navel or Valencia oranges. Blood oranges give better colour, Seville oranges give a delightful bitterness, but other oranges are delicious also.*

CHOCOLATE PEAR RUM PUDDING

Serves 6
(for a 3.2–3.5 litre slow cooker)

500g pears
1 tablespoon butter, softened
1 tablespoon golden syrup
¼ cup rum (any sort)

Topping
90g butter, chopped
125g dark chocolate, chopped
2 eggs
1 cup sugar
1½ cups self-raising flour
½ cup milk

Grease the slow cooker and turn to High to preheat for a few minutes.

Peel and core the pears and cut in half. Place the pears, cut side down, in the base of the cooker.

Combine the butter, golden syrup and rum in a small saucepan and heat until just boiling. Pour over the pears and stir to combine, then turn the pears to cut side down once more.

To make the topping, melt the butter and chocolate in a saucepan over low heat. Whisk together the eggs and sugar in a bowl, then all at once fold in the flour, milk and chocolate mixture. Pour evenly over the pears.

Place the lid on the cooker and cook for 2½–3 hours on High or until the chocolate topping is set.

Serve with vanilla ice-cream.

CHOCOLATE SELF-SAUCING PUDDING

Serves 6–8
(for a 3.5–4.5 litre slow cooker)

1½ cups self-raising flour
¾ cup sugar
3 tablespoons cocoa powder
¾ cup milk
90g butter, melted

Sauce
1¼ cups firmly packed brown sugar
3 tablespoons cocoa powder
90g choc chips or chocolate melts
3½ cups boiling water
vanilla ice-cream, to serve

Grease the slow cooker.

Mix together the flour, sugar, cocoa, milk and butter in a bowl until well combined. Spread evenly into the cooker.

To make the sauce, mix together the sugar and cocoa and sprinkle over the cake batter in the cooker, then sprinkle over the choc chips or chocolate melts. Slowly pour the boiling water evenly over the top.

Place the lid on the cooker and cook for 3½–4 hours on Low.

Serve with ice-cream.

CLAFOUTIS

Serves 4–6
(for a 3.5 litre slower cooker only)

125g fresh or frozen blueberries
125g fresh or frozen raspberries
2 eggs
½ cup sugar
½ cup milk
½ cup self-raising flour
½ teaspoon grated lemon rind
90g butter, melted
icing sugar, to dust
crème fraîche, cream or ice-cream, to serve

Grease the inside of the slow cooker with a little butter or spray with cooking oil.

Spread the berries evenly over the base. Whisk the eggs and sugar together until light and fluffy, then mix in all together the milk, flour, lemon rind and butter. Pour evenly over the berries.

Place lid on cooker and cook for 2 hours on High.

Dust with a little icing sugar and serve with crème fraîche, cream or ice-cream.

CLASSIC BAKED APPLES

Serves 4–8
(for a 3.5–4.5 litre slow cooker)

8 apples (such as Sturmer or Golden Delicious)
3 teaspoons butter
¼ cup dates
½ cup sultanas
1½ tablespoons brown sugar
½ teaspoon ground cinnamon
1 tablespoon golden syrup

Core the apples and run a sharp knife around the middle of the apple, just to break the skin. Grease the slow cooker with 1 teaspoon of the butter and place apples inside.

Chop the dates and combine with the sultanas, brown sugar and cinnamon. Spoon into the cavity of the apples (don't worry if a little spills over the sides), pressing down gently.

Drizzle over the golden syrup, then top each apple with the remaining butter. Pour ½ cup of water around the apples (not over the top).

Place lid on cooker and cook for 3–4 hours on Low, or until the apples are cooked.

COMPOTE OF FRUIT

Serves 4–6

(for a 3.2–3.5 litre slow cooker)

This is a handy way to prepare a healthy breakfast. It can be served with cereals and yoghurt. Use a variety of fresh seasonal, canned, bottled and/or dried fruit. The following is an example of what can be used. If you use dried apricots or other dried fruits, you may need to increase the water accordingly (add approximately an extra ½ cup).

The compote can also be served as a dessert, in which case you can add a little liqueur such as Cointreau. With or without liqueur, it matches perfectly with Rice Custard (recipe page 379).

> 1¼–1½ cups berries or cherries
> 12 apricot halves (canned or bottled)
> ½–¾ cup pitted prunes
> ⅓ cup sugar, approximately (optional)
> ¾ cup water

Place all the ingredients in the slow cooker and stir to combine. Place the lid on the cooker. Cook on Low overnight or for 5–8 hours. If needed, add sugar to taste.

CRÈME BRULÉES

Serves 4
(for a 3.2–4.5 litre slow cooker)

½ cup milk
½ cup cream
1 egg
1 egg yolk
¼ teaspoon vanilla extract
5 teaspoons sugar
⅓ cup caster sugar, approximately

To make the custard, heat the milk and cream in a saucepan until just boiling, then remove from the heat. Meanwhile, whisk together the egg, egg yolk, vanilla and sugar. Gradually whisk in the hot milk mixture, then strain through a sieve into a jug.

Grease four 100ml ramekins and pour in the custard. Place the ramekins in the slow cooker and pour warm water around them to come halfway up the sides. Cover with a piece of foil, place the lid on the cooker and cook for 1¼–1½ hours on Low until just set.

Remove the ramekins from the cooker and place in the fridge to cool.

At serving time, sprinkle the tops all over with the caster sugar and caramelise the sugar with a culinary blow torch or place under the grill for a few minutes until the sugar turns to golden toffee.

CRÈME CARAMELS

Serves 4

(for a 3.5 litre or larger slow cooker)

For this recipe it is a good idea to purchase 200ml metal dariole moulds. Four of these will fit comfortably into an oval 3.5 litre capacity slow cooker. If you have a large 8 litre capacity cooker, you could use 200ml ramekins instead, which are broader than metal darioles.

These puddings have just a hint of coconut flavour – however, it can be left out if preferred, in which case replace the coconut cream with cream.

Toffee
125g sugar
⅓ cup water

Custard
1½ cups milk
½ cup cream
½ teaspoon vanilla extract
3 eggs
2 egg yolks
60g sugar
½ cup coconut cream

Grease four 200ml metal dariole moulds or heatproof ramekins.

To make the toffee, place the sugar and water in a small saucepan and bring to the boil, stirring only until the sugar has dissolved. Boil, without stirring, until the mixture turns a caramel colour. Remove from the heat immediately and pour into the base of each mould or ramekin. Set aside.

To make the custard, place the milk, cream and vanilla in a saucepan and bring to the boil, stirring often. Meanwhile whisk together the eggs, egg yolks and sugar until well combined. Gradually whisk in the hot milk mixture, then whisk in the coconut cream. Strain through a sieve into a jug and pour over the toffee in the moulds.

Place the moulds in the slow cooker and pour in enough hot water to come halfway up the sides of the moulds. Place a piece of foil over the top – I just use one piece, folding in the edges. This helps keep moisture dripping from the lid into the custards.

Place the lid on the cooker and cook for 2½–3 hours on Low until the crème caramels are barely set.

Remove the moulds from the cooker and place in the fridge for several hours before turning out onto serving plates.

DAPPLED APPLE PUDDING

Serves 4–6
(for a 3.2–4 litre slow cooker)

60g butter
60g brown sugar
1 tablespoon golden syrup
300g apples, peeled and cored (such as Golden Delicious)

Batter

1 egg
60g sugar
½ cup milk
1 cup self-raising flour
60g butter, melted
1 teaspoon grated lemon rind (optional)
½ cup sultanas
300g apples, peeled, cored and diced (such as Granny Smith)

Grease the slow cooker.

Place the butter, sugar and golden syrup in a saucepan over low heat and melt. Meanwhile, cut the apple into 1cm cubes. Stir the apple into the butter mixture. Pour the mixture into the cooker.

To make the batter, whisk the egg and sugar in a bowl until well combined, then all at once fold in the milk, flour, melted butter and lemon rind, if using. Fold in the sultanas and apple.

Spoon the batter evenly over the apple mixture in the cooker.

Place the lid on the cooker and cook for 2 hours on High.

Serve with custard, cream or ice-cream.

FRUITY BREAD AND BUTTER CUSTARD

Serves 4–6
(for a 3.5 litre slow cooker only)

4 slices fruit bread
4 slices white or wholemeal bread
45g butter, softened, plus 2 teaspoons extra
½ cup sultanas
½ cup chopped dried apricots
½ teaspoon finely grated lemon rind
4 large or 5 smaller eggs
¾ cup sugar
2 cups milk
½ teaspoon vanilla essence
¼ teaspoon ground nutmeg
1 tablespoon brown sugar
½ teaspoon ground cinnamon

Cut the crusts from the bread and spread each slice thinly with the butter. Cut into 2cm squares and place in the slow cooker. Scatter over this the sultanas, apricots and lemon rind. Mix together gently.

Beat the eggs and sugar until well combined, then whisk in the milk and vanilla. Pour evenly over the bread mixture. Sprinkle with nutmeg.

Cut the extra butter into 8 pieces and dot over the top. Place lid on cooker and cook for 4 hours on Low or until the custard is set.

Combine the brown sugar and cinnamon and sprinkle evenly over the top of the pudding. Replace the lid and cook for a further 5 minutes, or until the sugar melts.

GINGERBREAD APPLE PUDDING

Serves 6
(for a 3.5–4.5 litre slow cooker)

This pudding can be served straight from the slow cooker or turned out onto a serving platter.

600g cooking apples (such as Granny Smiths)
5 tablespoons golden syrup
60g butter
30g sugar
1 egg
180g self-raising flour
1½ teaspoons ground ginger
½ teaspoon bicarbonate of soda dissolved in ¼ cup cold water

Grease the slow cooker.

Peel and core the apples and cut into 6mm slices.

Place 3 tablespoons of the golden syrup in the base of the cooker and add the apple slices. Stir to mix, then distribute the apple slices evenly over the base.

Combine the remaining golden syrup and the butter in a saucepan over low heat and stir until melted. Remove from the heat and whisk in the sugar. Allow to cool for about 3 minutes, then whisk in the egg and fold in the flour with the ginger. With a metal spoon, stir in the bicarbonate of soda and water mixture until well combined. Pour evenly over the apple.

Place the lid on the cooker and cook for 1 hour on High until the topping is cooked through.

Serve with vanilla ice-cream or custard.

HARLEQUIN PUDDING WITH RASPBERRY SAUCE

Serves 6
(for a 3.5–4.5 litre slow cooker)

This recipe uses raspberry jam in place of red food colouring. If a darker pink is preferred, add about three drops of red food colouring or a pinch of beetroot powder.

> 1½ cups self-raising flour
> 1¼ cups sugar
> ¾ cup milk
> 2 eggs
> 125g butter, melted
> 1½ tablespoons cocoa
> 1 tablespoon raspberry jam
> 1½ cups fresh or frozen raspberries
> ice-cream or sweetened whipped cream, to serve

Grease a 4- or 5-cup capacity metal pudding basin. Line the base of the pudding basin with a circular piece of baking paper to fit in place. Then grease the baking paper with butter or with spray cooking oil.

Place the flour, 1 cup of sugar, ½ cup of milk, eggs and melted butter into a bowl and beat with an electric beater for 2 minutes.

Divide the mixture into three even portions in separate bowls. Combine the cocoa and remaining milk and stir until smooth. Add to one portion and mix well. Add raspberry jam to another portion and mix well.

Place a spoonful of each mixture alternately into the pudding basin to make a pretty pattern (but do not swirl together). Cover the basin with two layers of foil and tie string around the basin just under the rim to secure the foil and ensure a good seal.

Place pudding basin in cooker and pour boiling water into the cooker until it reaches two-thirds of the way up the sides of the basin.

Place lid on cooker and cook for 3 hours on High.

Remove basin from the cooker and leave to stand for 5 minutes. Run a knife around the inside of the basin and invert the pudding onto a plate. Remove baking paper.

Place the raspberries in a small saucepan with 3 tablespoons of water and bring to the boil. Simmer for 5 minutes. Strain if desired. Add the remaining sugar, bring to the boil and cook for a further minute.

Serve slices of pudding with a little raspberry sauce and ice-cream or sweetened whipped cream.

LEMON AND APPLE BROWN BETTY

Serves 4–6
(for a 3.5 litre slow cooker only)

1.5kg cooking apples (such as Granny Smith, Sturmer or
   Bramley)
1 tablespoon lemon juice
2 tablespoons sugar (optional)
10 slices bread, crusts removed
¾ cup brown sugar, firmly packed
1 teaspoon ground cinnamon
½ teaspoon ground nutmeg
grated rind of 1 lemon
125g butter, melted

Grease the inside of the slow cooker with a little butter or spray with
cooking oil.

Peel and core the apples. Cut each apple into quarters, then each
quarter in half again. Place apple in the base of the cooker and drizzle
with lemon juice. If the apples are quite sour, mix through the sugar.

Layer half the bread on a board and cut into four, lengthways, then into
four, crossways. Repeat with remaining bread.

Place bread cubes in a large bowl and combine with the remaining
ingredients, using two metal spoons to mix together well. Place over
the top of the apple and spread out evenly.

Place lid on cooker and cook for 3–4 hours on Low.

Lemon Delicious

Serves 4

(for a 3.5–4 litre slow cooker)

This lemon dessert is truly delicious. In the slow cooker it performs very well, making a feather-light sponge on top with a lemon curd underneath.

90g butter, softened
250g caster sugar
4 teaspoons grated lemon rind
5 eggs, separated
60g self-raising flour
1 cup milk
½ cup lemon juice
vanilla ice-cream, to serve

Grease the slow cooker.

Beat the butter, sugar, lemon rind and egg yolks together in a bowl, then fold in the flour and combined milk and lemon juice (it doesn't matter if the juice mixture curdles). Fold in the stiffly beaten eggwhites.

Pour the batter into the slow cooker. Place the lid on the cooker and cook for 2 hours on Low until the sponge on top is set.

Serve with vanilla ice-cream.

LEMON MARSHMALLOW MERINGUE PUDDING

Serves 6
(for a 3.5–4.5 litre slow cooker)

This delicious recipe has a small, soft crust that perfectly encapsulates the tangy lemon filling. It is topped with a soft marshmallow meringue.

½ cup fresh breadcrumbs
1¼ cups sugar, plus 2 teaspoons extra
⅓ cup cornflour
¾ cup lemon juice
2 teaspoons finely grated lemon rind
4 egg yolks
1 egg
30g butter

Meringue
4 eggwhites
1 cup sugar
1 teaspoon cornflour

Grease the inside of the slow cooker with a little butter or spray with cooking oil. Mix together the breadcrumbs and 2 teaspoons of sugar and sprinkle over the base and 5cm up the sides of the cooker.

Mix the cornflour with about ½ cup of cold water to a smooth paste and set aside. Place the lemon juice, lemon rind and 1¼ cups of sugar in a saucepan and bring to the boil. Add the cornflour paste, stirring constantly until thickened, then cook for a further minute, still stirring. Remove from heat and leave to stand for 5 minutes. Whisk in the egg yolks and egg, then the butter. Spoon mixture over the breadcrumb base in the cooker. Turn the cooker setting to Low.

To make the meringue, beat the eggwhites until stiff peaks form, then add the sugar and cornflour and beat until stiff peaks form once more. Spoon over the lemon filling and spread out evenly, making sure it reaches right out to the sides and is slightly lower in the centre. Swirl the mixture with a spatula, knife or fork to form an attractive pattern. Alternatively, the mixture could be piped over the lemon filling.

Place lid on cooker and cook for 2 hours on Low.

Note: *If you have access to a culinary butane torch, you can use it to brown the top a little, but it is by no means necessary.*

LEMON SAGO

Serves 4–6
(for a 3.5–4.5 litre slow cooker)

90g sago or seed tapioca
2 teaspoons grated lemon rind
½ cup sugar
2 tablespoons golden syrup
juice of 1 large lemon

Place the sago, 2½ cups of water and lemon rind in the slow cooker and stir to combine.

Place lid on cooker and cook on High for about 45 minutes to 1 hour, or until sago is clear.

Turn off cooker and mix in the sugar, golden syrup and lemon juice.

MOIST APPLE AND SULTANA DESSERT CAKE

Serves 6
(for a 3.5–4.5 litre slow cooker)

1 egg
½ cup sugar
1 cup self-raising flour
125g butter, melted
cream, ice-cream or yoghurt, to serve

Apple and Sultana Filling
1 cup grated apple
¼ cup sultanas
½ teaspoon ground cinnamon
¼ teaspoon ground nutmeg
2 teaspoons cornflour
1½ tablespoons lemon juice
½ teaspoon grated lemon rind
1 tablespoon sugar

Topping
2 teaspoons melted butter
1½ teaspoons sugar
½ teaspoon ground cinnamon

Turn cooker setting to High to preheat for 10 minutes.

Grease a 16cm (or just slightly larger) round cake tin with butter or with spray cooking oil. Line the base of the tin with a circular piece of baking paper to fit in place. Then grease the baking paper with butter or with spray cooking oil.

To make the shortcake, whisk the egg and sugar together, then add the flour and melted butter and mix well.

Spread two-thirds of the shortcake mixture over the base and 1cm up the sides of the cake tin.

Mix together the apple, sultanas, cinnamon, nutmeg, cornflour, lemon juice, lemon rind and sugar. Spoon over the shortcake mixture in the tin.

Press spoonfuls of the remaining shortcake mixture into discs (just in your hands will do) and place over the apple mixture so that it covers it as much as possible.

Cover the cake tin with foil and tie a piece of string around the rim to ensure a good seal. Place cake tin in the slow cooker. Pour boiling water into the cooker to come 1cm up the sides of the cake tin.

Place lid on cooker and cook for 4 hours on High.

Remove foil from cake tin and leave to stand for 5 minutes. Invert cake onto a wire rack and leave upside down. Transfer to serving plate when cool.

For the topping, brush cake with the melted butter, then sprinkle with the sugar and cinnamon. Serve warm with cream, ice-cream or yoghurt.

MUD PUDDING WITH WHISKY SAUCE

Serves 6–8
(for a 3.5–4.5 litre slow cooker)

150g dark cooking chocolate
250g butter
2 cups brown sugar, firmly packed
1 cup water
2 eggs
¼ cup cocoa
2 cups plain flour
2 teaspoons baking powder
ice-cream or cream, to serve

Whisky Sauce
200g dark chocolate
200ml cream
¼ cup whisky

Grease the inside of the slow cooker with a little butter or spray with cooking oil.

Break the chocolate into small squares and cut the butter into several pieces. Place in a medium saucepan with the sugar and water. Stir over medium heat until the butter and chocolate are melted and the sugar dissolved. Remove from heat and allow to cool for 5 minutes.

Whisk in the eggs, then the cocoa, flour and baking powder. Pour the mixture into the cooker.

Place lid on cooker and cook for 3 hours on High.

To make the whisky sauce, break the chocolate into small pieces. Place the cream in a medium saucepan and bring to the boil. Remove from heat and add the chocolate, stirring until melted. Add the whisky and stir to combine.

Serve slices of the pudding with a generous amount of whisky sauce and ice-cream or cream.

Note: *Any leftover sauce from this decadent but delicious dessert can be stored in a jar in the fridge. To melt, simply remove lid and microwave on medium for 20-second bursts. Serve over ice-cream.*

MULLED PEARS

Serves 4–6

(for a 3.5–4.5 litre slow cooker)

1¼ cups red wine
¼ cup lemon juice
1 cup sugar
½ cinnamon stick
4 cloves
small strip of lemon rind
6–8 pears
1 tablespoon cornflour*

Place the red wine, lemon juice, sugar, cinnamon stick, cloves and lemon rind in the slow cooker. Turn cooker setting to High and stir occasionally until sugar is dissolved.

Meanwhile, peel the pears, leaving the stalks intact. When syrup is ready, place pears in cooker. Place lid on cooker and cook for 1½ hours on High or 3 hours on Low.

Remove pears from cooker and place in a serving dish.

Place a sieve over a medium saucepan and strain the liquid from the cooker into it. Pour 1½ cups of the liquid into a small saucepan and bring to the boil. Mix the cornflour with about 2 tablespoons of cold water to a paste and use a little or all of it to slightly thicken the sauce. Spoon sauce over the pears.

*   *If you have access to arrowroot, use this in place of the cornflour as it will make for a clearer sauce. However, remove the sauce from the heat as soon as it has thickened.*

PEARS IN RASPBERRY AND REDCURRANT SAUCE

Serves 4
(for a 3.2–3.5 litre slow cooker)

The juice that gathers during cooking can be poured off and reduced in a saucepan on the stovetop if desired, or serve each pear with the juice as it stands. Any excess juice, strained, makes a truly delightful after-dinner drink similar to mulled wine.

> 4 pears
> 5cm strip of lemon rind
> juice of ½ lemon
> 1 cup fresh or frozen raspberries
> ½ cup sugar
> ½ cup red wine (such as cabernet sauvignon, pinot noir
>   or merlot)
> 2 tablespoons redcurrant jelly
> pinch of freshly ground black pepper
> mascarpone or vanilla ice-cream, to serve

Peel the pears, leaving the stalks on, and place in the slow cooker with the lemon rind.

Combine the rest of the ingredients and pour over the pears.

Place the lid on the cooker and cook for 2½–3 hours on High or 5–6 hours on Low.

Serve with mascarpone or vanilla ice-cream.

Poached Quinces with Cinnamon Spice Dumplings

Serves 4
(for a 3.5–4.5 litre slow cooker)

1.2kg quinces (approximately)
¾ cup sugar
1 cup self-raising flour
2 teaspoons icing sugar
30g butter
½ teaspoon ground cinnamon
½ teaspoon ground mixed spice
¼ teaspoon ground ginger
2 teaspoons lemon juice
½ cup milk

Peel the quinces, cut into quarters and remove the inner cores. Cut each quarter in half and place in the slow cooker, together with the sugar and ½ cup of water. Stir to combine.

Place lid on cooker and cook overnight or for about 8 hours on Low, by which time the quince will have turned a deep scarlet colour.

Turn cooker setting to High while making the dumplings.

Place the flour, icing sugar and butter into a bowl (it is best to cut the butter into small pieces), then rub together with your fingertips until the mixture resembles breadcrumbs. Mix in the cinnamon, mixed spice and ginger. Make a well in the centre and add the lemon juice and half the milk. Mix them into the dry ingredients, adding more of the remaining milk as necessary to make a soft dough. Roll into walnut-size balls.

Take a sheet of baking paper slightly larger than the slow cooker and spray one side with cooking oil spray or grease with a little butter.

Place the dumplings on top of the quince, cover with the baking paper greased-side down and replace lid. Cook for 45 minutes on High.

Pumpkin Pudding with Lemon Cream

Serves 6
(for a 3.5–4.5 litre slow cooker)

This recipe is a variation of a pumpkin cake that was handed down to me by my grandmother. When she was young her family owned a bakery in Sandy Bay, and this cake was one of their regular products. Its flavour is truly delicious, and is one of the only things containing pumpkin that my young children would ever knowingly eat.

My father lived with us for many years. He had an extreme aversion to pumpkin, however this was his favourite cake. Mind you, we never did tell him about pumpkin being one of its major components. One day a visiting friend commented, 'You'd never think there was pumpkin in this cake would you?' Dad overheard her and immediately spat out the piece of cake he was chewing. He never touched pumpkin cake again; a true case of mind over matter.

The cake made as this pudding in the slow cooker is even better than when made in the oven. It is so flavoursome that it doesn't need a custard or sauce, but a little lemon cream or ice-cream complements it well.

125g butter
½ teaspoon lemon essence
½ cup sugar
1 egg
½ cup mashed pumpkin
½ cup self-raising flour
½ cup plain flour
250g dried mixed fruit

Lemon Cream
200ml cream
2 teaspoons caster or icing sugar
½ teaspoon finely grated lemon rind
2 teaspoons lemon juice

Grease a 4-cup capacity metal pudding basin. Line the base of the pudding basin with a circular piece of baking paper to fit in place. Then grease the baking paper with butter or with spray cooking oil.

Cream together the butter, lemon essence and sugar. Add the egg and whisk, then add the mashed pumpkin and whisk again until well combined. Mix in the flours and dried fruit.

Spoon the mixture into the pudding basin and cover with two layers of foil. Tie string around the basin just under the rim to secure the foil and ensure a good seal.

Place pudding basin in cooker and pour boiling water into the cooker until it reaches two-thirds of the way up the sides of the basin.

Place lid on cooker and cook for 2½ hours on High.

Remove basin from cooker and leave to stand for 10 minutes. Run a knife around the inside of the basin and invert pudding onto a plate.

To make the lemon cream, whisk together the cream and caster or icing sugar until soft peaks form. Fold in the lemon rind and juice. Serve slices of pudding with a little lemon cream.

RICE CUSTARD

Serves 4–6
(for a 3.2–3.5 litre slow cooker)

This rice custard is particularly nice with stewed or bottled fruits. For a simple dessert, ladle into a bowl and top with a spoonful of raspberry jam.

80g long-grain rice
4 cups milk
100g sugar
4 eggs
½ teaspoon vanilla extract
2 teaspoons cornflour mixed to a paste with ¼ cup milk
½ cup cream (optional)
½ teaspoon ground nutmeg (optional)

Spray the slow cooker with cooking oil spray.

Place the rice and milk in the cooker, stir, then cover with the lid and cook for 3–4 hours on Low until the rice is cooked through.

Whisk together the sugar, eggs and vanilla and stir into the cooker together with the cornflour paste. Replace the lid on the cooker and cook for 5 minutes more on Low.

Stir in the cream, if using, and then sprinkle the nutmeg over the top, if desired.

RICH FRUIT PUDDING

Serves 6–8
(for a 3.5–4 litre slow cooker)

This pudding is rich enough to be used as a last-minute Christmas pudding. It is delicious served anytime with custard.

125g butter
375g mixed dried fruit
juice and rind of ½ orange
1 cup sugar
1 teaspoon ground cinnamon
½ teaspoon ground nutmeg
2 teaspoons marmalade
1 teaspoon bicarbonate of soda
½ cup sherry (any sort)
½ cup water
1 apple, cored and coarsely grated
30g dark chocolate, chopped
2 eggs, lightly whisked
1 cup plain flour
1 cup self-raising flour

Spray the inside of the slow cooker with cooking oil spray or grease well.

Place the butter, dried fruit, orange juice and rind, sugar, spices, marmalade, bicarbonate of soda, sherry, water and apple in a large saucepan and bring to the boil, stirring often. Simmer for 1 minute. Stir in the chocolate until melted. Remove from the heat and leave to stand for

10 minutes. Quickly mix in the eggs and flour until well combined, then pour into the cooker.

Place the lid on the cooker and cook for 4–5 hours on Low until the centre of the pudding is firm to touch.

Serve with custard flavoured with a little sherry or brandy.

RUM AND RAISIN PUDDING

Serves 4–6
(for a 3.5–4.5 litre slow cooker)

¾ cup raisins
1½ tablespoons rum
125g butter
1 cup sugar
2 eggs
3 tablespoons cocoa
½ cup self-raising flour
cream or ice-cream, to serve (optional)

Chocolate Ganache
250g dark chocolate
1 cup cream
2 teaspoons butter (optional)

Soak the raisins in the rum for 30 minutes, if possible.

Grease a 4-cup capacity metal pudding basin. Line the base of the pudding basin with a circular piece of baking paper to fit in place. Then grease the baking paper with butter or spray with cooking oil.

Whisk the butter and sugar together until light and fluffy, then whisk in the eggs. Fold in the cocoa and flour, then fold in the rum and raisin mixture.

Spoon mixture into the pudding basin. Cover with two layers of foil and tie string around the basin just under the rim to secure the foil and ensure a good seal.

Place pudding basin in cooker and pour boiling water into the cooker to two-thirds up the sides of the basin.

Place lid on cooker and cook for 3 hours on High.

Remove basin from cooker, leave to stand for 10 minutes, then invert pudding onto a serving plate.

To make the chocolate ganache, break the chocolate into small pieces. Bring the cream to the boil, remove from heat and stir in the chocolate until melted and smooth. For an extra rich sauce and to give a lovely glossy finish, add the butter and stir until well combined.

Serve the pudding with the chocolate ganache for an extra rich dessert, or cream or ice-cream.

SAGO PLUM PUDDING

Serves 6–8
(for a 3.5–4.5 litre slow cooker)

⅓ cup sago or seed tapioca
1 cup milk
1 cup raisins
1 cup fresh breadcrumbs
½ cup brown sugar, firmly packed
1 teaspoon bicarbonate of soda
½ teaspoon vanilla essence
¼ cup melted butter
ice-cream, cream or custard, to serve

Mix the sago with milk and let stand for several hours or overnight.

When ready to make the pudding, grease a 4-cup capacity metal pudding basin. Combine the sago and milk with the raisins, breadcrumbs, brown sugar, bicarbonate of soda, vanilla and melted butter. Mix well and spoon into basin. Cover with two layers of foil and tie with string around rim of basin to secure foil and ensure a good seal.

Place pudding basin in slow cooker and pour boiling water into the cooker to two-thirds up the sides of the basin.

Place lid on cooker and cook for 4 hours on High.

Remove basin from cooker and leave to stand for 5 minutes before inverting pudding onto a serving plate.

This pudding is delicious served with ice-cream, cream or custard.

SELF-SAUCING STICKY DATE PUDDING

Serves 6
(for a 3.2–3.5 litre slow cooker)

1½ cups self-raising flour
½ cup sugar
1 teaspoon ground cinnamon
1 teaspoon mixed spice
1½ cups chopped pitted dates
¾ cup milk
1 cup brown sugar, firmly packed
1 tablespoon butter, diced
2 cups boiling water
vanilla ice-cream, to serve

Grease the slow cooker.

Mix together the flour, sugar, spices, dates and milk and spoon evenly into the cooker.

Mix together the brown sugar, butter and boiling water in a bowl and pour gently over the date mixture.

Place the lid on the cooker and cook for 2½–3 hours on High until the pudding topping is cooked through.

Serve with ice-cream.

STEAMED FRUIT PUDDING

Serves 6
(for a 3.5–4.5 litre slow cooker)

This recipe can quite easily serve as a Christmas pudding that can even be made just the day before it is needed. To lengthen its shelf life, brush the entire pudding with brandy while hot. When cool, wrap in foil. Place in the fridge where it will then keep well for a week or more.

1 cup dried mixed fruit
½ cup brown sugar, firmly packed
1 teaspoon mixed spice
¾ cup milk
1 tablespoon butter
1 tablespoon marmalade
2 tablespoons grated apple
1 teaspoon bicarbonate of soda
¼ cup brandy
1 cup self-raising flour

Brandy Custard
2 cups milk
½ cup sugar
2 tablespoons cornflour
2 egg yolks, whisked
1–2 tablespoons brandy

Grease a 4-cup capacity metal pudding basin. Line the base of the pudding basin with a circular piece of baking paper to fit in place. Then grease the baking paper with butter or spray with cooking oil.

Place the dried fruit, sugar, mixed spice, milk, butter, marmalade and apple in a medium saucepan. Bring to the boil, stirring, then simmer for 1 minute. Remove from heat, stir in the bicarbonate of soda and leave to cool for 10 minutes.

Fold in the brandy and flour until well combined. Pour mixture into the pudding basin. Cover basin with two layers of foil and tie with string around the rim of basin to secure foil and ensure a good seal.

Place pudding basin in cooker and pour boiling water into cooker to two-thirds of the way up the basin.

Place lid on cooker and cook for 3½ hours on High.

Remove basin from cooker, leave to stand for 5 minutes, then invert pudding onto a serving plate, or transfer onto a rack if it's to be used at a later date.

To make the brandy sauce, place the milk, sugar and cornflour in a saucepan and bring to the boil, stirring constantly. Cook until thickened. Remove from heat and quickly whisk in the egg yolks and brandy. Serve slices of pudding with brandy custard.

STEAMED JAM PUDDING

Serves 6
(for a 3.5–4.5 litre slow cooker)

A steamed jam pudding made in a slow cooker is an interesting thing. The jam is absorbed a little into the pudding and thus flavours the cake component to some extent, while still retaining its characteristic jam layer at the top. To allow for this, a generous amount of jam is used in this recipe.

90g butter, softened
½ cup sugar
1 egg
1½ cups self-raising flour
½ cup milk
½ teaspoon vanilla essence
2½ tablespoons raspberry or other dark jam*
cream, to serve (optional)

Custard
2 cups milk
½ cup sugar
2 tablespoons cornflour
2 egg yolks, whisked

Grease a 4-cup capacity metal pudding basin. Line the base of the pudding basin with a circular piece of baking paper to fit in place. Then grease the baking paper with butter or with spray cooking oil.

Whisk the butter and sugar together, then whisk in the egg until well combined. Fold in the flour, milk and vanilla essence (all at once).

Place the jam in base of pudding basin and spoon the flour mixture over it.

Cover basin with two layers of foil and tie with string around the rim to secure foil and ensure a good seal.

Place pudding basin in cooker and pour boiling water into the cooker until it reaches two-thirds of the way up the sides of basin.

Place lid on cooker and cook for 3½ hours on High.

Remove basin from cooker and leave to stand for 3 minutes, then invert pudding onto a serving plate.

To make the custard, place the milk, sugar and cornflour in a saucepan and bring to the boil, stirring constantly. Cook until thickened. Remove pan from heat and quickly whisk in the egg yolks. Serve slices of pudding with the custard or cream.

*   *Use any type of jam or even marmalade as a variation.*

STICKY FIG AND DATE PUDDING WITH COFFEE TOFFEE SAUCE

Serves 6
(for a 3.5–4.5 litre slow cooker)

½ cup chopped dried figs, firmly packed
½ cup chopped dates, firmly packed
¾ cup sugar
30g butter
1 teaspoon bicarbonate of soda
1 egg
1 teaspoon mixed spice
1 cup self-raising flour

Coffee Toffee Sauce
2 teaspoons instant coffee powder or granules
90g butter
250g golden syrup
180g sugar
150g soft dark brown sugar
¾ cup cream

Grease a 4-cup capacity metal pudding basin. Line the base of the pudding basin with a circular piece of baking paper to fit in place. Then grease the baking paper with butter or with spray cooking oil.

Place the figs, dates, sugar, butter and 1 cup of water in a saucepan and bring to the boil. Simmer for 1 minute. Remove from heat and add the bicarbonate of soda. Stir and leave to cool for 10–15 minutes.

Whisk the egg and add to the mixture along with the mixed spice and flour. Mix well.

Pour into the pudding basin and cover with two layers of foil. Tie string around the basin just under the rim to secure the foil and ensure a good seal.

Place the pudding basin in cooker and pour boiling water until it reaches two-thirds of the way up the outside of the basin.

Place lid on cooker and cook for 4 hours on High.

Meanwhile, to make the coffee toffee sauce, mix the coffee with 3 teaspoons hot water. Place in a medium saucepan with the butter, golden syrup and sugars. Stir over medium heat until the mixture comes to the boil. Simmer, while still stirring, for 5 minutes.

Remove from heat, gradually add the cream and stir well. Return to heat, bring to the boil, stirring, then simmer for 3 minutes more. Allow to cool for a few minutes before serving.

Remove pudding basin from cooker and leave to stand for 5 minutes. Run a knife around the inside of the basin and turn the pudding out onto a serving plate.

Cut the pudding into wedges and place on serving plates. Drizzle the coffee toffee sauce in and around the pudding wedges. For a truly special effect, place drops of cream about 2cm apart in the sauce, then drag a skewer through them to make tiny hearts.

Note: *Any leftover coffee toffee sauce can be poured into jars and kept in the fridge. Reheat in the microwave, uncovered and in 20-second bursts, for an excellent sauce to serve with ice-cream or pancakes.*

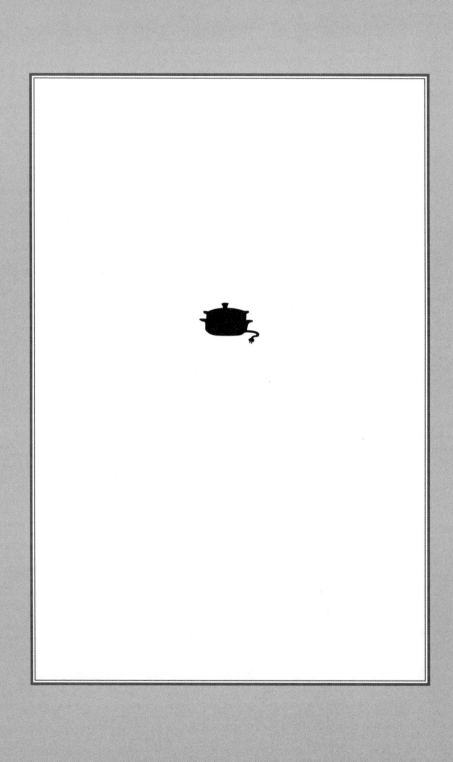

BREADS

Breads made in the slow cooker do not brown
but on the other hand they are deliciously moist.
They are wonderful served with soups or
casserole-style dishes as 'gravy soakers'.

ANTIPASTO PULL-APART BREAD

Serves 4—6
(for a 4 litre [round] or larger [round or oval] slow cooker)

You will need a wire rack or upturned saucer to fit in the base of your slow cooker for this recipe.

1 ½ cups plain flour
1 ½ teaspoons dried yeast
¾ teaspoon salt
1 teaspoons sugar
1 tablespoon oil (light olive, canola or peanut)
¾ cup warm water, approximately
¼ cup chopped roasted red capsicum
¼ cup chopped semi-dried tomatoes
¼ cup chopped black olives
¼ cup shredded fresh basil
¼ cup freshly grated parmesan, optional

Mix together the flour, yeast, salt and sugar in a medium bowl. Make a well in the centre and pour in the oil and almost all the water. Mix to a soft dough, adding the rest of the water if necessary and even a little more if needed. Cover the bowl with a tea towel and leave to stand until doubled in size (about 1 hour).

Grease a 16cm round deep sided cake tin and line the base with baking paper, grease again.

Pour 1 cup hot water into the base and turn the slow cooker to High.

Turn the dough out onto a lightly floured surface and knead for about 3 minutes until smooth and elastic. Press out into a rectangle 20 x 30cm approximately and sprinkle evenly with the capsicum, tomatoes, olives and basil. Roll up from the long side (Swiss-roll style), enclosing the filling.

Cut the roll into 5 equal slices and place in the prepared tin, cut side up. Leave to rise almost to the top of the tin. Place the tin on the rack or upturned saucer in the cooker and cook for 2½ hours on High. Sprinkle the cheese over the loaf if liked, then replace the lid and cook for 15 minutes more.

Remove from slow cooker, leave to stand for 5 minutes, then turn out onto a wire rack to cool for 20 minutes at least before serving.

FLOWER POT BREADS

Makes 6 small flowerpot loaves
(a 4.5 litre slow cooker to hold 6 clay pots
6.5cm diameter across the top by 6cm tall)

Guests are always stunned at the novelty of these little flower pot loaves. The flavour of the clay lingers on the bread, which is really delicious.

Unglazed clay pots are necessary for this recipe, but they must first be sealed by deep frying them in cooking oil for 30 minutes at 140°C, after which they are drained and cooled. They only need to be treated once; thereafter, simply spray the insides well with cooking oil or grease them.

For this recipe so that the water doesn't get into the bread through the hole in the base of the pot, roll out 42cm of foil on the bench top and cut into six 14 x 14cm squares. Wrap each piece of foil up and around the base of the pot — it will almost reach up to the rim.

> 1 cup plain flour
> 1 teaspoons dried yeast
> ½ teaspoon salt
> ¾ teaspoon sugar
> 3 teaspoons oil (light olive, peanut or canola)
> ½ cup warm water, approximately
> 1 small egg, lightly beaten with 1 tablespoon water
> 2 teaspoons poppy or sesame seeds, optional

Mix together the flour, yeast, salt and sugar in a medium bowl. Make a well in the centre and pour in the oil and almost all the water. Mix to a soft dough, adding the rest of the water if necessary and even a little more if needed. Cover the bowl with a tea towel and leave to stand until doubled in size (about 1 hour). Turn out onto a lightly floured surface and knead until smooth and elastic – about 3 minutes.

Divide the dough into 6 pieces and shape each into a ball. Spray the inside of the pots well with cooking oil and place one ball of dough in each. Leave to rise to the top of the pots.

About 10 minutes before the dough has reached the top of the pots, pour ¾ cup of hot water into the base of the slow cooker and turn on to High. Place an upturned flat based plate in the bottom or a small wire rack. Place the lid on cooker.

When the breads have risen, brush them carefully with the egg mixture and sprinkle with poppy or sesame seeds, if using. Place the pots on the plate or rack in the slow cooker, cover with the lid and cook for 2½ hours on High.

Cover with a tea towel, remove from slow cooker and turn out onto a wire rack (you may need to run a knife around the inside so the bread comes out easily).

PAN CROCK BREAD

Serves 4
(for a 3.5–4.5 litre slow cooker)

This is a wonderful light and moist loaf of bread, which is delicious with soups. The recipe was invented quite by accident one day when a friend came to visit. Noticing a bowl of bread dough on the kitchen bench, he commented, 'And this is for the crock pot too?' Although I had not planned for it to be, I thought 'Why not?'

 2 cups plain flour*
 2 teaspoons dried yeast
 1½ teaspoons sugar
 1 teaspoon salt
 1 tablespoon olive (or other) oil

Grease a 16cm round cake tin with butter or spray with cooking oil. Line the base of the tin with a circular piece of baking paper to fit in place. Then grease the baking paper with butter or spray with cooking oil.

Mix the flour, yeast, sugar and salt in a bowl. Make a well in centre and add the oil and enough lukewarm water (see note) to make a soft dough. Mix well, cover with a tea towel and leave to rise until doubled. Turn out onto a lightly floured board and knead the dough briefly.

Place dough in prepared tin and set aside to rise for approximately 20 minutes, until it reaches the top of the tin.

About 15 minutes before the bread is fully risen, preheat the slow cooker on High, adding hot water to a depth of 1 cm. Place a small wire rack in the base of cooker. Once the bread has risen, place cake tin on top of rack.

Place lid on cooker and cook for 2 hours on High.

*   *You can substitute $^1/_2$ cup of wholemeal flour for $^1/_2$ cup of the plain flour, if you like.*

Note: *It is not possible to specify a set amount of water, as flour moisture content can vary and can also be affected by the moisture in the atmosphere. Just make sure your dough is soft so that the yeast can do its work.*

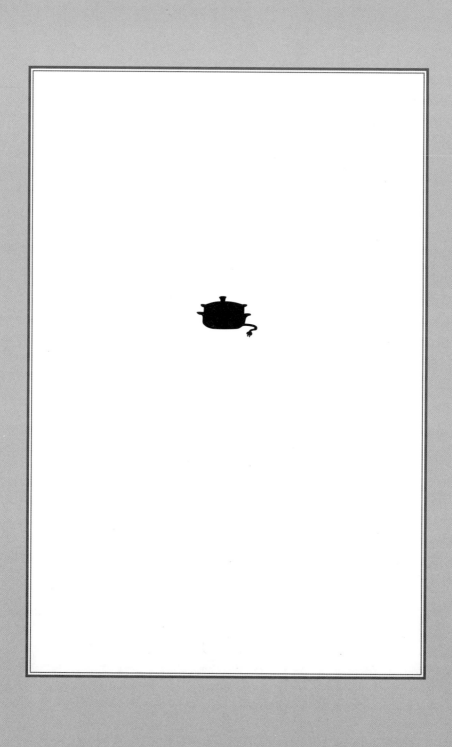

HANDY EXTRAS

FAMILY PORRIDGE

Serves 4
(for a 3.2–3.5 litre slow cooker)

It is absolutely necessary to obtain steel cut oats for this slow-cooked porridge. The regular rolled oats will cook to a horrible sludge. Steel cut oats are available from most health food stores.

If you can get hold of a 1 or 1.5 litre capacity slow cooker, use half the amount specified here for an ideal healthy breakfast for two.

    1 cup steel cut oats
    5 cups water
    pinch of salt
    honey and milk, to serve

Place all the ingredients in the slow cooker and stir to combine.

Place the lid on the cooker and cook for 8 hours on Low.

Serve each bowlful with a splash of honey and milk.

GARLIC BREAD

Serves 4
(for a 3.2–3.5 litre slow cooker)

Although garlic bread cooked in the slow cooker will not be crisp, it is deliciously soft and moist. It is also very convenient and saves all the preparation of cooking at the last minute. You can, of course, crisp the bread by removing the foil and placing the bread under a hot grill or in the oven for just a few minutes at the end of cooking time.

If the recipe is doubled, you could easily use a 4.5 litre capacity cooker.

    2 tablespoons water
    30cm French bread stick
    90g butter, softened
    2 cloves garlic, crushed
    1 tablespoon chopped parsley

Place the water in the base of the slow cooker.

Cut the bread stick into 2cm slices.

Mix the butter, garlic and parsley in a bowl.

Spread each side of the slices of bread with the garlic butter and join back together. Wrap half the bread in foil and place in the cooker, seam side up. Repeat with the remaining bread.

Place the lid on the cooker and cook for 1 hour on High or 2 hours on Low.

STEAMED RICE

Serves 6–8

(for a 3.2–4.5 litre slow cooker)

2 cups long-grain rice
¼ teaspoon salt
5½ cups warm water

Place all the ingredients in the slow cooker, stir to combine and then cover with the lid and cook for 2 hours on High or 4 hours on Low.

Fluff up the rice with a fork and serve as an accompaniment to savoury dishes.

BEEF STOCK

Makes 1 litre, approximately
(for a 4–5.5 litre slow cooker)

This beautiful stock is so deliciously rich that it usually forms a jelly when it gets cold – a sure sign of its excellent quality.

1kg beef bones, approximately
1 carrot, chopped
1 onion, chopped (no need to peel)
1 small stalk celery or 10 celery leaves, chopped
1 bay leaf
1½ teaspoons salt
1 sprig thyme (optional)
5 cups water

Wash the beef bones and place in the slow cooker with the rest of the ingredients.

Cover the cooker with the lid and cook for 4–6 hours on High or 10–12 hours on Low.

Strain the stock through a sieve and place in the fridge to cool. If you want a clearer stock, line the sieve with muslin.

Next day, remove the fat layer from the stock. It is now ready to use.

Store in the fridge for up to 5 days, or in the freezer for up to 3 months.

CHICKEN STOCK

Makes 1 litre, approximately
(for a 4–5 litre slow cooker)

2 chicken carcasses or 500g chicken wings, necks or the
   carcass and trimmings from a roasted chicken
1 carrot, chopped
1 onion, chopped
1 small stalk celery or 10 celery leaves, chopped
1 bay leaf
1½ teaspoons salt
1 sprig thyme (optional)
5 cups water

Wash the chicken bones and place in the slow cooker with the rest of the ingredients.

Cover the cooker with the lid and cook for 4–6 hours on High or 10–12 hours on Low.

Strain the stock through a sieve and place in the fridge to cool.

Next day, remove the fat layer from the stock. It is now ready to use.

Store in the fridge for up to 4 days, or in the freezer for up to 3 months.

VEGETABLE STOCK

Makes 1 litre, approximately
(for a 4–5.5 litre slow cooker)

You can use virtually any vegetables or vegetable scraps to make this stock. If you are aiming for colour, include some well-washed onion skins. Be careful of using vegetables with an overpowering flavour, such as swedes and turnips.

It is best to leave out potatoes as they will make the stock cloudy.

> 5 cups of a range of chopped vegetables or scrubbed
>   vegetable skins
> 1 onion, chopped
> 1 sprig thyme
> 1 bay leaf
> 1 teaspoon salt
> 5 cups water

Place the vegetables or peelings in the slow cooker with the rest of the ingredients.

Cover the cooker with the lid and cook for 4–6 hours on High or 10–12 hours on Low.

Strain the stock through a sieve, add salt to taste if desired and place in the fridge to cool. Store in the fridge for up to 4 days, or in the freezer for up to 6 months.

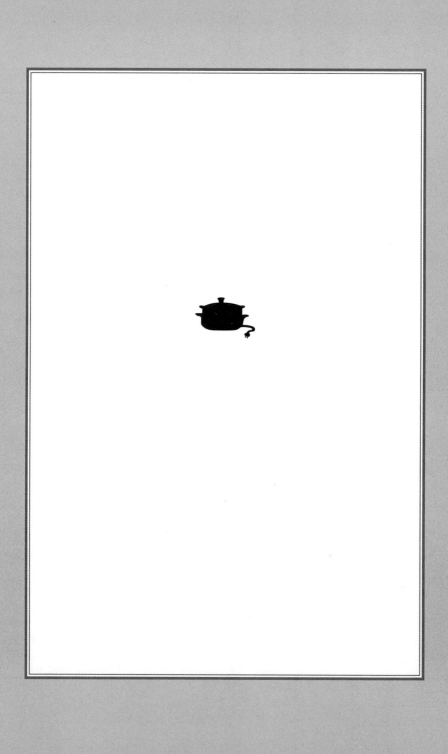

PRESERVES

I love making the most of a summer's abundance of fruit so I was delighted recently when I discovered that the slow cooker can be a great asset for preserving. I found that the preserves made in the slow cooker have slightly different characteristics to those made on the stovetop; for instance the flavours are slightly stronger and pleasingly sharper.

The slow cooker is perfect for softening the fruit for jam or marmalade and this slow cooking process seems to help in extracting maximum pectin, which means the jam will set well and more quickly. It is best to use fruits that do not oxidise, such as berries or dark plums. However, you can combine fruits that tend to go brown when exposed to air, such as nectarines and peaches, with non-oxidising fruit, such as raspberries, to make jams such as the delicious peach and raspberry jam in this section.

When the fruit is soft, transfer it to a large saucepan on the stovetop, add the sugar and boil for 20–30 minutes until setting point is reached.

Savoury preserves such as chutney and relishes can be made entirely in the slow cooker. They just need a little extra thickening at the end.

Setting point and sterilising jars and bottles

To know when you have reached setting point, place 2 teaspoons of the hot mixture on a cold saucer, place in the fridge for a few minutes. Run your finger through the cold jam; if the surface is quite firm and wrinkles when you pull your finger through it, the jam has reached setting point.

To sterilise the jars, wash in hot soapy water, rinse and place upside down on a clean cloth or dish drainer to drain. Place on a tray in a cold oven. Turn the oven to 110°C (fan forced) or 130°C (not fan forced). When the oven reaches this temperature, turn off the heat and leave the bottles for 10 minutes. To make sure the lids are sterile, thoroughly wash and dry them. When the lid is placed on the jar of hot jelly, turn the jar briefly upside down – the heat of the jelly will sterilise the lid.

Peach and Raspberry Jam

Makes approximately 1.1 litres
(for a 3.2–3.5 litre slow cooker)

You will need about 650g peaches for this recipe as 500g of peach flesh is needed. You can double the quantities in this recipe if you have a larger cooker.

> 500g sliced or diced peach flesh, chopped
> 500g fresh or (thawed) frozen raspberries
> 1kg sugar

Place the raspberries and peaches in the slow cooker and stir to combine. Place lid on cooker and cook on Low for 5 hours until the peaches are soft.

Allow to cool slightly (for ease of handling), then transfer the mixture to a large saucepan. Bring to the boil, then stir in the sugar. Bring back to the boil, stirring until the sugar is dissolved, then boil over medium heat until setting point is reached (see page 410).

Pour into warm sterilised jars (see page 410) and seal immediately.

Store in a very cool, dry, dark place or in the fridge. Refrigerate after opening.

BERRY JELLY

Makes approximately 900ml
(for a 3.2–3.5 litre slow cooker)

This jelly is delicious served on scones, fresh bread, pikelets or toast. It can be melted as needed and used as a glaze over berry tarts. Add ½ teaspoon to a cup of gravy for a lovely subtle fruitiness or add I teaspoon to a casserole-style dish.

> 1kg fresh or (thawed) frozen berries
> juice 1 lemon
> 1 cup water
> sugar

Place the berries, lemon juice and water in the slow cooker. Place the lid on the cooker and cook on Low for 5 hours. Leave until cool enough to handle, then strain though a fine sieve, pressing the berries down to break them up to extract maximum liquid. Strain the resulting juice through a sieve lined with a single layer of muslin (or even a thin cloth).

Measure the resulting liquid and place in a large saucepan. Add 1 cup of sugar for each cup of juice and bring to the boil, stirring. Boil until setting point is reached (see page 410). Pour into warm sterilised jars and seal immediately (see page 410).

Store in a very cool, dry, dark place or in the fridge. Refrigerate after opening.

MARMALADE

Makes approximately 1.4 litres
(for a 3.5–5 litre slow cooker)

The peel softened in the slow cooker leads to a delicious tart marmalade, much like Seville orange marmalade, with the convenience of being able to make it any time of the year using any type of orange. I like to cut the fruit by hand for this recipe — it leads to a lovely, somewhat chunky, texture.

> 500g oranges
> 1 lemon
> 5 cups water
> 1.5kg sugar

Finley slice or chop the oranges and lemons and place in the slow cooker with the water. Place the lid on the cooker and cook on Low for 5–6 hours until the skins are soft. When the cooker is cool enough to handle, pour the contents into a large pot and add the sugar. Bring to the boil, stirring until the sugar is dissolved.

Boil for 20–25 minutes over medium heat until setting point is reached (see page 410). Pour into warm sterilised jars and seal immediately (see page 410).

Store in a very cool, dry, dark place or in the fridge. Refrigerate after opening.

PLUM OR BERRY SYRUP

Makes approximately 1.5 litres
(for a 3.5 –4.5 litre slow cooker)

You can use any type of plums to make this syrup. I like the dark skins and flesh of blood plums which make the colour of the finished syrup sensational and the flavour intense.

It can be served as a cordial, mixing one part syrup with 4 parts chilled water, soda water or lemonade. It is also delicious served over ice cream or panna cotta.

> 1kg blood or Japanese plums or berries
> 3 cups water
> sugar
> 2 level teaspoons citric or tartaric acid

Place the plums or berries and water in the slow cooker with the water. Cover with the lid and cook for 8 hours on Low.

Pour the mixture through a sieve (without pressing any of the pulp through), and if a really clear syrup is desired, pour the resulting liquid through another sieve lined with muslin or fine cloth.

Pour into a large saucepan. For each cup of the resulting liquid add 1 cup of sugar. Bring to the boil, stirring to dissolve the sugar and simmer for two minutes only. Stir in the citric acid. Pour into warm sterilised bottles and seal immediately (see page 410).

Store in the fridge or in a very cool, dry, dark place. Refrigerate after opening.

TOMATO RELISH

Makes approximately 1 litre
(for a 3.5 to 4.5 litre slow cooker)

You can peel the tomatoes for this recipe if you like but I never do. If you choose to do so, plunge the whole tomatoes into boiling water for a few seconds, then into iced water, after which the skins should slip off easily.

This recipe can also be used as a tomato sauce (ketchup) by simply puréeing the mixture at the end of the process with a stick blender. In this case use one teaspoon less of the cornflour.

1kg ripe tomatoes
250g onions
1 cooking apple (such as Granny Smith or Golden
    Delicious), cored and grated
250g sugar
1½ teaspoons curry powder
1½ teaspoons mustard powder
1 tablespoon salt
1¼ cups white vinegar
6 teaspoons cornflour mixed to a paste with
    1½ tablespoons white vinegar

Dice the tomatoes and onions and place in the slow cooker with the rest of the ingredients, except the cornflour paste. Place the lid on the cooker and cook on High for 6 hours. Stir in the cornflour paste, cover with the lid and cook for 10 minutes more.

Pour into warm sterilised bottles (see page 410) and seal immediately.

Store in a very cool, dry, dark place or in the fridge. Refrigerate after opening.

QUINCE CHEESE

(for a 3.2–3.5 litre slow cooker)

unblemished quinces (however many your slow cooker will
    hold)
¾ cup water
sugar

Rub the quinces with a dry cloth to remove any remaining furry 'bloom'. Place the whole quinces into the slow cooker and pour over the water. Place the lid on the cooker and cook on Low for 8–10 hours or until very soft. Leave to cool, then cut the flesh (including the skin) from the core and press through a sieve or food mill. For each cup of the resulting purée, add 1 cup of sugar. Place in a large pot and bring to the boil stirring constantly. Reduce heat and cook over low heat, stirring almost constantly with a wooden spoon until the stage when the spoon is dragged through the middle of the mixture it leaves a clear trail to the base of the pan.*

Line a square or rectangular tin with foil and pour mixture in (the size of the tin will depend on the amount of mixture – the cheese should be about 1.25cm thick). Leave to set, then cut into squares to serve as part of a cheese platter. Small squares are also very nice coated in chocolate for a special sweet treat, or even simply rolled in castor sugar.

* *If you tire of stirring before the mixture reaches this 'cheese' stage, simply pour the mixture into small wide-mouthed containers, in which case it is technically quince paste which can also be served as part of a cheese platter.*

INDEX